Reel Romance

Reel Romance

The Lovers' Guide to the 100 Best Date Movies

Leslie Halpern

Taylor Trade Publishing

Lanham New York Dallas Toronto Oxford

Published by Taylor Trade Publishing
An imprint of The Rowman & Littlefield Publishing Group, Inc.
4501 Forbes Boulevard, Suite 200
Lanham, Maryland 20706

Distributed by National Book Network

Library of Congress Cataloging-in-Publication Data
Halpern, Leslie, 1960-
Reel romance : the lovers' guide to the 100 best date movies / Leslie
Halpern.—1st Taylor Trade Pub. ed.
p.   cm.
Includes bibliographical references and index.
ISBN 1-58979-064-2 (pbk. : alk. paper)
1. Love in motion pictures. 2. Motion pictures—United States—Plots,
themes, etc. I. Title.
PN1995.9.L6 H35 2003
791.43'6543—dc22
2003017898

In love, one always begins by deceiving oneself,
and one always ends by deceiving others;
that is what the world calls a romance.
OSCAR WILDE

Contents

Contents

Contents

Contents

Acknowledgments

MANY THANKS to my agent Linda Konner for initiating the project and to Ross Plotkin at Taylor Trade Publishing for his editorial assistance and helpful suggestions. In addition to writing the foreword, Jay Boyar reviewed the manuscript and offered creative ideas for which I'm very grateful. Others who helped along the way: Jim Leibson, Dr. Robert Smither, Sarah Asher, and Michelle Margol. My sincere appreciation also is extended to Jackie Lynn Clement, Linda Saracino, and Patricia Sporer of Professional Freelancer Writers of Orlando for their longtime friendship and support and to my husband, Steven, for watching all 100 movies (and some that didn't make the cut) with me, to provide a male perspective.

Foreword

IN THE GRAND, early days of the movies, couples would spoon in the picture-palace balcony. By the 1950s, you'd find them making out at the drive-in theater—the "passion pit."

These days, an amorous pair might hook up in front of a plasma-screen TV, the DVD player on pause, perhaps, as the offscreen action accelerates.

Whatever the era, whatever the setting, people have always intuitively understood that watching a movie is the best thing (or maybe the second-best thing) to do on a date. It's no accident that film critic Pauline Kael used sexually tinged titles for many of her books: *Kiss Kiss Bang Bang*, *Taking It All In*, and *I Lost It at the Movies*. In just about any film, the intensity of the close-ups and the intimacy of the experience carry an erotic charge. And if the plot is at all romantic, why, then, all the better.

Throughout *Reel Romance*, Leslie Halpern offers cinematic suggestions that further blur the already fuzzy line between lovers and movie lovers. Whatever your taste, and your partner's taste, in romantic cinema, there's something here that the two of you ought to enjoy together.

Groundhog Day (1993), for example, might at first seem an odd choice to include in a book about romance. On one level, it's a zany comedy about a TV weatherman, played by Bill Murray, who, for reasons left unexplained, is condemned to relive the same day over and over again. But the more he repeats the day, the more he is able to perfect his romance with his fetching producer, played by Andie MacDowell. And what could be more purely romantic than a film about the quest for a perfect romance?

Casablanca, a 1942 film included here, is a far less surprising choice. The movie's subject is the love that got away, the love that grows stronger and more idealized with each passing year. Humphrey Bogart is the wartime saloon owner who is trying to get on with his life when his old flame, played by Ingrid Bergman, suddenly comes through the door. "Of all the gin joints in all the towns in all the world, she walks into mine," he fumes. Another quote from the film, "We'll always have Paris," has become the very motto of lost love.

Then there is *Moonstruck*, a film from 1987 that makes the point that true romance is often truly inconvenient. Early in the film we meet Loretta Castorini (Cher), a young widow who is determined that everything concerning her upcoming marriage to the unexciting Johnny Cammareri (Danny Aiello) go just right. And so it might have if, while Johnny was out of the country on family business, Loretta had not met and fallen madly in love with Johnny's brother, Ronny (Nicolas Cage). How terribly awkward! How completely romantic! As the movie begins, the words of the song that Dean Martin sings say it all: "When the moon hits your eye like a big pizza pie, that's amore!"

Amore, of course, existed long before the movies came along. And moviegoing need not always be romantic. But as *Reel Romance* suggests, and as we all somehow know, something special happens when pictures and passion combine. Like moonlight and romance, movies and romance can be irresistibly potent.

With a little imagination and this helpful book as a guide, you and your partner should soon be swept away. You'll find yourselves viewing—if not also doing—what comes naturally.

JAY BOYAR
movie critic for the
Orlando Sentinel

Introduction

*I*N SOME WAYS, selecting the right date movie is like selecting the right date. Will you rent it for a few days or buy it to last a lifetime? Will you enjoy it over and over at first and then lose interest? Will the critics influence your decision? Will the contents be as exciting as the packaging promises? Will the love story still seem romantic after repeated viewings?

Reel Romance is intended to help you answer these important questions . . . at the video store. This book was created for romantic couples—anywhere from the first date through the fiftieth wedding anniversary—to find date films that satisfy the viewing preferences of both partners. Grouped by common themes, these 100 selections will help you make the right choice for that perfect date night at home.

In the 2000 independent film *Love & Sex*, written and directed by Valerie Breiman, a romantic couple, Kate and Adam (Famke Janssen and Jon Favreau), browse through a video store looking for a date movie. She wants the 1922 F. W. Murnau German Expressionist film *Nosferatu* so she can think deep thoughts about passion and death. He holds a copy of *Ninjeta*, a martial arts action film that promises swift kicks and bare breasts. Their argument in the video store is echoed by real-life couples in similar venues around the globe.

Though a night at the movie theater provides a needed sense of community for horror, suspense, and comedy films, romantic date movies—which can be horror, suspense, or comedy films that include a strong romantic element—are best enjoyed at home snuggling on the sofa while sipping your beverage of choice. Or in cases of life imitating art imitating life, you can watch classic date movies in the park as in *The Wedding Planner* or go to retro theaters as in *Children of a Lesser God*, where they watch *Some Like It Hot*.

When magazine and newspaper film critics recommend "a perfect date movie," they usually mean a romantic comedy or tearful drama that women

1

love and men tolerate. While most women would enjoy a week-long film festival of bodice-ripping romances, most men would not. To state it simply: Woman prefer adjectives; men prefer verbs.

Although men certainly like romance, what they really crave is action and adventure with a sprinkling of romance. So when Bruce Willis, Vin Diesel, or The Rock beds a bimbo and cracks a joke, does this really qualify as romantic comedy? At least half the population would say no.

Identifying a Reel Romance

Reel Romance is a guide for couples who want to enjoy really romantic films together. This book identifies 100 entertaining films from every genre that have enough romance to satisfy women, enough action (most of the time) to satisfy men, and enough clever dialogue, interesting characters, memorable moments, and involving story developments to satisfy both. While some films lean toward a female audience (e.g., *Crossing Delancey*), others appeal more to male viewers (e.g., *True Lies*). However, all 100 films contain something for both sexes, and unlike other movie guidebooks currently on the market, *Reel Romance* is devoted exclusively to romantic films that meet three criteria:

- ❤ They appeal to women and men; no strictly chick flicks or macho movies are included.
- ❤ They contain a plausible romance, either as the main story or an important subplot in a genre film.
- ❤ They leave the audience feeling romantic.

Reel Romance focuses mainly on films from the 1980s, 1990s, and 2000s because of their physical availability (movies from the late 1960s, 1970s, and early 1980s can be hard to find for rental or purchase) and emotional accessibility, although one similarly themed pre-1965 classic selection is included in each chapter. Some of these classics may cause culture shock to contemporary viewers: Politically incorrect characterizations that seem sexist, racist, and ageist now were permitted then, while today's explicit sex and violence are absent from these movies of earlier generations.

In addition, watching old black-and-white romantic comedies where the characters talk incessantly, chain-smoke, keep their clothes on in every circumstance, avoid four-letter words, work on typewriters instead of computers, and dress formally for all three meals can seem unsophisticated to viewers accustomed to quick cuts, special effects, and computer-generated images. Some of these early talkies from the 1940s and 1950s provide quite a contrast to the action-oriented movies produced today. Even so, a representative classic in each chapter will give you a sense of the foundation on which current date films are based.

For example, the Katharine Hepburn–Cary Grant screwball comedy *Bringing Up Baby* (1938), the classic date movie selection for Chapter 5, inspired countless date movies throughout the years. Just a few famous scenes and situations re-created in contemporary movies from this classic include a woman tearing a man's formal jacket at a party (*Blind Date* [1987]), a woman delivering an exotic jungle cat (*Who's That Girl?* [1987]), a man wearing a woman's frilly bathrobe to the door (*Meet the Parents* [2000]), and the couple—one at a time—falling down a mud slide (*Romancing the Stone* [1984]). As you watch the other classic date movie selections, look for more characters and scenes that have been "borrowed" for today's films.

Whether classic or modern, the movies in this book provoke, tease, and stimulate, but never feature explicit nudity or prolonged sexual encounters. Romantic date movies are not about instant gratification, but about two people who have an overpowering sexual attraction to each other that is impeded by seemingly insurmountable obstacles. These barriers include misconceptions, superstitions, differences in class, race, religion, or species, unresolved internal conflicts, opposite beliefs or priorities, prejudices, violent or criminal tendencies, physical and emotional wounds, fate or supernatural occurrences, physical threats, false impressions or dangerous secrets, and the ever-popular mix-and-match obstacle: a previous attachment, engagement, or marriage.

Like any good romance novel that keeps its readers eagerly turning pages, a good romantic date movie holds on to its viewers (and keeps its viewers holding on to each other) by generating some sexual heat. Two attractive idealized characters meet in an exotic setting, dangerous situation, or unusual circumstance, and although they fight against their enormous attraction to each other, they inevitably experience the universally recognizable feelings of love and lust. Some movies emphasize the sensual characteristics of love, the pleasuring of characters' senses through touch, taste, smell, sight, and hearing their loved ones, such as *French Kiss* and *The Bridges of Madison County*. Other movies produce sexual tension through a conflict that leads to unexpressed or unfulfilled physical desires, such as *You've Got Mail* and *Out of Sight*. Other films, including

The English Patient, combine sensual pleasuring with sexual tension for an extremely stimulating experience.

Although romance novels written for women always have happy endings, great romantic date movies don't necessarily end that way. The lack of a storybook ending, however, doesn't lessen the romance in movies such as *Crouching Tiger, Hidden Dragon, Witness, Out of Sight,* and *The Bridges of Madison County.*

How to Use This Book

The 100 selected movies—divided thematically (rather than ranked) into groups of ten movies per chapter—were chosen because they incorporate the right mix of romance in an overall entertaining movie. Chapter 1: Always a Wedding Planner, Never a Bride examines date movies in which weddings represent more than the union of two people for the characters involved. Chapter 2: Literate Ladies in Love looks at journalists, broadcasters, bookstore employees, and editors who misuse the language of love. Chapter 3: Once Upon a Time takes you long ago and far away to romances requiring some kind of transformation. Chapter 4: Planes, Trains, Automobiles, and Ships lets you journey into the lives of lovers to whom transportation symbolizes something other than travel. Chapter 5: Opposites Attract (Then Repel, Then Attract Again) brings you opposing sides that long to be side by side.

The last five chapters provide fifty more romantic date movies sure to tease and please. Chapter 6: In the Eye of the Beholder looks at romances that go beneath surface beauty. Chapter 7: Is That a Pistol/Knife/Nunchak in Your Pocket? explores using love as a weapon. Chapter 8: Love Is a Supernatural Thing presents romances that venture beyond the laws of nature. Chapter 9: Watch Out for That Tree! branches out to date movies where the environment brings lovers together. And, finally, Chapter 10: Love in Disguise uncovers romances in which at least one partner has something to hide.

Obviously, more than 100 great romantic date movies from more than 100 years of filmmaking line the shelves of video stores around the world. *Reel Romance* features some of the best films from a variety of genres. Are you most comfortable with romances that leave something to the imagination (e.g., waves crashing in the ocean and trains roaring through tunnels), or do you like a little more explicitness? Do you prefer light romantic comedies and dramas where the other elements are secondary to the romance? Or maybe you like action films where necking couples take a (figurative) backseat to the rest of the story.

Do you require a happy ending to be satisfied? This guidebook provides the information you need to find romantic films you can watch as a couple.

Reel Romance introduces each of the ten chapters with a description of common themes. These introductions are followed by ten alphabetized movie listings that contain basic credit information, a story synopsis, and a review based on each film's romantic appeal to men and women; in addition, cross-references to other related films listed (and sometimes not listed) in the book are included for your information.

Contained within each of the 100 film descriptions are five tools to help you decide whether the movie is right for you:

1. The **Intimacy Comfort Level** classifies the movie's sexual explicitness and relationship complexities for a general level of physical and emotional intimacy and suggests stages in your relationship most appropriate for watching each particular movie. A rating of *First Date* means the film is terrific for first dates and newly formed couples; a rating of *Going Steady* recommends the film for more established dating couples; and *Committed/Married* suggests the film is enjoyable for romantic couples in long-term relationships. Films fall into more than one category, and just because a movie is directed toward one particular level of intimacy doesn't mean that it can't be enjoyed by couples in other kinds of relationships.

2. Next comes the film's total on the **Make-Out Meter**, a ranking of 1-5 candles for the sexual heat generated by the film. The Make-Out Meter is not a rating for the quality of the movie, but a points award based on the mixture of onscreen chemistry, offscreen rumors, risqué dialogue, sensuality, sexual tension, love scenes, and romantic inspiration, with the lowest rating of one candle representing a romantic spark and the highest rating of five candles representing a blaze of unremitting passion. Low ratings on the Make-Out Meter indicate that the film's emphasis is on something other than romance: You'll find an intricate plot, laugh-out-loud comedy, or hard-hitting action that provides a different kind of excitement.

3. Each movie description also includes a brief section listing something in the film **Just for Her** and **Just for Him**. These lighthearted tips and quotes on what women and men might find particularly amusing will give you something to watch for as you enjoy these films together.

4. Completing each description is a **Do Try This at Home** section that provides a spicy suggestion or gentle gesture inspired by the movie that you can try at home (or anywhere else that's legal).

5. Each chapter also includes fun **trivia questions** about popular stars of date movies. Test yourself about lesser-known facts regarding the stars you love to love. Is it Jim Carrey or John Cusack? Harrison Ford or Brendan Fraser? Richard Gere or Hugh Grant? Drew Barrymore or Sandra Bullock? Gwyneth Paltrow or Michelle Pfeiffer? Julia Roberts or Meg Ryan? Check the answers beginning on page 205 to see if you're right.

The ten chapters are also followed by references and an index so you can conduct your own searches and gain maximum usefulness from the book.

Be warned! Not all of these movies are five-star, two-thumbs-up, Academy Award winners. These 100 films were chosen because they entertain men and women involved in romantic relationships, dazzle with lush cinematography or sparkling dialogue, and forge new ground in portraying erotic encounters. They engage your senses until you can almost taste the chocolate nipples of Venus offered by Juliette Binoche (*Chocolat*) and the lemonade dripping down Harrison Ford's strong, muscled throat (*Witness*) or smell the bottles of earthy spices (*French Kiss*) and the scent of Leslie Mann's hair as Brendan Fraser playfully sniffs it (*George of the Jungle*). You experience the characters almost as if they were your own lovers.

So the next time you visit the video store, bring along your copy of *Reel Romance* if you want to feel the characters' breathless anticipation, melt under their gazes of desire, and feel those same tingles of desire. You won't have to argue over whether to rent *Nosferatu* or *Ninjeta*. You'll be able to find movies about love and sex that even Kate and Adam could enjoy together.

Chapter 1

Always a Wedding Planner, Never a Bride

In all the wedding cake, hope is the sweetest of the plums.
Douglas Jerrold

HEN YOU WATCH most movies, wedding scenes can be taken at face value. They represent a shift in the family structure, a flurry of activities and expenses, and a demarcation of time in the life cycle. In *Father of the Bride* (either the 1950 original or the 1991 remake), a father adjusts to the marriage of his only daughter by planning an elaborate wedding. Although the occasion represents his wealth and stature in the community and marks an important rite of passage, its primary function is to serve as an exciting backdrop for the father's emotional growth. In the animated feature *Rugrats in Paris* (2001), a little boy's wish for a new mom finally comes true when his father remarries. This wedding brings together different families and different cultures in a climactic scene that signals a new beginning for the motherless boy. In these films (and in countless other nondate movies), the inclusion of a wedding scene represents the emotional and financial crescendo for characters other than the wedding couple, making the union funny, poignant, or dramatic, but not necessarily romantic.

In date movies, however, weddings often take on a greater role than the actual marriage of two people. The wedding evolves from merely a ritualistic romantic union to an anxiety-producing symbol of the conflict within the central character. In the best date movies—like the ten that follow—this conflict finds a resolution. The wedding then loses all its frightening associations for the character, frazzled nerves become rejuvenated, and he or she becomes free to enjoy romance, love, passion, and all those wonderful wedding gifts.

Improving his lot from a drum-beating airhead and a witless waterboy, Adam Sandler becomes a romantic leading man in *The Wedding Singer*. He plays a freelance singer and voice coach whose musical abilities are exceeded by his enthusiasm for and cultivation of romance. After he is jilted at the altar, however, he turns his back on what he once embraced. His repertoire changes from tender love songs to equally heartfelt, hard-rock classics such as the J. Geils Band's "Love Stinks."

Sandler's character, Robbie Hart, hates weddings because he wants everyone else to be miserable, too. Formerly representing love and commitment, weddings come to symbolize all the happiness that lies just beyond his grasp. He can sing about true love and train others to sing about it, but can't experience it for himself. But with the help of his friends, the love of a new woman (Drew Barrymore), and the courage to attempt the seemingly impossible, Robbie learns to enjoy weddings again.

In *The Wedding Planner*, Jennifer Lopez plays Mary Fiore, a compulsive workaholic addicted to creating perfect weddings for others. Romantic by nature, she nevertheless has given up on love since her fiancé betrayed her two years earlier. She says, "Those who can't do, teach; and those who can't wed, plan." A self-described magnet for unavailable men, she has a chance meeting with Steve (Matthew McConaughey), a handsome pediatrician, that incites a mutual attraction until they learn that Mary is the wedding planner for his upcoming wedding. While he tries to convince himself that he's feeling anxiety, not chemistry, she forges ahead with wedding plans that will make her career, but break her heart.

Pursued by a man she doesn't love and unable to make a romantic appointment with the doctor, Mary is ready to give up on romance and weddings. She tells her matchmaking father (Alex Rocco) that "love isn't like some enchanted evening from a fairy tale." To symbolize her loss of belief in the magic of marriage, Mary agrees to a simple arranged wedding at the justice of the peace to the man she doesn't love. Through some last-minute, quirky (okay, contrived) coincidences, and two canceled weddings, Mary and Dr. Steve work together to restore her belief in love, romance, and weddings.

In another case of nuptial neurosis, Julia Roberts plays a small-town, man-eating flirt named Maggie Carpenter who abandons five men at the altar in *Runaway Bride*. Although the townspeople jokingly say that she is always a bride, never a bridesmaid, she is neither: Her character's fear of marriage forces her to run away from all commitments. Until she conquers this fear, Maggie is destined to be alone, unhappy, and the butt of every joke in her community.

There's a reason why these characters are always wedding planners (or wedding singers, matchmakers, best men, or invited guests), but not brides and grooms. With names such as Robbie "Hart" and "Mary" Fiore, it's obvious that love is central to them, yet some inner obstacle keeps them from saying "I do."

Though not a particularly action-packed category in terms of guns, car crashes, and military action, date movies about weddings come with a few surprises for skeptical male viewers. Strong, well-developed characters such as caustic newspaper columnist Richard Gere (*Runaway Bride*), well-dressed, well-spoken Jeremy Northam (*Emma*), and angry opera lover Nicolas Cage (*Moonstruck*) may resonate with men who have endured the inevitable struggle of pitting logic against love.

Whatever their particular type of mental anguish, however, these characters must walk away from their fears in order to walk down the aisle. In losing one thing, they gain another. American author Helen Rowland once wrote: "In olden times sacrifices were made at the altar—a custom which is still continued." Luckily for us, date movies are all about the customs surrounding love and sex. And date movies about weddings concern the fear of these customs and lovers' countless schemes for overcoming the debilitating effects of nuptial neurosis.

❧ *Blind Date* (1987)

Bruce Willis, Kim Basinger, John Larroquette, Mark Blum
DIRECTED BY BLAKE EDWARDS
95 minutes; in color; PG-13
Intimacy Comfort Level: First Date, Going Steady
Make-Out Meter: ▌
Just for Her: A very special box of chocolates
Just for Him: Car chases; the ripped-pocket look

One year before he became foul-mouthed, tough-guy cop John McClane in *Die Hard*, Bruce Willis made his big-screen debut as the soft-spoken workaholic Walter in *Blind Date*. Needing an escort for an important company party, Walter

In *Blind Date*, Walter (Bruce Willis) and David (John Larroquette) put on their own exhibit during a visit to an art gallery, while Nadia (Kim Basinger) expresses shock. (Copyright © 1987 TriStar Pictures; courtesy of Photofest)

gets more than he bargained for when he takes out beautiful blind date Nadia (Basinger).

Warned that she "gets wild" when she drinks alcohol, he interprets this to mean promiscuous, when in fact Nadia has a chemical imbalance that produces a severe allergic reaction. (Coincidentally, Basinger has the same affliction in the 1992 thriller *Final Analysis*, although with far more drastic consequences.)

A nice, quiet, "one-concubine-kind of guy," Walter finds his entire life turned upside down when he eagerly shares a bottle of champagne with his lovely date and then encourages her to continue drinking throughout the evening.

Larroquette plays the psychotic ex-boyfriend who coerces Nadia into a Disney-style wedding that signifies the end of her happiness and her inability to control her alcohol intake. When she resigns herself to the wedding, she dooms herself to a life of unhappiness. But as the wedding looms nearer, help is on the way.

Formerly married to his job, Walter does some soul-searching and discovers new priorities. But can he arrive in time to stop the wedding armed with only a box full of chocolates and a heart full of love?

Blind Date is a fun mix that includes great supporting roles by Mark Blum as a sleazy coworker and Phil Hartman as Walter's car salesman brother. The emphasis on silliness rather than sensuality makes it especially good for a first date or early date rental, although the lack of any real intimacy may disappoint more established couples.

For another uncomfortable blind date scenario, see *Crossing Delancey* in Chapter 2.

Do Try This at Home: Sip champagne while listening to live music.

Emma (1996)

Gwyneth Paltrow, Jeremy Northam, Toni Collette, Alan Cumming
DIRECTED BY DOUGLAS MCGRATH
121 minutes; in color; PG
Intimacy Comfort Level: First Date, Going Steady, Committed/Married
Make-Out Meter: ▮▮▮
Just for Her: Elegantly phrased barbs to the deserving; a real gentleman
Just for Him: Décolletage; ungentlemanly behavior

Based on Jane Austen's 1816 novel, lovely twenty-one-year-old Emma Woodhouse (Paltrow) is always a matchmaker, never a bride. Her family's wealth and position guarantee that she will retain her status even if she stays single. "A single woman of good fortune is always respectable," she claims. Having never experienced love, she is content arranging the marriages of others, although she's not particularly good at it.

This well-meaning busybody has all the wrong instincts for matchmaking. She plays the pianoforte beautifully, sings sweetly, and paints lovely portraits. As an artist she excels, but at the art of love, she's strictly an amateur. She can't recognize loving feelings in herself, much less in other people. Yet that never keeps her from trying, despite her protests of "It's not my place to intrude" and "I am determined never to interfere."

Emma's meager matchmaking skills start to slip, however, when she unexpectedly feels pangs of jealously and lustful urges herself. She admires the flam-

In *Emma*, two friends (Gwyneth Paltrow as Emma and Jeremy Northam as Mr. Knightley) practice target shooting. As a matchmaker, Emma is way off target. (David Appleby/Copyright © 1996 by Miramax Films; courtesy of Photofest)

boyant Frank Churchill (Ewan McGregor) and also feels something for her life-long friend Mr. Knightley (Northam). She wonders if any of her emotions could be signs of love, or *should* be signs of love considering that her less fortunate friend Harriet (Collette) also needs some romance in her life.

While Frank is daring and flashy, he lacks some of Knightley's nobler qualities. Indeed, "not one in a hundred men have 'gentleman' so plainly written across them as Mr. Knightley," she says. But then again, exactly whom does Knightley fancy? His angry admonishments certainly make it appear that he feels neither admiration nor love for the fickle little matchmaker who changes her mind as often as she changes her beautiful gowns, and who freely gives charity, but not kindness.

Paltrow looks lovely as Emma and proved to the world that she could handle an English accent with aplomb. This comes in handy for her 1998 role as Lady Viola in *Shakespeare in Love* (see Chapter 10).

This sophisticated comedy has laughter and tears, but not much in the way of action. Rent *Emma* when you're in the mood for some cerebral foreplay and you won't be disappointed. Collette gives a fine performance as Emma's highly suggestible friend Harriet Smith; Cumming plays the shallow Mr. Elton; and Greta Scacchi is convincing as Emma's kindly friend, Mrs. Weston. After watching this movie, you'll surely agree that "the most beautiful thing in the world is a match well made."

For an updated version of the story, try the 1995 comedy _Clueless_, starring Alicia Silverstone, Stacey Dash, and Paul Rudd. Faster paced and far less subtle, _Clueless_ will satisfy anyone who likes Austen's intricately tangled web of romantic relationships, but doesn't enjoy watching period pieces.

For another film based on an Austen novel, see _Sense and Sensibility_ in Chapter 6; see _Bridget Jones's Diary_ in Chapter 2 for another updated version of an Austen classic.

Do Try This at Home: Remember your lover's favorite foods.

Paltrow or Pfeiffer?
1. Did Gwyneth Paltrow or Michelle Pfeiffer star in a movie about a homely waitress who can't find love?
Answer on page 206

❧ _Four Weddings and a Funeral_ (1994)

Hugh Grant, Andie MacDowell, Simon Callow, Kristin Scott Thomas
DIRECTED BY MIKE NEWELL
118 minutes; in color; R
Intimacy Comfort Level: Going Steady, Committed/Married
Make-Out Meter: ▮▮▮
Just for Her: A lovely nonproposal in the rain; MacDowell's intimidating list of lovers
Just for Him: Best man speeches

Charming Englishman Charles (Grant) develops a strange relationship with Carrie (MacDowell), an elusive American beauty. With the help of his friends during four weddings and a funeral in England, the sworn bachelor begins to rethink his pledge of no allegiance.

Though she remains a woman of mystery, Carrie—the lady in the big black hat—charms Charles at first sight, despite their various entanglements with other people. He is a highly indiscreet serial monogamist who is always at weddings, but never the one getting married. She is a fashionable socialite who goes too far in the heat of the moment. Both of them have exceptionally bad timing.

Even so, Charles stays hopelessly committed to the idea of their getting together permanently. As he attends Carrie's wedding to someone else, he still refuses to give up his fantasy.

Charles's perpetual foot-in-the-mouth scenarios continue from his early speech as best man to his later admission of love, when he quotes singer David Cassidy from the song "I Think I Love You." In awe of commitment but unable to do it himself and symbolically arriving late to every wedding, Charles muddles his way through until he finally offers Carrie a nonproposal she can't refuse.

Although we don't learn much about MacDowell's character, the strange circle of friends surrounding Charles bears close examination for its own bizarre romances, such as his tart-tongued friend Fiona (Thomas), who secretly loves him as he loves someone else. And Rowan Atkinson makes a welcome appearance as a tongue-tied new priest officiating at the ceremonies.

Clever and romantic, *Four Weddings and a Funeral* was a big hit with audiences and critics, winning numerous awards in the United States and overseas and ranking as one of the highest grossing movies in Great Britain's history. The sex scenes are a little more explicit than the average date movie, and plenty of profanity flies from the characters' mouths, rightfully earning the film its R rating.

For more romantic British comedies also written by Richard Cutis (and not-so-coincidentally starring Hugh Grant), see *Notting Hill* in this chapter and *Bridget Jones's Diary* in Chapter 2. Grant's character in *Four Weddings and a Funeral* is decidedly more likeable than in *Bridget Jones's Diary*, though a little less likeable than in *Notting Hill*. Watch them all and decide for yourself.

Do Try This at Home: Wait for the thunderbolt before committing to someone.

Gere or Grant?
1. Before he played romantic leads, did Richard Gere or
Hugh Grant first appear on screen as a street thug?
Answer on page 206

CLASSIC DATE MOVIE SELECTION

❧ *June Bride* (1948)

Bette Davis, Robert Montgomery, Fay Bainter, Debbie Reynolds
DIRECTED BY BRETAIGNE WINDUST
97 minutes; in black and white; not rated, comparable to G
Intimacy Comfort Level: First Date, Going Steady, Committed/Married
Make-Out Meter: ❙❙
Just for Her: Lamp games
Just for Him: Slapstick comedy, guy talk over "apple cider," and those Bette
    Davis eyes

Mr. Carey Jackson, a well-respected, hard-hitting journalist (Montgomery),
gets reassigned to a fluffy women's magazine called *Home Life*, which is coincidentally edited by his former girlfriend, Linda Gilman (Davis), whom he abandoned three years earlier because of his fear of commitment. Underneath his
nonstop wisecracks, he displays the softer side of the former top foreign correspondent for Allied Magazine Syndicate who now finds himself professionally
displaced after the war.

Sparks fly, tempers flare, and typewriters pound as the two big-city dwellers
come to a (temporary) mutual agreement about how to manage their June cover
story about an all-American wedding held in rural Indiana in the dead of winter.

As spectators at the wedding, they are outsiders longing to be inside—atten-
dees dreaming of being participants. Their simmering romance is barely con-
cealed by the frantic wedding preparations going on around them. The quaint
Brinker family of Indiana is hiding a few secrets of its own, however, that com-

plicate the issue. Luckily a little sister with a big mouth (Reynolds in her debut role) is willing to share what she knows . . . for a price.

Linda discovers that the big June cover story she'd planned has become an entirely different story. Through Carey's meddling antics, she learns that the bride actually is in love with the groom's brother and the bride's sister is in love with the groom. Somehow she must resolve this sticky situation and her own romantic dilemma as well.

Witty dialogue comes almost as fast as the slapstick, making this comedy enjoyable for women and men. Linda and Carey use this wit, however, to protect themselves from becoming attached again. She protests that they talk too much and have probably talked away all the romance between them, making a long-term commitment nearly impossible. But despite the crisp Indiana air, the big chill soon melts for these inevitable lovers. Keep in mind that the sexist ending was appropriate for 1948, and try to lose yourself in the movie rather than find yourself in the present.

For more editors, reporters, and other annoying media types trying to guard themselves against romance, see Chapter 2. If you like *June Bride*, try watching *Woman of the Year* (Chapter 2), another classic similar in tone and story.

Do Try This at Home: Go for an evening hayride in a horse-drawn wagon, or skip the hay and try a horse-drawn carriage. (Or skip the wagon and the carriage and just go for the hay.)

❧ *Kate & Leopold* (2001)

Meg Ryan, Hugh Jackman, Liev Schreiber, Breckin Meyer
DIRECTED BY JAMES MANGOLD
118 minutes; in color; PG-13
Intimacy Comfort Level: First Date, Going Steady, Committed/Married
Make-Out Meter: ▐▐▐▐▌
Just for Her: A horseback rescue
Just for Him: Sparring over dinner; dating tips from a nineteenth-century
    duke

It's 1876 in New York City, and on the night of his thirtieth birthday, Leopold (Jackman), a technically savvy English duke, must announce his wedding engagement. The handsome future inventor of the elevator, however, is far more concerned with his inventions than with choosing a bride from the ugly stepsisters who attend the ball set up by his guardian uncle.

Through a portal in time (and the magic of motion pictures), Stuart (Schreiber), a man from the future, appears and piques the interest of the bored duke. Leopold hitches a ride to the future with him and meets the woman he wants to marry: Kate (Ryan), an aggressive, career-oriented market researcher on the brink of a big promotion. Tired of manipulative game players, she falls for the gentlemanly charms of the duke as he hides out with her time-traveling ex-boyfriend, whose apartment is conveniently located right above hers.

Poor Stuart suffers an elevator accident (linked to the time displacement of Leopold) and winds up hospitalized with serious injuries. While there, he shares his theory of time travel and is promptly sent to the mental ward. Kate and Leopold use his absence to get acquainted . . . very acquainted.

Kate's sleazy boss (Bradley Whitford) makes an appropriate foil for the suave duke, and her brother Charlie (Breckin Meyer) breaks the romantic rhythm for some comic relief. Throughout their brief time together, Leopold repeatedly comes to Kate's rescue using his quick-witted verbal jibes as easily as his well-muscled physical alacrity.

Convinced that her "love Santa keeps getting stuck in the chimney," Kate is required to make an enormous leap of faith to find true happiness. Although she firmly believes that you can't live a fairy tale, that's exactly what happens to the modern-day Cinderella.

Despite Ryan's porcupine haircut and masculine attire (apparently reflective of her infiltration of a male-dominated field), she still manages to look great. Dressed in form-fitting clothes worthy of his noble birth, Jackman has no such obstacles to overcome, combining poise, charm, and virility to establish a regal presence. Sure, the time-traveling portal premise is ludicrous and the characters unbelievable stereotypes, but *Kate & Leopold* still manages to amuse, entertain, and, more important, arouse.

For more tales of courtly love, see Chapter 3. If you accept this movie's conclusion that time is "a 4-D pretzel of inevitability," you might also enjoy *Serendipity* in Chapter 8.

Do Try This at Home: Plan a private dinner for two on a rooftop, violinist optional.

Chapter 1

Roberts or Ryan?
1. In a popular romantic comedy of the late 1990s, did Julia Roberts or Meg Ryan fall in love with a bookstore owner?
Answer on page 207

Moonstruck (1987)

Cher, Nicolas Cage, Danny Aiello, Olympia Dukakis
DIRECTED BY NORMAN JEWISON
102 minutes; in color; PG
Intimacy Comfort Level: First Date, Going Steady, Committed/
    Married
Make-Out Meter: ▌▌▌▌▌
Just for Her: Cher's submission to the "wolf"
Just for Him: A question to ponder: "Why do men chase women?"

Bad luck, curses, full moons, and wolves seem to follow Loretta Castorini (Cher), a young Italian widow who is engaged to a longtime friend (Aiello) whom she doesn't really love. Days before the wedding, she meets his younger brother Ronny (Cage) and they fall for each other at first sight. Afraid of the bad luck that plagued her first marriage to a husband she loved, Loretta is sure that it's safer to marry a man she only likes.

A safer choice doesn't make a great date movie, however. While her concerns are understandable, sometimes watching her make the wrong decisions over and over makes you want to slap her and shout: "Snap out of it!"

Ronny is an angry, one-handed baker who has just a few days to persuade Loretta to marry him instead of his brother. Quickly he tries to convince her of his own philosophy: We aren't here to make things perfect. We're here to ruin ourselves, break our hearts, and love the wrong people.

Loretta goes from frumpy to fabulous as she blossoms in his loving embrace. Cher, Dukakis (who plays Loretta's mother, Rose), and screenwriter John Patrick Shanley received Academy Awards for their contributions to this beautiful tribute to love, family, Little Italy, and New York. Vincent Gardenia plays her philandering plumber father, Cosmo, and John Mahoney has a small part as a professor who likes to "inspire" young women.

Simultaneously funny, bittersweet, passionate, and moving, *Moonstruck* strikes a chord with men and women looking for romance. The film also seems to have struck a chord with the creators of *My Big Fat Greek Wedding*, the delightful 2002 romantic comedy that surely takes its inspiration from the frumpy ethnic character created in the earlier film.

For other cosmetic transformations, see *Ever After: A Cinderella Story* in Chapter 3; *America's Sweethearts*, *Miss Congeniality*, and *Shallow Hal* in Chapter 6; *Bedazzled* and *The Mask* in Chapter 8; and *Fletch*, *Shakespeare in Love*, and *Some Like It Hot* in Chapter 10.

Do Try This at Home: Buy something flashy to wear, change your hair, and completely revamp your look for a night out at the opera (or ballet, theater, symphony, etc.).

❧ *Notting Hill* (1999)

Julia Roberts, Hugh Grant, Rhys Ifans, Hugh Bonneville
DIRECTED BY ROGER MICHELL
124 minutes; in color; PG-13
Intimacy Comfort Level: First Date, Going Steady, Committed/Married
Make-Out Meter: ▮▮▮▮
Just for Her: The final press conference
Just for Him: William's roommate

A charming, yet tongue-tied Englishman (Grant) develops a relationship with an elusive American beauty (Roberts) with the help of his friends. Sound like *Four Weddings and a Funeral*? Actually, it's *Two Books and an Orange Juice*. That's what it takes to bring together the handsome bookseller, William Thacker, and the famous American film star, Anna Scott.

Business at William's travel bookstore seems to have flown south for the winter, and he's taken a permanent vacation from the dating scene. In fact, he lives a strange half-life that involves nothing other than work at the bookshop and dinner with friends. Yet, through a set of strange coincidences, ruthless paparazzi, a ridiculous roommate, an unexpected visit from Anna's boyfriend

(Alec Baldwin), a jar of honeyed apricots, one erotic encounter, and, of course, two books and an orange juice, the unlikely pair get together.

William is a "fairly level-headed bloke" who until recently went by the nickname of "Floppy" and still uses phrases like "whoopsie daisies." He politely goes to work each day in his modest little bookshop with the blue door and returns to his modest little house with the blue door each night until that fateful day when Notting Hill meets Beverly Hills. In addition, William is only partially recovered from an earlier broken heart that has made him fearful of love.

Conversely, Anna has international fame and enormous riches, plus a checkered past with a string of boyfriends, nude photos, and explicit film footage of her. Admittedly rash and stupid, she isn't sure what she wants, but she's beginning to figure things out.

Both need to overcome their personal obstacles in order to settle down in any permanent relationship, and in this particular relationship, they must get past her fame and his obscurity to make a marriage work.

Anna is not one of Roberts's most endearing roles because it's hard to sympathize with the rich, beautiful international star who has everything but happiness (and privacy). She's far more sympathetic than in her role as Jules in *My Best Friend's Wedding* (Chapter 2) but slightly less so than as Vivian in *Pretty Woman* (Chapter 5).

It's really William's story anyway. Grant has never been more lovable than as the poor guy shot with love heroin who can't get another fix. He bumbles his way through this stylish film with a strong sense of place and humor, ranging from subtle to slapstick.

Richard Curtis wrote *Notting Hill* and *Four Weddings and a Funeral*, both of which are packed with charm, wit, and warmth. The idea of the world's most famous movie star falling for an average guy who runs an unsuccessful little bookshop isn't the most plausible, but is certainly enjoyable, thus making the characters of *Notting Hill* "surreal, but nice."

For another lonely bookstore owner who always says the wrong thing, see *You've Got Mail* in Chapter 2, and for another movie star falling in love under the spotlight of media scrutiny, see *America's Sweethearts* in Chapter 6.

Do Try This at Home: Engrave something in honor of your relationship.

❧ *Runaway Bride* (1999)

Julia Roberts, Richard Gere, Joan Cusack, Rita Wilson
DIRECTED BY GARRY MARSHALL
116 minutes; in color; PG
Intimacy Comfort Level: First Date, Going Steady, Committed/Married
Make-Out Meter: ▮▮▮▮
Just for Her: His idea of a marriage proposal
Just for Him: Her idea of a marriage proposal

New York newspaper columnist Ike Graham (Gere) regularly writes bitter diatribes against women, which essentially alienate him from half the readers of *USA Today*. A last-minute man who waits for inspiration to hit right before deadline, he hears a story in a bar about Maggie Carpenter (Roberts), a woman living in Hale, Maryland, who entices men to marry her then abandons them at the altar.

Nearing his deadline with no other prospects in sight, he latches on to this idea and makes Maggie the focus of his column. When the published article is revealed to contain numerous inaccuracies, Ike gets fired by his editor/ex-wife (Wilson). Seeking vindication, he visits the town where Maggie lives so he can prove the story's validity. On the brink of another wedding, she is basking in her self-absorbed glory until the brash reporter comes to Hale in anticipation of another humiliated groom left standing alone in the church.

The man-eating Maggie "may not be Hale's longest running joke, but she's certainly the fastest," her father likes to say. In fact, her irrational fear of weddings and her apparent lack of remorse make her such a popular topic of gossip that the mayor tells the entire town to quit talking about her for awhile.

Maggie flits and flirts through town, bragging of her abilities to "charm the one-eyed snake." Despite his dislike for her, Ike finds himself fighting a growing attraction. He warns her that she's going to run away again—and, of course, he'll be there to report it. In addition, their conflicts include his goading her into deciding her egg preference and her chiding him for not really *seeing* women.

The small town includes some peculiar residents, including Joan Cusack as Peggy Fleming (not the skater), Maggie's long-suffering best friend since childhood, Paul Dooley as her alcoholic father, and Laurie Metcalf as Betty Trout, the local baker who prepared all the various wedding cakes for the bride-to-be.

Maggie's anxiety with everything connected to weddings is fun to watch, and you can take some comfort in knowing that she suffers for the pain she inflicts on her jilted suitors. But even so, you'll want her to succeed in spite of herself.

You'll also be rooting for Ike as his hard-hearted approach to love softens into mush. His appreciation of music and ability to make friends easily in the small town help make him seem more human and less of the hard-nosed stereotype that he is when in New York. Eventually, Ike and Maggie form a bond, recognize their weaknesses, and bring the film to a highly satisfying ending.

Although the conclusion is wildly romantic and just what you're hoping for, one niggling question remains: How did Maggie get away with keeping all those engagement rings from the guys she jilted?

For more sizzling chemistry between Roberts and Gere (and another fine supporting role for Hector Elizondo) see *Pretty Woman* in Chapter 5.

Do Try This at Home: Snuggle on the floor drinking wine in front of the fireplace.

❧ *The Wedding Planner* (2000)

Jennifer Lopez, Matthew McConaughey, Bridgette Wilson-Sampras, Alex Rocco

DIRECTED BY ADAM SHANKMAN

104 minutes; in color; PG-13

Intimacy Comfort Level: First Date, Going Steady, Committed/Married

Make-Out Meter: ▮▮▮▮▮

Just for Her: Ballroom dancing; the limestone statue scene; Steve's confession

Just for Him: Manly bonding in the gym; gratuitous shots of Lopez's famous backside

Detail-oriented Mary Fiore (Lopez) seems destined to remain always a wedding planner, never a bride, because of her cynical attitude. She says that selecting the song "I Honestly Love You" or teal bridesmaids' dresses are sure signs of a doomed marriage.

Living alone in her ridiculously neat apartment where she eats TV dinners

Mary (Jennifer Lopez) proves to Dr. Steve (Matthew McConaughey) that she's an excellent planner and dancer, but she still needs help with romantic commitments in *The Wedding Planner*. (Ron Batzdorff/Copyright © 2001 Columbia Pictures; courtesy of Photofest)

on TV trays in front of the TV each night, she watches others find love and happiness—in real life and on television. Disillusioned by her own broken engagement, she compulsively plans romantic weddings for others, yet secretly believes that "love is just love." That is, until she meets Dr. Steve (McConaughey), a down-to-earth pediatrician who is "NID" (not into details).

After her life (and Gucci shoe) are saved from a runaway dumpster by Dr. Steve, this compulsively organized wedding planner becomes unraveled and somewhat NID herself, deliriously telling him that he smells like "sweet red plums and grilled cheese sandwiches." The doctor's engagement to a beautiful woman named Fran (Wilson-Sampras) and Mary's job as their wedding planner make the situation a little complicated.

Add her father's frantic attempts to find her a husband and Mary's quest for a full partnership at her company to the mix, and you've got two confused couples, the bride's eccentric parents, one unhappy father, one greedy boss, and one frazzled assistant in a warm, fuzzy film that will keep you smiling.

As the wedding planner, Mary hides a wedding emergency kit inside her jacket at all times. The only emergency she can't handle is her rush of romantic feelings. Lopez fully embraces the role with a sweet vulnerability beneath her control-freak exterior that makes it easy to overlook some of the story's many contrivances.

Rocco lays it on a little thick as her meddling, Italian father who would do anything to see his daughter married (happily or otherwise). Likewise, Kathy Najimy overplays Mary's boss a little, wringing cloying emotion from scenes that don't carry much weight within the story.

So don't examine the movie too closely; just sit back, get ready to laugh, and feel the love. *The Wedding Planner* is a perfect union of comedy and romance; just don't peek under the veil looking for something else.

For more parents trying to push their children into loveless marriages, see *Crouching Tiger, Hidden Dragon* in Chapter 3, *George of the Jungle* in Chapter 9, and *Coming to America* and *Shakespeare in Love* in Chapter 10.

Do Try This at Home: Plan A: Watch a romantic movie outdoors (if any parks in your area do this). Plan B: Toast marshmallows over candlelight.

❧ *The Wedding Singer* (1997)

Adam Sandler, Drew Barrymore, Christine Taylor, Alan Covert
DIRECTED BY FRANK CORACI
96 minutes; in color; PG-13
Intimacy Comfort Level: First Date, Going Steady, Committed/Married
Make-Out Meter: ❙❙❙
Just for Her: The "educational purposes" kiss; Sandler's serenade on the
    airplane
Just for Him: The slow dance at the bar mitzvah

Wedding singer Robbie Hart (Sandler) is a born romantic who lives up to his name as someone whose heart was robbed of love. He adores his fiancée so much that he overlooks her obvious faults. He enjoys giving singing lessons so much that he takes payment in meatballs from an elderly pupil. He takes so much pride in his work as a wedding singer that he saves wedding parties from jealous best men, drunken teenagers, and others who threaten to ruin the blessed event.

In fact, Robbie's life is one continually playing silly love song from the 1980s until he's left at the altar on his wedding day. Suddenly, he hates everything associated with weddings—especially that his close friend Julia (Barrymore), a cute wedding waitress, is engaged to marry a rich, two-timing *Miami Vice* wannabe.

Robbie's new attitude is reflected in this conversation with a father footing the bill at a wedding reception. The dissatisfied father loudly complains to the wedding singer, who makes the crowd miserable with his lovesick ramblings onstage. "Hey buddy," the man yells, "I'm not paying you to share your thoughts on life. I'm paying you to sing."

The wedding singer replies with an answer that increases in volume as it increases in hostility. "Well, I have a microphone and you don't, so you will listen to every damn word I have to say."

As Robbie reluctantly helps Julia plan her wedding, he can't help falling in love with her, despite the odds. Also complicating the situation is Julia's sleazy cousin (Taylor), who decides that Robbie is her soul mate—or at the very least bedmate. Then Robbie's disillusioned best friend has an emotional meltdown and his repentant former fiancée comes to call. How much can a starving wedding singer who lives in his sister's basement and survives on meatballs take?

Sandler is surprisingly lovable as the wedding singer. His vulnerable character and pained expression may even feel a bit too familiar for anyone who's experienced a similar last-minute wedding cancellation. The unevenly paced film keeps us wondering what comes next: a lively song, clever one-liner, angry display, or romantic encounter?

Highlights include the 1980s-based soundtrack, cultural references to Madonna, Michael Jackson, and Freddy Krueger, Sandler's furious rendition of "Love Stinks," and cameos by Steve Buscemi, Jon Lovitz, Billy Idol, and Kevin Nealon. After an hour and a half of hearty laughs, the tears-to-the-eye ending is most welcome.

For more singers in love, see *Annie Hall* in Chapter 5, *The Mask* in Chapter 8, and *Some Like it Hot* in Chapter 10.

Do Try This at Home: Give up the window seat for your lover on long trips.

Barrymore or Bullock?
1. Did Drew Barrymore or Sandra Bullock make her feature film
acting debut as a little girl in the psychedelic sci-fi
adventure *Altered States* in 1980?
Answer on page 205

Want more weddings? See a restaurant reviewer longing to taste her own wedding cake in *My Best Friend's Wedding* in Chapter 2, a beautiful princess engaged to a gruesome prince in *The Princess Bride* in Chapter 3, a clumsy boyfriend who longs to be a groom in *Meet the Parents* in Chapter 4, a monstrous love affair in *Shrek* in Chapter 3, two weddings put on hold because of a chance meeting in *Serendipity* in Chapter 8, and one man with two weddings in *Coming to America* in Chapter 10.

Chapter 2

Literate Ladies in Love

I sound my barbaric yawp from the rooftops of the world.
Walt Whitman

WHETHER THEY WRITE for magazines, deliver broadcast news, or work at bookstores, literate ladies enjoy words almost as much as they enjoy men. This professional mastery of words makes for some delightful repartee between the women and their equally educated men. But for every clever comeback that advances the romance, there are two outbursts or insults dragging it back.

You see, these independent thinkers have something in common besides their intelligence and wit. Literate ladies have a knack for selecting precisely the right words while on the job and precisely the wrong words while talking to the men they love.

Take the self-absorbed, internationally renowned journalist Tess Harding (Katharine Hepburn) in the 1942 comedy *Woman of the Year*. Despite her condescending attitude and belittling behavior toward her husband (Spencer Tracy), she is awarded Woman of the Year. As she leaves home to attend the awards dinner, her long-neglected husband decides not to attend because of a commitment made to an orphaned child. To calm her fears about what people will think of his absence from the big event, her husband tells her to say that he had something important to do instead. She snaps back that no one would ever believe that he could have anything more important in his life. Her demeaning remark has the intended effect . . . and more.

In *Crossing Delancey*, bookstore community relations manager Isabelle Grossman (Amy Irving) is simultaneously attracted to and repulsed by traditional pickle man Sam Posner (Peter Riegert). After he woos her with a polite invitation, family history, and a new hat, she pays a visit to his store, apparently to accept his romantic overtures. However, after seeing his hairy hands and wrists immersed in barrels of stinky pickle juice, she blurts out that she only came by to say thanks and that he should expend his good romantic energy on some other girl who might appreciate it. After her meandering speech, she apologizes for not being able to express herself.

Angrily, Sam responds, "You did fine."

Isabelle also does a fine job expressing her desire for Sam to go out with a close friend, only to discover, once the words are spoken, that she really wants him for herself. Throughout *Crossing Delancey*, this literate lady's mouth is one page ahead of her heart.

In an unexpected twist from the typical talkative literate lady, magazine columnist Andie Anderson (Kate Hudson) purposely says the wrong things to break up her romance in just over a week in the 2003 comedy *How to Lose a Guy in 10 Days*. In researching an article about what not to do, she tries baby talk, whiny complaints, jealous rages, emasculating nicknames, and rushed commitment in order to get her new boyfriend to dump her within the allotted time. As if her words weren't bad enough, her actions are just as irritating. Andie combines her street smarts, dating experience, manipulation of words, and master's degree to produce a thoroughly obnoxious woman who is charming only when her beautiful mouth is smiling, pouting, or better yet closed.

And pity television news reporter Bridget (Renée Zellweger) in the 2001 romantic comedy *Bridget Jones's Diary*, who spends most of the film apologizing to people for her inappropriate comments. Or bookstore owner Kathleen Kelly (Meg Ryan) in *You've Got Mail*, who laments her inability to shoot zingers yet finds her flapping trap nearly ruins the best relationship she's ever had. Ryan's character also has trouble expressing herself in *Sleepless in Seattle*, where she plays a newspaper reporter who stands in the middle of the road, speechless, when called upon to talk to the man she's been longing to meet. She finally musters up enough courage and poise to mutter "hello." And in *When Harry Met Sally*, Ryan, a reporter yet again, always says too much or too little.

Male reporters in the movies are an entirely different breed. Their preoccupation concerns getting the job done at any cost, rather than manipulating their words both on and off the job. In *Runaway Bride* (Chapter 1), columnist Ike Graham (Richard Gere) forges ahead with his newspaper articles even though he's destroying an emotionally troubled woman's life. Likewise in *Roman Holiday* (Chapter 3), a reporter for the American News Service, Joe Bradley (Gregory Peck), pursues a hurtful behind-the-scenes story without the subject's knowledge.

In *One Fine Day* (Chapter 5), a popular newspaper columnist (George Clooney) goes to great lengths to track down a source and seek out his new love. In *Breakfast at Tiffany's* (Chapter 6), an author (George Peppard) continues to write despite his breaking heart. And in *Fletch* (Chapter 10), investigative reporter Irwin Fletcher (Chevy Chase) researches an article for his "Jane Doe" column that will wreck a woman's marriage and put her husband in jail. Sure they're preoccupied, but with male reporters the problem usually relates to their actions rather than their words.

But you can always count on literate ladies to say something stupid to lose (or at least alienate) their men before they learn to keep their oh-so-educated opinions to themselves once in a while. Remember that old journalistic motto: Who? What? When? Where? and Why? For some reason, these particular women always forget to ask that final question about their personal lives. Yes, the pen may be mightier than the sword, but with literate ladies in love, the pen is not as mighty as the mouth. Luckily, love is the mightiest of all.

❧ *Bridget Jones's Diary* (2001)

Renée Zellweger, Colin Firth, Hugh Grant, Sally Phillips
DIRECTED BY SHARON MAGUIRE
92 minutes; in color; R
Intimacy Comfort Level: Going Steady, Committed/Married
Make-Out Meter: ▮▮▮
Just for Her: The concept of "comfort food" during times of emotional crisis
Just for Him: Fistfight; Bridget in her underwear

Thirty-something, overweight, and unhappily single, Bridget Jones (Zellweger) leaves her publishing job after a disastrous fling with her lustful boss, Daniel Cleaver (Grant), and moves on to broadcast journalism to become a news presenter for *Sit Up Britain*, a current-affairs show. In addition to the trauma of a failed relationship and a career shift, she endures a family crisis in which her mother leaves her father for a home shopping channel marketer.

During the tumultuous year chronicled in the film, Bridget continually meets and insults the handsome human rights lawyer Mark Darcy (Firth), who has some unfinished personal business with handsome human rights violator

Daniel. Mark isn't exactly complimentary toward her either; he describes her as a "verbally incontinent spinster who drinks like a fish, smokes like a chimney, and dresses like her mother." Without question, Bridget, a self-described lunatic, is an appallingly bad public speaker and isn't really that adept at private conversations either.

Despite their awkward first meeting and subsequent unpleasant encounters, they temporarily form a bond when Mark uses his legal connections to help her get an exclusive interview with a political refugee.

Eventually, Bridget and Mark acknowledge a growing attraction for each other, but the relationship gets sidelined by Daniel's intrusion, a misunderstanding, and a careless diary entry. Bridget relies on cigarettes, desserts, booze, and her dysfunctional friends until she learns that she can rely on Mark. We can only hope that someday she'll rely on herself.

Based on Helen Fielding's bestselling novel of the same name (and loosely adapted from Jane Austen's *Pride and Prejudice*), the film reportedly required Zellweger to gain nearly twenty-five pounds for the role, all of which are evident in her scantily clad final scene in the snow. As Bridget, Zellweger is funny, endearing, and enormously irritating, as is her love interest, Mark.

Although Fielding's fans initially objected to an American actress playing the role, Zellweger mastered the accent and soon won them over with her feisty performance as the bloated Brit. The actress actually worked at a British publishing house incognito, using her feigned accent in order to prepare for the role.

Richard Curtis, who cowrote the screenplay, also wrote the English romances *Notting Hill* and *Four Weddings and a Funeral*, both in Chapter 1. For more adaptations of Jane Austen novels, see *Emma* in Chapter 1 and *Sense and Sensibility* in Chapter 6.

Do Try This at Home: Keep romantic diary entries or sexy books in places where they might be "accidentally discovered" by your partner.

Gere or Grant?
**2. Did Richard Gere or Hugh Grant receive a Golden Globe award
in 1994 for best actor in a comedy?**
Answer on page 206

❧ *Crossing Delancey* (1988)

Amy Irving, Peter Riegert, Jeroen Krabbe, Reizl Bozyk
DIRECTED BY JOAN MICKLIN SILVER
97 minutes; in color; PG
Intimacy Comfort Level: First Date, Going Steady, Committed/Married
Make-Out Meter: **▎▎▎**
Just for Her: A meddling grandma
Just for Him: A nice guy gets the girl without getting beat up, publicly
    humiliated, or kicked in the crotch

A modern, independent, thirty-something Jewish woman, Isabelle Grossman (Irving), is determined to enjoy her single status and respected position organizing readings and signings at an upscale independent bookstore on the Upper West Side of New York City. Her matchmaking grandmother (Bozyk) enters the scene and helps set up a date for her granddaughter with a traditional pickle maker (Riegert).

A suave, egotistical novelist (Krabbe) who also pursues Isabelle (and just happens to be gentile) makes a nice contrast to the simple Jewish pickle man who needs to soak his hands in vanilla every night to combat the smell of garlic on his fingers. The novelist represents everything that Isabelle thinks she wants out of life.

Teasing from her coworkers, pressure from her grandmother, attention from a male friend, and that ever-ticking biological clock sometimes make her protestations about the joys of single life ring a little hollow. The question is whether this intelligent, educated, well-spoken woman can find the right road to happiness.

Adapted from a play by Susan Sandler, the story pits tradition against change, old against young, simplicity against complexity, and natural against artificial. A definite sense of place, several highly memorable surrealistic scenes, and lively background music by The Roches (plus Suzzy Roche in a featured role as one of Isabelle's in-your-face friends) add some needed edge to this otherwise sweet romance.

Granted, *Crossing Delancey* has some chick-flick tendencies, but the peek behind the New York literary scene, the senior citizen's self-defense class, the grandmother's scheming, the pompous authors, and Isabelle's a-little-too-late revelation make this a fun date movie for men and women—and no, you don't have to be Jewish to enjoy it.

For more date movies in which ethnicity plays a role, see *Moonstruck* in Chapter 1, *Crouching Tiger, Hidden Dragon* in Chapter 3, *Meet the Parents* in Chapter 4, *Annie Hall* in Chapter 5, *Rocky* in Chapter 6, *Big Trouble in Little China* and *Witness* in Chapter 7, and *Coming to America* and *Maid in Manhattan* in Chapter 10.

Do Try This at Home: Send a surprise gift to your lover when he or she least expects it (and perhaps doesn't even deserve it).

❧ *How to Lose a Guy in 10 Days* (2003)

Kate Hudson, Matthew McConaughey, Bebe Neuwirth, Robert Klein
DIRECTED BY DONALD PETRIE
116 minutes; in color; PG-13
Intimacy Comfort Level: Going Steady, Committed/Married
Make-Out Meter: ❙❙❙
Just for Her: Stuffed animals; stuffed medicine chest
Just for Him: Motorcycle rides; boys' poker night

To write an article about how to lose a guy in ten days, *Composure* magazine columnist Andie Anderson (Kate Hudson) must research common mistakes made by women early in the dating relationship. She could interview various women about their dating disasters, scrutinize their behavior, analyze the material, and synthesize the findings. But it's so much more entertaining to watch Andie get hands-on experience trying to sabotage a relationship all by herself.

One minute, she's sexy and adoring; the next, she's plotting with his mother and planning their family album. As the target of her seemingly psychotic attentions, Benjamin Barry (Matthew McConaughey) has a secret agenda of his own; he has bet his boss (Klein) that he can make a woman fall in love with him in the same amount of time. If he proves that she's truly in love, he wins a lucrative diamond account that his advertising agency recently secured.

Like frustrated advertising copywriter Nick Marshall (Mel Gibson) in *What Women Want* (see Chapter 8), Ben must show that he can get inside the mind of women and make them believe that they want what he wants—in this case, for them to buy diamonds. Unfortunately, Ben lacks Nick's supernatural ability to read women's minds. And unbeknownst to him, Andie is doing everything in

If only their motives were as beautiful as their smiles. Kate Hudson and Matthew McConaughey lie and scheme to get what they want in *How to Lose a Guy in 10 Days.* (Paramount Pictures/Michael Gibson; courtesy of Photofest)

her power to ruin the relationship that he is doing everything in his power to preserve.

Andie has much in common with the other literate ladies in this chapter. Beautiful, brainy, and incapable of keeping her big mouth closed when it would serve her best interests to do so, she is a role model of what not to do while dating (see Julia Roberts in *My Best Friend's Wedding* in this chapter for more inspiration). Then again, if you look like Kate Hudson or Julia Roberts, a guy might be more willing to put up with such annoying behaviors as piling stuffed animals on his bed or dragging him to a Celine Dion concert.

The beginning of the movie where they set up the ridiculous premise takes too much time to get some laughs, and the ending is all too predictable. However, the bulk of the movie features very funny scenes, light romance, and appealing stars. Based on a book by Michele Alexander and Jeannie Long, *How to Lose a Guy in 10 Days* should please anyone who's made it past ten days in a relationship.

For McConaughey in another amiable role as a boyfriend who deceives and gets deceived, see *The Wedding Planner* in Chapter 1.

Do Try This at Home: Don't be afraid to try couples therapy if a troubled relationship is worth saving.

❧ *L.A. Story* (1991)

Steve Martin, Victoria Tennant, Richard E. Grant, Marilu Henner
DIRECTED BY MICK JACKSON
98 minutes; in color; PG-13
Intimacy Comfort Level: First Date, Going Steady, Committed/Married
Make-Out Meter: ▮▮▮▮
Just for Her: The weatherman's confession that he would alter all of nature
    to keep his love from flying back to England
Just for Him: Sarah Jessica Parker as the ultimate Valley Girl

Despite previous bad luck with relationships, Los Angeles weatherman Harris K. Telemacher (Martin) is convinced that there's someone out there for him, even if he needs a pick axe, compass, and night goggles to find her. Bored beyond belief with his current job and preening girlfriend (Henner), he flips over an intelligent, tuba-playing Brit (Tennant), a reporter who has come to L.A. to write an article. Unknown to Harris, she also uses the visit for a possible reconciliation with her ex-husband (Grant).

Undergoing a personal and professional crisis, Harris briefly finds comfort with a sexy Valley Girl (Parker), who enters the unhappy group with delightful consequences that culminate in a painfully funny scene at a romantic little inn, reminiscent of the switched pairs of lovers from William Shakespeare's *Midsummer Night's Dream*, a play that is loosely adapted here. In fact, if you're a fan of the Bard, look for references and inside jokes throughout the entire movie.

In a clever script written by Martin, the film uses humor, insight, and supernatural events to offer a tribute to love and Los Angeles, a city where the weather apparently never changes. In an unusual variation, this particular literate lady in love says too little instead of too much. But even when there's nothing to talk about, these two can always discuss the weather.

Light and whimsical, *L.A. Story* adds museum performance art, a talking billboard, New Age parodies, and comments about human nature in general and superficiality in L.A. in particular to the eclectic mix. This truly romantic film was Martin's response to the 1989 trio of shorts *New York Stories*.

For another supernatural love story with Martin and (former wife) Tennant see *All of Me*, and for another strange tale of a weatherman in love see *Groundhog Day*, both in Chapter 8. For more L.A. stories, see *Speed* in Chapter 4, *Pretty Woman* in Chapter 5, *Kindergarten Cop* in Chapter 7, and *Fletch* in Chapter 10.

Do Try This at Home: Kiss outside in the pouring rain.

❧ *Love & Sex* (2000)

Famke Janssen, Jon Favreau, Noah Emmerich, Ann Magnuson
DIRECTED BY VALERIE BREIMAN
82 minutes; in color; not rated, comparable to R
Intimacy Comfort Level: Going Steady, Committed/Married
Make-Out Meter: ❚❚❚❚
Just for Her: Risk-free, vicarious thrills from a very promiscuous
 lifestyle
Just for Him: Janssen's long, skinny legs; a visit to Earl's Pornorama

The story begins with a flashback to young Kate Welles (Janssen) on the school playground (see *Miss Congeniality* in Chapter 6 for a similar beginning). She ruins her first secret love affair by blabbing about it to the class gossip, thus establishing her penchant for saying the wrong thing at an early age.

The story then flashes forward to the present where Kate is now a writer for a major women's magazine. Assigned to write a "perfect relationship" story, she instead turns it into a how-to sex article. Under the threat of termination, she is forced to rewrite the article by the end of the day as a squeaky clean take on modern relationships.

In researching the article, she reflects on her own sordid past, which includes a much-older high school teacher, a married man, a basketball player, an action-movie star, and an artist named Adam Levy (Favreau). Kate's reverie makes a few things perfectly clear: she talks too much, has sex too soon, thinks about death too often, and has very large feet.

Although Kate and Adam share great love for each other, they also share insecurities. She worries so much about saying the wrong thing that she talks nonstop during times when silence would be more appropriate. He is uncomfortable with his relative lack of sexual experience. (See *Four Weddings and a Funeral* in Chapter 1 for a similar scenario.) Even though they engage in romantic endeavors like aiming for the longest kiss ever, they agree that the timing isn't quite right for this relationship to work.

Breiman also was the screenwriter for the film, which is semiautobiographical. Filled with many funny moments, *Love & Sex* also examines the unfunny complications that arise from equating love with sex and from trying to make any long-term relationship work. Watch for a cameo by *Friends* star David Schwimmer.

For another mismatched neurotic couple, see *Annie Hall* in Chapter 5.

Do Try This at Home: Create nicknames for each other.

❥ *My Best Friend's Wedding* (1997)

Julia Roberts, Dermot Mulroney, Cameron Diaz, Rupert Everett
DIRECTED BY P. J. HOGAN
105 minutes; in color; PG-13
Intimacy Comfort Level: Going Steady, Committed/Married
Make-Out Meter: ▌▌▌
Just for Her: An anatomically correct ice sculpture
Just for Him: "Cat fight" in the ladies room

This is not your typical date movie. Jules (Roberts), an aggressive Chicago restaurant reviewer with an acidic tongue, has an agreement with her best friend Michael (Mulroney) that if neither finds their true love by age twenty-eight, they will marry each other. As the deadline looms ahead in the not-too-distant future, Michael suddenly announces his engagement to someone else. Only then does Jules realize that she is in love with Michael and always has been.

Naturally, Jules decides a few days before his wedding to the most perfect woman on earth that she needs to break up their relationship at any cost. She attempts several devious methods of breaking up the happy couple, such as publicly embarrassing the bride, sending a deceptive email, and even enlisting the help of her gay friend George (Everett) to serve as her own fake fiancé.

A restaurant critic (Julia Roberts) is highly critical of her friend's (Dermot Mulroney) fiancée in *My Best Friend's Wedding*. Here, she invites Kimmy (Cameron Diaz), her rival, to sing at a karaoke club. (Suzanne Tenner/Copyright © 1997 TriStar Pictures; courtesy of Photofest)

As Kimmy, the lovely bride-to-be, Diaz provides an example of the right way to behave; she sincerely tries to embrace everything and everyone in Michael's life, including Jules, whom Michael has placed on a pedestal all these years. We're about to see exactly how far she can fall off that pedestal.

As the insanely jealous best friend of the groom-to-be, Jules provides the opposite example. Though quick-witted, it's a dark humor she possesses. Poor Jules seems incapable of controlling her harsh words and callous deeds. Her wild antics range from comedic to malicious.

Too late she realizes what might have been if she had shown more love, been less selfish, and valued relationships more. In fact, if she had said those three little words early and often, her best friend would not be marrying someone else.

As a food critic always ready to take the next bite out of something (or someone), Jules eventually learns to keep her mouth shut. Funny, sexy, and sad, this film may or may not have the traditional storybook ending (depending upon your perspective). Yet it still stirs up romantic feelings, and the ensemble cast is terrific.

For Diaz in another role as the perfect woman, see *There's Something About Mary* in Chapter 10. For more nuptial neurosis, see Chapter 1.

Do Try This at Home: Take pleasure in your partner's public displays of affection toward you.

Roberts or Ryan?
2. Was Julia Roberts or Meg Ryan the highest paid actress in Hollywood in 2001?
Answer on page 207

❥ *Sleepless in Seattle* (1993)

Tom Hanks, Meg Ryan, Bill Pullman, Rob Reiner
DIRECTED BY NORA EPHRON
105 minutes; in color; PG
Intimacy Comfort Level: Going Steady, Committed/Married
Make-Out Meter: ▐▐▐
Just for Her: Sentimental discussions of fate, love, and romance
Just for Him: Advice on modern dating; men making fun of chick flicks

Lonely widower Sam Baldwin (Hanks) is unwillingly placed on a national radio talk show by his equally lonely son. Under the call-in name "Sleepless in Seattle," he confides to the host that he would like to find the right woman. His first marriage was so blissfully happy that he doubts ever finding a comparable relationship.

Newspaper reporter Annie Reed (Ryan), who's already engaged and living in Baltimore, hears him on the radio and decides to research his story with the help and encouragement of her editor and best friend (Rosie O'Donnell). Her professional interest in the article, however, is merely a disguise for her personal obsession.

Annie writes a letter suggesting they meet on top of the Empire State Building on Valentine's Day like the lovers do in the 1957 film *An Affair to Remember* (which you might also want to rent if you're in the mood for a good cry). When Sam decides not to meet with her, his son travels there alone.

In New York for her bridal registry, this usually decisive reporter must decide whether or not she really wants to marry her fiancé (Pullman) or keep searching for the "magic" that might be waiting for her on top of the Empire State Building. Sam and Annie seem so right for each other that it's almost painful waiting to see what happens.

Tension and excitement build throughout the movie, but the delayed meeting might disappoint those craving upfront action, and the dead wife/cute kid scenario could be a little uncomfortable for a first date. With its idyllic romanticism and clever insights into relationships, *Sleepless in Seattle* provides a modern love story complete with computer background checks, long-distance love, and blended families.

For more cute kids playing cupid, see *The American President*, *Jerry Maguire*, and *One Fine Day* in Chapter 5; *Kindergarten Cop*, *Me, Myself & Irene* (if you consider three foul-mouthed, obese eighteen-year-olds cute), *True Lies* and *Witness* in Chapter 7; *The Birds* and *Chocolat* in Chapter 8; and *Maid in Manhattan* in Chapter 10.

Do Try This at Home: Arrange to meet in interesting places to break the routine and create an air of anticipation.

Roberts or Ryan?
3. Does Julia Roberts or Meg Ryan own the production company
Prufrock Pictures, named after a T. S. Eliot poem?
Answer on page 207

Harry (Billy Crystal) finally finds a way to keep Sally's (Meg Ryan) mouth shut for a while in *When Harry Met Sally*. (Courtesy of Photofest)

❧ *When Harry Met Sally* (1989)

Billy Crystal, Meg Ryan, Carrie Fisher, Bruno Kirby
DIRECTED BY ROB REINER
96 minutes; in color; R
Intimacy Comfort Level: Going Steady, Committed/Married
Make-Out Meter: ▌▌▌▌
Just for Her: How to fake a sexual response
Just for Him: Harry's explanation of why men and women can't be friends; rules for "holding"; dating advice

It takes twelve years and three months for *New York* magazine reporter Sally Allbright (Ryan) and political consultant Harry Burns (Crystal) to fall in love, but hey, it's worth it. The insightful screenplay by Nora Ephron, who was nominated for an Academy Award for her efforts, follows the perennially perky Sally and dark-sided Harry through their ever-changing relationship from the college years in 1977 through their present-day situation. Woven throughout their story are clips of interviews with older married couples who describe how they met each other.

She's always bright and happy (as implied by her last name), though so structured that she alphabetizes her videotapes on index cards. Like other literate ladies in love, she blurts out embarrassing comments at restaurants, talks too much, and says things like "I'm not your consolation prize" to Harry when he sincerely expresses affection. In short, Sally is a high-maintenance woman who believes that she's low maintenance.

Nicknamed "the angel of death," Harry reads the last chapter first in case he dies before finishing a book and mourns his failed marriage long past the normal grieving period. Another huge obstacle in their relationship is her belief in serial monogamy and his belief in sleeping with anyone who says yes.

Through Harry and Sally's relationships with other people and with each other, and the developing romance between their best friends, *When Harry Met Sally* explores the beginnings, middles, and endings of various love stories. Harry examines the crucial question, surely debated by the ancient Greek philosophers and every great mind since, "Can men and women really be friends without sex getting in the way?"

Funny, intelligent, and romantic, this terrific date film features a soundtrack by Marc Shaiman with special musical performances by Harry Connick Jr. and great supporting roles for Fisher and Kirby. It's so good you might want to alphabetize this DVD on an index card.

For another "Harry" who finds that the love of his life has been right in front of him all these years, see *True Lies* in Chapter 7. For another lesson in "faking it," see *All of Me* in Chapter 8.

Do Try This at Home: Develop a real friendship first.

CLASSIC DATE MOVIE SELECTION

❧ *Woman of the Year* (1942)

Katharine Hepburn, Spencer Tracy, Fay Bainter, Reginald Owen
DIRECTED BY GEORGE STEVENS
114 minutes; in black and white; not rated, comparable to PG
Intimacy Comfort Level: First Date, Going Steady, Committed/Married
Make-Out Meter: ❙❙
Just for Her: Tracy's witty, well-dressed wolf in disguise
Just for Him: Football and baseball

The first of nine movies that Hepburn and Tracy made together, *Woman of the Year* already exhibits the easy camaraderie that will last through many years to come. She plays Tess Harding, a much-admired political columnist who writes for the *New York Daily Chronicle* and appears on a radio show. He is Sam Craig, a lesser-known sportswriter for the same publication.

They meet after she ridicules sports on the radio show, saying that baseball is merely a worthless distraction from the country's war effort. He writes an angry rebuttal in his column, which she answers in her column. When their editor calls a truce between them, they celebrate by attending a baseball game together.

After a brief courtship, they marry and (against his wishes) live in her apartment. She speaks many different languages with her international admirers who frequently stop by to visit without notice. Sam feels out of place in his own home and increasingly out of place as Tess's husband. Her busy schedule, rude friends, and self-absorption damage the marriage seemingly beyond repair.

Attending the wedding of her father and maiden aunt, however, Tess has an epiphany and goes running back to Sam with a new attitude. But is a new attitude enough to compensate for her complete ineptitude in domestic matters?

Today's feminists might take issue with this movie, but should find some comfort in noting that Tess has a male secretary. Try putting yourself in a 1942 frame of mind in order to appreciate why *Woman of the Year* received an Academy Award for best original screenplay and Hepburn for best actress. Hepburn reportedly objected to the sexist ending herself, but was overruled by Stevens and producer Joseph L. Mankiewicz.

For other Katharine Hepburn films, see *Bringing Up Baby* in Chapter 5 and

The African Queen in Chapter 9.

Do Try This at Home: Send a short note with a bottle of wine for your small mistakes.

❧ *You've Got Mail* (1998)

Tom Hanks, Meg Ryan, Greg Kinnear, Parker Posey
DIRECTED BY NORA EPHRON
119 minutes; in color; PG
Intimacy Comfort Level: First Date, Going Steady, Committed/
    Married
Make-Out Meter: ▮▮▮▮▮
Just for Her: Mother–daughter twirling
Just for Him: An explanation of why *The Godfather* is so meaningful

What kind of people can you meet in an over-thirty chat room? Rooftop killers, the dangerously obese, married partners looking for extramarital affairs, and maybe—just maybe—the love of your life.

In *You've Got Mail*, enchanting independent children's bookshop owner Kathleen Kelly (Ryan), a.k.a. Shopgirl, has an anonymous, though progressively romantic, e-mail correspondence with ruthless chain bookstore owner Joe Fox (Hanks), a.k.a. NY152. They dislike each other intensely in person, but unknowingly fall in love with each other online.

When Joe first discovers the truth, he hides it from Kathleen in order to win her heart privately although he is destroying her business publicly. Meanwhile Kathleen, "a lone reed in the corrupt sands of commerce," watches helplessly as her mother's forty-two-year-old bookshop is run out of business by Fox & Sons Books. Her "small, but valuable life" is thrown into complete turmoil by the one man she hates the most, but unknowingly loves the most too.

The frequency and intensity of their e-mails increase as the sexual tension builds. Their lives and loves parallel each other as they decide whether to take their online romance to the next level. Ryan and Hanks are great together, and their flailing relationships with their current partners, the egomaniacal Frank (Kinnear) and cutthroat Patricia (Posey), are interesting reflections of themselves. Under the circumstances, their own love–hate relationship is believable, expected, and enormous fun.

Ultimately, their business conflict releases the trapped novelist inside her and their personal relationship restores her faith in love. Professionally and personally, the tongue-tied Shopgirl finds her voice.

Throughout the movie, we know far more than the characters do about their growing relationship. When Joe eventually learns the identity of his email correspondent, he is in on our secret. Watching Kathleen's growing awareness becomes more and more pleasurable as Joe continues to gently manipulate the situation in his favor.

You've Got Mail has cute kids, furry dogs, red roses, fresh daisies, hidden identities, mystery dates, chance meetings, initial hatred, good chemistry, clever dialogue, descriptive music, a much-delayed first kiss, and an excellent supporting cast. It's hard to match this kind of romanticism, except perhaps in the earlier two versions (*The Shop Around the Corner* [1940] starring Margaret Sullavan and James Stewart and *In the Good Old Summertime* [1949], a musical version starring Judy Garland and Van Johnson).

For other romantic notes and letters, see *A Knight's Tale* in Chapter 3, *Say Anything* in Chapter 5, *Roxanne* in Chapter 6, and *Shakespeare in Love* in Chapter 10.

Do Try This at Home: Send each other romantic e-mails.

Still longing for more literate ladies in love? Enjoy an editor and a writer on assignment in Indiana in *June Bride* in Chapter 1, a newspaper reporter and an Australian adventurer in *Crocodile Dundee*, a librarian seeking love (and an ancient book) in *The Mummy*, a romance novelist and a mercenary seeking buried treasure in Colombia in *Romancing the Stone*, and a feisty magazine editor stranded on a deserted island with a crusty pilot in *Six Days, Seven Nights*, all in Chapter 9.

Chapter 3

Once Upon a Time

*I've had several years in Hollywood and I still think the movie
heroes are in the audience.*
Wilson Mizner

IF YOU THOUGHT LOVE was only true in fairy tales, these next ten
movies will make a firm believer out of you. Incorporating elements from classic children's fairy tales, these films playfully mix and match familiar fables and
fantasies to create exotic new love stories.

Although characters and stories are unique, the basic plot goes something
like this: A young man and woman of unequal status, or incompatible species,
fall in love with each other. (This romance often plays off the parallel subplot of
an older couple also falling love.) In order to pursue the romance, one of the
young lovers must don a disguise and enlist the help of an enchanted or magical helper. Ultimately, a magical transformation takes place, wherein one character changes from animal to human, dead to alive, peasant to noble, ugly to
beautiful or vice versa.

Take Cinderella, for instance. This classic children's story inspired *Ever After: A Cinderella Story*, *Pretty Woman* (Chapter 5), *Maid in Manhattan*, and *Working Girl* (Chapter 10) among countless others, including a reversed-sex version
in *Notting Hill* (Chapter 1). According to the story, a young woman lives in an
abusive household with her stepmother and two stepsisters. Forced to work as
a servant in her own home, Cinderella gets trapped in the house while her stepsisters attend the royal ball where the prince will seek his bride.

Cinderella has no hope for the future until her fairy godmother magically
appears, ready to grant her wishes. She then makes her grand appearance at the

ball in disguise and wins the prince's heart. After a countrywide search for the slender-footed woman who dropped her glass slipper, the prince finds Cinderella and they marry and live happily ever after. She transforms from the dirty girl in the cinders to the lovely woman in the castle.

Contrary to popular belief, fairy tales aren't just for children and don't always have happy endings. They began as oral traditions in the prescientific age meant to calm the fears of prepubescent children unable to understand nature, life, death, and most of all love. As the Brothers Grimm (and others) began to write these stories down for future generations, they edited, rewrote, and improvised to make the tales more interesting to a variety of readers.

With young women pricking their sensitive little fingers on revolving shafts of spinning wheels, carelessly wandering through wolf-filled woods, and awakening to love's first kiss, these stories often seem directed more at the parents than the children. (For an erotic retelling of the Little Red Riding Hood story that would make Sigmund Freud blush with its use of phallic symbols and birthing rites, try renting the 1984 Neil Jordan–directed horror film *The Company of Wolves* sometime.)

Whether historical or contemporary, great date movies display a creative use of fairy-tale imagery. A lovely young woman is forced into an arranged marriage with someone she hates (*Crouching Tiger, Hidden Dragon, Don Juan DeMarco, Ever After: A Cinderella Story, A Knight's Tale, Ladyhawke, Mannequin, The Princess Bride, Shrek*). Reliant on outside forces, she is the helpless female archetype who needs a hero, a little magic—and sometimes both—to help her survive.

A wretched villain, often an older woman in a motherly, nanny, or governess role (*Crouching Tiger, Hidden Dragon, Ever After: A Cinderella Story, Roman Holiday*) or an evil male rival (*Don Juan DeMarco, A Knight's Tale, Ladyhawke, Mannequin, The Princess Bride, Shrek, Splash*) emerges early and inflicts emotional and often physical pain on the woman and the newly introduced hero.

This hero, a brave young man who must leave home and endure various trials to establish himself, willingly (or through a change of heart) rises to the ultimate challenge of transforming himself for (or enabling the transformation of) the woman he loves (*Crouching Tiger, Hidden Dragon, Don Juan DeMarco, A Knight's Tale, Mannequin, The Princess Bride, Shrek, Splash*). Additional fairy-tale elements including magic potions, wishes, evil stepmothers, clever thieves, missing or dead parents, lucky numbers (three, seven, twelve), and triumph of good over evil usually work their way into these movies as well.

One of the most common elements, however, is the struggle with the pyramidal social class structure. In rural life before the French Revolution in 1789, 70 percent of the populace lived at the bottom of the pyramid as peasants. Above them were the bourgeoisie, and at the top were the aristocracy. As many of the fairy tales were collected by the Brothers Grimm from the peasants of this period, they reflect the frustration of being at the bottom of the heap and don't necessarily end happily.

Roman Holiday (1953), the classic date movie selection in this chapter, is a reverse fairy tale in which a beautiful princess longs to be a peasant—well, an average woman at any rate. After escaping from her room and disguising her appearance, she flirts with a handsome stranger and dances under the stars. So happy in her holiday from royal responsibilities, she fears the moment when the magic will dissolve and life will return to normal.

Although the times, places, characters, situations, and inevitable fight scenes differ, one characteristic remains the same in all of these Once Upon a Time romances: A miraculous transformation is needed for true love to flourish.

❧ *Crouching Tiger, Hidden Dragon* (2000)

Chow Yun Fat, Michelle Yeoh, Chang Chen, Zhang Ziyi
DIRECTED BY ANG LEE
120 minutes; in color; in Mandarin with English subtitles; PG-13
Intimacy Comfort Level: Going Steady, Committed/Married
Make-Out Meter: ▌▌▌
Just for Her: A long, lustful flashback
Just for Him: Rooftop chases; treetop martial arts

Long ago and far away in nineteenth-century China, a magical 400-year-old sword called The Green Destiny helps bring together two sets of lovers. Li Mu Bai (Chow) and Yu Shu Lien (Yeoh) are master warriors secretly in love with each other, but kept apart by a sacred promise.

Jen Yu (Zhang), a gifted young martial artist and daughter of the governor, must prepare herself for an arranged marriage to a man she doesn't love. Lo (Chang), a.k.a. Dark Cloud, is a hunted bandit in love with Jen. An evil murderer who goes by the name Jade Fox torments both sets of lovers throughout their adventures.

Two warriors (Chang Chen and Zhang Ziyi) decide to stop crouching and hiding for a while so they can put their energy elsewhere in *Crouching Tiger, Hidden Dragon*. (Chan Kan Chuen/Sony Pictures Classics; courtesy of Photofest)

The story begins two weeks before the arranged marriage is scheduled to take place. The plot is set into motion when Li Mu Bai gives up the sword and decides to retire from his life as a warrior, presumably to pursue his love life with Yu Shu Lien. The cycle of bloodshed continues, however, when The Green Destiny is stolen by a masked thrill seeker, who inadvertently sets a series of tragic events into motion.

Part martial arts flick, part exploration of ancient Chinese culture, and part love story, *Crouching Tiger, Hidden Dragon* has breathtaking martial arts choreography by Yuen Wo Ping, famous for his work on *The Matrix*. The movie, based on Wang Du Lu's epic five-part novel, won Academy Awards in 2000 for best foreign language film, choreography, art direction, and original score.

Legends, magic, disguises, wishes, promises, wicked witches, good versus evil, aristocracy versus commoners—this movie has all the fairy-tale elements except the usual happy ending (consider yourself warned). Men especially will enjoy the many action sequences, and women will love the entire stolen-comb scenario.

For another romantic movie directed by Ang Lee, see *Sense and Sensibility* in Chapter 6. For more martial arts action, see *Big Trouble in Little China* in Chapter 7.

Do Try This at Home: Give each other a personal keepsake when you'll be apart for a while.

❧ Don Juan DeMarco (1994)

Johnny Depp, Marlon Brando, Faye Dunaway, Rachel Ticotin
DIRECTED BY JEREMY LEVEN
92 minutes; in color; PG-13
Intimacy Comfort Level: Going Steady, Committed/Married
Make-Out Meter: ▮▮▮▮▮
Just for Her: "Singing" manhood
Just for Him: Sword fights; a Rorschach test

In one of the most erotic PG-13 films you're likely to watch, a twenty-one-year-old man (Depp) wearing a mask and cape and claiming to be Don Juan attempts suicide because of unrequited love. Admitted to a state mental hospital, he is assigned to burned-out psychiatrist Dr. Jack Mickler (Brando), who is a few days away from retirement.

The reluctant patient requests permission for ten days to tell his entire story to the doctor, without medication and without judgment. Sensing the depth of the man behind the mask, Mickler listens with increasing interest to the romantic adventures of the famed lover who claims to have bedded 1,502 women.

As Don Juan relates his many trials, which began in childhood and include narrow escapes from jealous men and living among harem girls, he urges Mickler to look beyond what is visible and see the beauty within. As he listens intently, the doctor applies this concept to his patient and to himself. An exotic blend of fantasy and fact, Don Juan's story changes everyone with whom he comes into contact.

Told almost entirely through flashback, *Don Juan DeMarco* contains rich cinematography, a beautifully written story by director Leven, and creative casting of Brando and Dunaway (as Mickler's wife). Portraying the world's greatest lover, the perfectly cast Depp utters Castilian-accented lines so seductive they make nuns swoon and embraces women with such sensitivity that they respond like rare musical instruments under the direction of a maestro.

Bryan Adams had a huge hit with the theme song "Have You Ever Really Loved a Woman." In keeping with the fairy-tale tradition, look for at least one amazing transformation at the end of the film.

For other sexy men in masks, see *The Princess Bride* in this chapter and *The Mask of Zorro* in Chapter 10.

Do Try This at Home: Keep the number of previous lovers you've had a secret from your current lover (especially if it's more than 1,500).

❥ *Ever After: A Cinderella Story* (1998)

Drew Barrymore, Dougray Scott, Anjelica Huston, Patrick Godfrey
DIRECTED BY ANDY TENNANT
122 minutes; in color; PG-13
Intimacy Comfort Level: First Date, Going Steady, Committed/Married
Make-Out Meter: ▮▮▮▮
Just for Her: The arrival at the ball
Just for Him: Sword fights with gypsies

A thoughtful, romantic, feminist retelling of the Cinderella story, *Ever After* discards the helpless female archetype in favor of an intelligent, brave, outspoken girl of the cinders who is trapped by circumstances out of her control. Told within the framework of an old woman revealing the "true" account of her great, great grandmother to the Brothers Grimm, this story within a story puts a new spin on the old classic.

The movie begins with the cryptic line: "Once upon a time there was a girl who loved her father very much." Naturally, the father dies a few minutes into the movie, and poor Danielle (Barrymore) is left with her new stepmother (Huston) and two stepsisters (one beautiful, but mean; one plain, but kind). Her life of misery under her stepmother's rule is prompted in part by her father's dying words of "I love you" directed toward his daughter rather than his new wife.

After her stepmother takes over the house, Danielle's only remaining possessions include her father's book *Utopia* and her mother's wedding dress with

An abused young woman from the cinders (Drew Barrymore) hopes to live happily ever after with a handsome, spoiled prince (Dougray Scott) in *Ever After: A Cinderella Story.* (Stephen F. Morley/Copyright © 1998 Twentieth Century-Fox; courtesy of Photofest)

matching glass slippers. Danielle unwillingly becomes a servant to her abusive stepfamily.

One day, while disguised as a countess in order to buy back a servant sold by her stepmother, Danielle encounters the handsome Prince Henry (Scott), who likens himself to a bird trapped in a gilded cage. Dreading the upcoming marriage forced upon him by his father, Prince Henry finds himself so intrigued by the outspoken young countess that he spends all his available time with her.

Through integrity and loyalty, rather than magic, Danielle manages to escape her stepmother's imprisonment and attend the prince's bride-seeking ball in her mother's dress. The king has commanded that a bride be announced by midnight—the magical stroke of twelve. When her true identity is revealed publicly, Danielle is devastated. The prince, who previously had admired her passion and conviction, decides he's not so sure he wants to spend his life and share his crown with a common cinder girl.

A range of emotions are represented in this well-cast film, from frustration and rage to passion and joy. This truly romantic story remains full of surprises, regardless of how many times you've seen the Walt Disney animated feature.

For more rags-to-riches romances, see *Pretty Woman* in Chapter 5 and *Maid in Manhattan* and *Working Girl*, both in Chapter 10.

Do Try This at Home: Establish a secret meeting place.

Barrymore or Bullock?
2. Does Drew Barrymore or Sandra Bullock have a famous opera singer for a mother?
Answer on page 205

❧ *A Knight's Tale* (2001)

Heath Ledger, Shannyn Sossamon, Rufus Sewell, Paul Bettany
DIRECTED BY BRIAN HELGELAND
132 minutes; in color; PG-13
Intimacy Comfort Level: First Date, Going Steady, Committed/Married
Make-Out Meter: ▌▌▌▌
Just for Her: "Losing" for love; William's prize
Just for Him: Jousting; sword fights; a father's love

William Thatcher (Ledger) is sent away as a young boy by his peasant father, who is determined for his only son to "change his stars" and have a better life as a knight's squire. Twelve years later, the knight dies unexpectedly between games at a jousting tournament and William (with the help of fellow squires played by Mark Addy and Alan Tudyk) disguises himself in the knight's armor and successfully competes in his place.

Buoyed by this first win, William talks the other squires into pooling their money for training, so he can joust in other competitions. Training will be costly and time-consuming because William has more enthusiasm and drive than natural ability. His winning philosophy, however, is that losing only proves one thing: that he's a loser.

Along the way, they encounter a flamboyant gambler and astonishing word-smith named Geoffrey Chaucer (Bettany) and a lovely young woman with many hairstyles named Jocelyn (Sossamon). They also meet Count Adhemar (Sewell), a cruel knight who takes an instant dislike to William and becomes an increasing threat to the young squire posing as a knight, wearing another man's armor, and stumbling over his assumed name.

Director Helgeland, who also wrote and produced the film, bridges the ages with this fourteenth-century fairy tale that features 1970s rock music, modern slang, appealing characters, terrific acting, and a father-son scene that will touch your heart. Quirky supporting characters give the story more depth by showing how William affects those around him.

Filled with joy, sadness, passion, tension, action, dancing, love, friendship, loyalty, and deceit, *A Knight's Tale* will make you believe in a peasant squire who becomes a knight in his heart, but not on paper.

The movie doesn't take itself too seriously, as evidenced by a surprising scene for those dedicated enough to sit through all the end credits. Rent or buy the DVD version and you'll hear an extraordinary story about how the director lost his front tooth, find out why the Geoffrey Chaucer character was included, and learn the secrets about staging the jousting tournaments.

For another fictional tale of how a famous writer found inspiration, see *Shakespeare in Love* in Chapter 10. The final chapter also contains more characters who, like William Thatcher, hide their true identities to get ahead in life.

Do Try This at Home: Dress to match at parties.

❧ *Ladyhawke* (1985)

Michelle Pfeiffer, Rutger Hauer, Matthew Broderick, Leo McKern
DIRECTED BY RICHARD DONNER
121 minutes; in color; PG-13
Intimacy Comfort Level: First Date, Going Steady, Committed/Married
Make-Out Meter: ▮▮
Just for Her: Anguished twilight scene
Just for Him: Swords and crossbows

This film supplies a variety of fairy-tale elements: magic curses, star-crossed lovers, a clever young thief without parents, an evil male rival, enchanted animals, peasant versus royalty, and good versus evil all wrapped up in a long ago, faraway medieval fantasy. Young Phillipe Gaston, a.k.a. Phillipe the Mouse (Broderick), escapes from the dungeon of the cruel bishop, where he has been imprisoned for stealing.

This nervous young man who claims he has no honor becomes something of a local hero for his daring escape and hooks up with the mysterious swordsman Laval (Hauer), who saves him from angry prison guards searching for the escaped convict. Known as a pickpocket and a liar, Phillipe is stunned when he turns away from his life of crime only to learn that living within the law and telling the truth provide little safety during these magical times.

Many years ago, Laval was cursed by the bishop, who was jealous that his former captain of the guards fell in love with the beautiful Isabeau (Pfeiffer), whom the bishop also loved. The bishop called upon the powers of darkness to curse the lovers with this unholy union: by day Isabeau is a hawk; by night Laval is a wolf, thus ensuring that the couple never has more than a few fleeting seconds together during the twilight of each day.

Phillipe must call upon his own powers—though of a nobler nature—as he travels with the strange duo. Figurative and literal transformations occur throughout the entire film, as Phillipe and the unhappy couple try to devise a plan for lifting the curse. Will they ever become man and woman again, at the same time, that is? Either way, hawks mate for life.

Watch for authentic period costumes and anachronistic Alan Parsons music throughout this romantic fantasy, making a strange yet intoxicating mix.

For another story in which our feathered friends play a part in the romance, see *The Birds* in Chapter 8.

Do Try This at Home: Appreciate each other's animal instincts.

Paltrow or Pfeiffer?
2. Did Gwyneth Paltrow or Michelle Pfeiffer once work as a court reporter?
Answer on page 207

❧ *Mannequin* (1987)

Andrew McCarthy, Kim Cattrall, James Spader, Estelle Getty
DIRECTED BY MICHAEL GOTTLIEB
90 minutes; in color; PG
Intimacy Comfort Level: First Date, Going Steady, Committed/Married
Make-Out Meter: ▮▮▮
Just for Her: Trying on clothes and accessories in your own private
   department store
Just for Him: Creating the perfect woman

You could call it *Sex and the City Department Store*. Emmy, a beautiful young woman (Cattrall) born in Edfu, Egypt, in 2514 B.C., runs away before her arranged marriage to a camel-dung dealer. She makes a wish for the gods to solve her problem. Emmy is magically transported through time (briefly courting Christopher Columbus and Michelangelo) before landing in present-day Philadelphia as a department store mannequin that comes to life only for the man of her dreams.

In this case, the unlikely hero is Jonathan Switcher (McCarthy), a lost soul who (as his last name suggests) switches jobs as frequently as a mannequin changes clothes. As he shrewdly observes just before his girlfriend dumps him, "Reality is very disappointing."

The would-be artist gets fired from jobs as a balloon sculptor, landscaper, and pizza maker. Before getting axed at a mannequin shop, however, he builds the perfect woman, who just happens to look exactly like Emmy. Though Jonathan hardly resembles the traditional romantic hero, he possesses a kind, sensitive, loyal nature that attracts his female Pinocchio.

Most important, Jonathan is fun. When he discovers Emmy in the store window of Prince and Company, a failing department store celebrating its centennial anniversary, he gets a job there and begins a romance that takes him to every corner of the store, from the boardroom to the ladies dressing room.

At night, he and Emmy cavort through the aisles, playing games, making love, and searching for merchandise to decorate the store window. Emmy's dream of finding true love and Jonathan's dream of being a real artist collide in one enjoyable dance sequence. Now if only the gods would grant her one more wish. . . .

From the moment the animated opening credits start, you know there's nothing subtle or sophisticated about *Mannequin*. Over-the-top supporting roles by Spader as a smarmy store employee, Getty as a feisty store owner, Meshach Taylor as a flamboyant gay window dresser, and G. W. Bailey as an idiotic security guard help keep the story light. Jefferson Starship contributes to the soundtrack, which gives the film a 1980s kind of feel.

Like Jonathan, this movie is fun. This is pure romantic fluff—window dressing, you might say. There's nothing for you to figure out after the movie is over, except, of course, how you want to spend your time together.

If you enjoy this particular fairy tale, don't be tempted to rent the silly sequel *Mannequin Two: On the Move* with Kristy Swanson and William Ragsdale. Instead, watch the similarly themed *Splash* (in this chapter), which served as an inspiration for *Mannequin*.

Do Try This at Home: Role play with costumes and props.

❧ *The Princess Bride* (1987)

Cary Elwes, Robin Wright, Mandy Patinkin, Chris Sarandon
DIRECTED BY ROB REINER
98 minutes; in color; PG
Intimacy Comfort Level: First Date, Going Steady, Committed/Married
Make-Out Meter: ❚❚❚❚❚
Just for Her: "As you wish"
Just for Him: Pirates; swashbuckling; Iñigo Montoya's revenge

Told within the framework of a grandfather (Peter Falk) reading a fairy tale to his sick grandson (Fred Savage), *The Princess Bride* includes all the traditional fairy-tale elements, plus some unexpected thrills and chuckles, such as a commentary-filled duel, a rhyming giant, a chocolate-coated miracle pill, a six-fingered man, and an impressive clergyman with a speech impediment.

Despite several interesting subplots, such as war and revenge, and well-developed supporting characters such as Fezzik the giant (Andre the Giant) and the evil Prince Humperdinck (Sarandon), the story concerns itself first and foremost with true love—the kind of love that survives time, separation, and even death.

A beautiful young woman, Buttercup (Wright), and her handsome farm boy

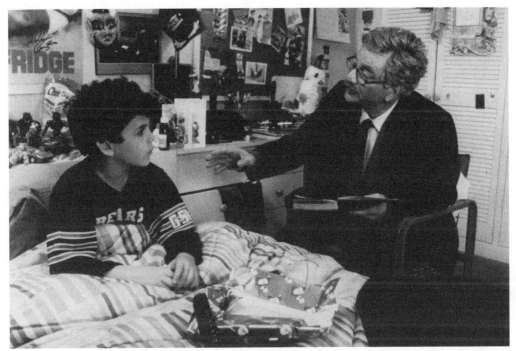

In *The Princess Bride*, a grandfather (Peter Falk) reads his skeptical grandson (Fred Savage) a favorite fairy tale, otherwise known as "a kissing book." (Clive Coote/Copyright © 1987 The Princess Bride Ltd.; courtesy of Photofest)

servant, Westley (Elwes), fall in love but cannot marry until he goes out into the world to change his station in life. After a tearful farewell, he is presumably killed by pirates, and five years later, she, a commoner, becomes engaged to marry "the slimiest weakling ever to walk the earth," that is, the cowardly Prince Humperdinck.

During her engagement, Buttercup is kidnapped by a calculating Sicilian (Wallace Shawn), a giant from Greenland, and a vengeful Spaniard (Patinkin). Despite their combined skills of mind, body, and spirit, respectively, they are no match for The Dread Pirate Roberts, a masked man who single-handedly steals the princess bride from them in three separate tests of skill.

After a terrifying trip through the fire swamp and an encounter with some rodents of unusual size, Buttercup is stolen again by Count Rugen, the six-fingered man (Christopher Guest), and Prince Humperdinck, who plans to force her into marriage so he can start a war.

The final rescue attempt from the castle brings about satisfying conclusions for all the interwoven subplots. Unlike so many movies that fall apart at the end with ridiculous contrivances, *The Princess Bride* wraps its story within a story using logic, wit, and love.

Look for cameos by Mel Smith, Billy Crystal, Carol Kane, and Peter Cook. Based on the novel by William Goldman, *The Princess Bride* is cleverly written, well acted, and beautifully directed. Repeated viewings will reveal something new each time.

For another movie presented as a bedtime story, see *Edward Scissorhands* in Chapter 6.

Do Try This at Home: Attempt one of the world's five most passionate kisses.

CLASSIC DATE MOVIE SELECTION

❧ *Roman Holiday* (1953)

Gregory Peck, Audrey Hepburn, Eddie Albert, Hartley Power
DIRECTED BY WILLIAM WYLER
118 minutes; in black and white; not rated, comparable to G
Intimacy Comfort Level: First Date, Going Steady, Committed/Married
Make-Out Meter: ❙❙
Just for Her: High heels; nightgowns; men's pajamas
Just for Him: Police chase; melee at the dance

The beautiful young Princess Ann (Hepburn in her first starring role) goes on a goodwill tour of Europe but while in Rome sneaks out so she can escape her tiresome schedules and royal duties. Bored with the uncomfortable clothes, stilted smiles, sweaty handshakes, and polite greetings, she runs away from the embassy one night to mingle with the commoners and experience their way of life for a while.

The first person she meets is a rude newspaper reporter named Joe Bradley (Peck), who's hungry enough to do anything for a saleable article. When he secretly learns that she is an escaped slumming princess, he plots to use this situation to his advantage. With the promise of $5,000 from his editor at the American News Service for an exclusive article on the private side of the princess, Joe goes undercover himself and disguises his true identity from Princess Ann, who goes by the name of Anya Smith during her adventure.

Joe then enlists the help of his friend (Albert), a dim-witted photographer, to accompany them while they explore the city, fulfilling her every wish for twenty-four hours. At the same time manipulating and patronizing, they set up the princess for a terrible fall from her heightened status as royalty.

Her regal attitude and his ungentlemanly behavior provide most of the laughs in this comedy, shot mainly on location in Rome. She explores the outdoor marketplace, visits a hair salon for a makeover, drinks champagne at a sidewalk café, rides around on a motor scooter, gets arrested, goes dancing under the stars, and visits the wall of wishes during her action-packed day with Joe.

As time passes, she becomes a little less regal and he becomes more gentlemanly until they inevitably fall in love. Ann likens herself to Cinderella, fearing that she will "turn into a pumpkin and drive away in a glass slipper at midnight." Joe remains more scoundrel than prince, but he also undergoes a transformation of sorts.

The film received several Academy Award nominations, and Hepburn won an Oscar for best actress. *Roman Holiday* charms, and Hepburn delights, but the story proves much milder than most modern fairy-tale renditions.

For more couples with something to hide, see Chapter 10.

Do Try This at Home: Take candid photographs of your dates together.

❧ *Shrek* (2001)

Voices of Mike Myers, Cameron Diaz, Eddie Murphy, John Lithgow
DIRECTED BY ANDREW ADAMSON AND VICKY JENSON
90 minutes; in color; animated; PG
Intimacy Comfort Level: First Date, Going Steady, Committed/Married
Make-Out Meter: ❘❘
Just for Her: Princess Fiona's initial response to her knight in shining armor
Just for Him: Sword fights; star gazing; ear-wax candles

Can cursed Princess Fiona (Diaz), obsessed with external beauty and the stereotypical knight in shining armor, find true love and eternal happiness with diminutive Lord Farquaad (Lithgow), who must marry to become king, or with a big, smelly ogre (Myers) who suffers from low self-esteem? That's the question posed throughout this amusing animated spoof of fairy-tale romance.

Charged with rescuing Fiona from her dragon-guarded tower in order to save his private swamp from invading fairy-tale creatures, Shrek the ogre grudgingly employs the aid of a magic talking "donkey on the edge" (Murphy) for the journey. Shrek's mission is delivery boy; he must bring the princess back to Lord Farquaad so he can marry her and become king.

While Shrek considers the rescue necessary business in securing his home, Fiona holds on to her lifelong dream that her savior must be her one true love. When her reality doesn't mesh with her illusion, she has a less-than-regal display of bad temper.

The princess desperately needs to find this hero so she can be freed from a secret curse. The more we get to know Princess Fiona, the more we see that she has little in common with a traditional princess. She burps, performs martial arts, sings off-key, and enjoys a well-cooked weed rat on occasion. But that's not all.

Based on a book by William Steig, *Shrek* is a multilayered movie, much like its title character. Underneath the rapid-fire jokes lie the deeper issues of superficial beauty, prejudgment, self-acceptance, friendship, trust, and the nature of love.

The animated characters take on lives of their own, yet also contain hints of the facial features and mannerisms of the actors portraying them. Constant cultural references, special appearances by beloved fairy-tale characters, fast-moving action, a lively soundtrack, and a standout performance by Murphy make *Shrek* a movie to be watched and enjoyed many times by lovers of all ages.

For more stories about inner beauty see Chapter 6.

Do Try This at Home: Make each other gifts by hand.

❧ *Splash* (1984)

Tom Hanks, Daryl Hannah, Eugene Levy, John Candy
DIRECTED BY RON HOWARD
110 minutes; in color; PG
Intimacy Comfort Level: First Date, Going Steady, Committed/Married
Make-Out Meter: ▮▮▮
Just for Her: Shopping at Bloomingdale's
Just for Him: The dropped-coin trick

This literal and figurative fish-out-of-water story begins twenty years earlier in Cape Cod when an eight-year-old boy is saved from drowning by a mermaid. She rescues him again as an adult when he has a boating accident and becomes so smitten that she follows him home to New York City. Well-versed in the mermaid's magic rulebook, she knows that she can live on dry land only for six days and that if she chooses to trade in her fins for legs, the change will be permanent.

Tom Hanks plays Allen Bauer, an athletic (though nonswimming) produce supplier who has been drawn to the water all his life. He finds himself equally drawn to the beautiful young naked woman (Hannah) who pulls him out of the water.

When she shows up in New York—again naked—he is perfectly willing to supply her with credit cards, lobster meals, and a nice saltwater bath. Nakedness aside, Hannah has little to do in this movie except swim, squeak, and look confused.

A feeble subplot surrounds a crazed scientist (Levy) who tries to exploit the interspecies couple. A better subplot involves Allen's older brother, Freddy (Candy), who uses sleazy tactics in his professional and personal life with disastrous results.

Small physical and emotional transformations occur throughout the movie, but the ending provides a whale of a transformation. Winner of an Academy Award for best screenplay, *Splash* offers a nice combination of romance, comedy, and fantasy.

For more tales of extraordinary love, see Chapter 8. For other movies in which lovers are in a New York state of mind, see *Moonstruck* and *Kate & Leopold,* both in Chapter 1; *Crossing Delancey, How to Lose a Guy in 10 Days,*

Sleepless in Seattle, You've Got Mail, When Harry Met Sally, and *Woman of the Year* in Chapter 2; *The Thomas Crown Affair* in Chapter 4; *Annie Hall* and *One Fine Day* in Chapter 5; *Breakfast at Tiffany's* in Chapter 6; *Ghost* and *Serendipity* in Chapter 8; *Crocodile Dundee* in Chapter 9; and *Coming to America, Maid in Manhattan, Spider-Man, Tootsie,* and *Working Girl,* all in Chapter 10.

Do Try This at Home: Go ice skating together at an outside rink.

Also see a time-traveling fairy-tale romance in *Kate & Leopold* in Chapter 1, a modern-day monster of Frankenstein with a heart of gold and a hand of scissors in *Edward Scissorhands* in Chapter 6, a magical woman who transforms a town in *Chocolat* in Chapter 8, a prince who hides his true identity in *Coming to America,* and updated retellings of the Cinderella story in *Maid in Manhattan* and *Working Girl,* all in Chapter 10.

Planes, Trains, Automobiles, and Ships

Methods of locomotion have improved greatly in recent years, but
places to go remain about the same.
Don Herold

IN THE LAWRENCE KASDAN–DIRECTED romantic comedy *French Kiss*, two strangers sitting next to each other on an airplane have a conversation. Luc Teyssier (Kevin Kline) suggests that anxiety-ridden Kate's (Meg Ryan) fear of flying is really a fear of something else. "Did you ever think that maybe it is not the airplane?" he asks. "That maybe it is something else you're afraid of. . . . You are afraid to live, really live. You are afraid of life. You are afraid of love. You are afraid of sex." Of course, he's right. And, of course, she denies it.

Similarly, in James Cameron's tragic romance *Titanic*, when Rose Dewitt Bukater (Kate Winslet) dines on board the doomed ship during its fateful maiden voyage in 1912, she becomes annoyed by a tablemate's constant boasting about the majestic size of the vessel. She asks if he has ever heard of Sigmund Freud's theories about overly large inanimate objects compensating for manly inadequacies. While other passengers snicker at her remarks, the confused braggart asks if Mr. Freud is a fellow passenger.

These seemingly dissimilar movies (and others reviewed in this chapter) have one unifying theme: They use transportation as a symbolic form of risk, often a sexual one. It's no coincidence that Cameron referenced Freud in his *Titanic* screenplay. The Viennese psychiatrist and coiner of the "Freudian slip" had much to say about the relationship between transportation and sex, in addition to his theories about compensation for inadequate endowment.

The father of current psychoanalytic thought, Freud seemed a little fixated on the subject of transportation issues. For instance, in his 1900 book *The Interpretation of Dreams*, he describes bodies of water as dream symbols for the mother's womb and the act of birth. He also associates dreams and daydreams of water with an exploration of the unconscious mind.

Then in 1910, Freud expanded the sexual associations of transportation from the water to the air by equating a dream about flight to a disguised wish for improved sexual performance. The plane or bird represents the stork that children associate with the mysterious birth process. As they get older, children learn the truth about sex and birth, but continue to hold on to their earlier beliefs in the dark recesses of their minds. Therefore, Freud decisively concludes that everything related to aviation has infantile erotic roots.

Sure, traveling by water and air might be sexy, but what did Freud have to say about land? From an essay he wrote on infantile sexuality and mechanical excitation comes this startling revelation: Adolescent boys take an extraordinarily intense interest in things connected to railways because the nucleus of this symbolism is sexual. He finds a compulsive link between railway travel and sexuality that is clearly derived from the pleasurable sensations of movement.

So when the young lovers in *Titanic* sneak away for a rendezvous and wind up in the backseat of a car in storage, we are vicariously aroused by the romance, the watery associations, and the mechanical excitation, according to Freud anyway. His well-known ideas about repressed sexuality emerging through dream symbolism have become part of our cinematic culture today. When a filmmaker includes a tense moment between a couple then cuts to a shot of a train plunging into a tunnel, it's pretty easy to decipher the intended meaning.

Freudian theories and sexual connotations aside for a moment, travel does represent more than mere transportation for the characters in these date movies. It means bridging the distance between two people who are physically or emotionally separated; they take risks by escaping, moving, growing, or arriving. Their literal journeys on water, air, and land become figurative journeys into themselves and their relationships.

In *Top Gun*, Pete Mitchell, a.k.a. Maverick (Tom Cruise), uses transportation to exemplify his risk taking. The overly confident pilot willingly takes risks in the air, but not with his relationships on the ground. In *Speed*, SWAT team expert Jack Traven (Keanu Reeves) uses speeding transportation (car, bus, train) for the same purpose as Maverick. He prides himself on being tough, strong, brave, and prepared for any situation. In *The Thomas Crown Affair*, daredevil billionaire Thomas Crown (Pierce Brosnan) also takes physical risks in planes, boats, and cars, but receives professional counseling for his fear of intimacy. Once you remove danger-craving Pete, Jack, and Thomas from their respective speeding vehicles and place them in the arms of beautiful women, they become less willing to take risks.

Exotic (and expensive) travel by water, air, or land that requires great speed and great distances necessarily requires more risk. In *Casablanca,* the characters use transportation as a means of escape; roaring airplanes in the background signify the comings and goings of refugees fleeing Nazi-occupied territories. In *Risky Business*, teenage Joel Goodsen (Tom Cruise) transitions from playing with his toy trains to a more adult form of play on a real train. Great risk implies great danger, an unsettling situation that produces a tingling rush of adrenaline much like sexual excitement.

Common and inexpensive forms of public transportation by bus and taxi show local scenes and landmarks, thus providing the unique flavor of the area. These more familiar scenes also reduce the risk factor and, especially in the case of bicycles, scooters, and motorcycles, make the audience part of the scene. We can all relate to Greg Focker (Ben Stiller) wanting to drag race against his overbearing father-in-law-to-be in *Meet the Parents*. Though familiar, this kind of everyday risk also conveys a certain element of danger.

During the ten journeys described in this chapter, at least one character in each film starts at one place emotionally and arrives at another by the end credits. Travel and transportation provide metaphors for their personal searches for fulfillment, and the cinematic manipulation of travel and transportation provides fulfillment for the audience.

CLASSIC DATE MOVIE SELECTION

❧ *Casablanca* (1942)

Humphrey Bogart, Ingrid Bergman, Claude Rains, Paul Henreid
DIRECTED BY MICHAEL CURTIZ
102 minutes; in black and white; PG
Intimacy Comfort Level: First Date, Going Steady, Committed/Married
Make-Out Meter:

Casablanca's final scene at the airport is among the most famous—and most romantic—ever filmed. (Courtesy of Photofest)

Just for Her: "Kiss as if it were the last time"
Just for Him: Tough-guy Bogart as a "rank sentimentalist"

Soft-hearted cynic Rick Blaine (Bogart) runs a fancy gin joint called Rick's Café Americain where an international crowd gets drunk, listens to Sam on the piano, and clandestinely tries to obtain exit visas during the Nazi occupation. Rick prides himself on remaining neutral. "I stick my neck out for nobody," he says. That is, until old flame Ilse Lund (Bergman) appears, along with her heroic husband, Victor Lazlo (Henreid), who escaped from a concentration camp and leads an underground movement.

The former lovers recall their Paris romance and talk about why she left him waiting alone at the train station when they had planned to escape together. Escape is a major issue for all involved; the refugees want safe haven in America, Ilse seemingly wants to escape from her marriage (based more on respect than love), and Rick wants to escape from himself. The buzzing of planes overhead serves as a constant reminder of the lucky few who obtain visas or letters of transit in order to flee the violence and persecution.

Casablanca is a hub of activity, with people arriving and departing en route to somewhere else. Maps, tickets, passports, papers, planes, plans, and deals mark everyday life in this international setting, which was actually filmed entirely in California at the Van Nuys Airport and Warner Bros. Studios in Burbank.

If you haven't seen *Casablanca* (or haven't seen it lately), enjoy the romance, humor, and intrigue with your current partner. See if you get goose bumps from hearing so many famous lines said in their original context.

Because of difficulties with the script, *Casablanca* was shot in sequence, unlike most films, which shoot scenes according to the availability of locations and actors. Even so, the film won an Academy Award for best screenplay, in addition to best picture and director wins.

It's a classic film that earns the distinction not from its age, but from its quality. After you rent the videotape or DVD, you'll immediately want to play it . . . and play it again.

For more lovers with something to hide see Chapter 10.

Do Try This at Home: Plan A: Establish "our song" early and play it often. Plan B: Establish "our toast" early and say it often. (Sorry, but "As Time Goes By" and "Here's looking at you, kid" have been taken already.)

❧ *French Kiss* (1995)

Meg Ryan, Kevin Kline, Timothy Hutton, Jean Reno
DIRECTED BY LAWRENCE KASDAN
111 minutes; in color; PG-13
Intimacy Comfort Level: First Date, Going Steady, Committed/Married
Make-Out Meter: ❘❘❘❘
Just for Her: The provocative pout; Luc's advice on temptation and suffering
Just for Him: A very important question: "Can you urinate with someone standing right behind you?"

Kate, a repressed, lactose-intolerant, nonsmoking history teacher (Ryan), meets Luc, a "nicotine-saturated and hygiene-deficient" Frenchman (Kline), on an airplane to Paris. Extremely fearful of flying, she is traveling abroad to find

Charlie, her fiancé (Hutton), who flew to Paris on business but fell in love with a French goddess and called off his engagement to Kate. Luc is returning from the United States with a stolen diamond necklace that he intends to sell for enough money to buy back his birthright, a vineyard that he lost to his brother in a poker game.

Once in Paris, Kate must realize her worst fears as she loses her man, money, possessions, and citizenship. Things aren't going too well for Luc either, as he chases his necklace as it moves among various purses, bags, and suitcases. Along the way, Kate encounters some very unfriendly—and very funny— Frenchmen with anti-American sentiments.

But life with a criminal isn't easy. Luckily, as they travel through the country in cars, motorcycles, and trains following Charlie and his "goddess," a kind policeman (Reno) is looking out for them.

Unhappy Kate makes some cruel comments to Luc, but otherwise Ryan plays her characteristically perky romantic female lead. Kline displays a sweet vulnerability beneath his roguish character. As they explore the City of Love, Kate and Luc realize some things about themselves. Both Kate and Luc do a fair amount of transforming during their long journey together.

The dialogue is quick and clever and the characters fun to watch. Helping secure its place among great date movies, *French Kiss* engages the senses with detailed discussions of kissing, scenes of the beautiful French countryside, an olfactory challenge, and mouthwatering descriptions of food. Watch this one with dimmed lights and glasses of wine.

For more lovable thieves and scoundrels see *The Thomas Crown Affair* in this chapter, *Out of Sight* in Chapter 7, and *Romancing the Stone* in Chapter 9. For another romantic journey on a train, see *Me, Myself & Irene* in Chapter 7.

Do Try This at Home: Show your partner an old class project that proves you weren't a nerd in high school (even if you were).

Roberts or Ryan?
4. Was Julia Roberts's or Meg Ryan's first movie role playing
Candice Bergen's eighteen-year-old daughter?
Answer on page 207

❧ *Meet the Parents* (2000)

Ben Stiller, Teri Polo, Robert De Niro, Blythe Danner
DIRECTED BY JAY ROACH
108 minutes; in color; PG-13
Intimacy Comfort Level: First Date, Going Steady, Committed/Married
Make-Out Meter: ▮▮▮
Just for Her: Cat teats; tiny Speedos
Just for Him: Drag race; volleyball smash

Poor Gaylord Focker. Not only is he stuck with an unfortunate name for a heterosexual man, but he also suffers from contradictory characteristics: He's a nicotine-addicted nurse and a truth-challenged nice guy. Worst of all, he's in love with Pamela Byrnes (Polo), a beautiful schoolteacher with a perfect ex-fiancé (Owen Wilson) and an impossible-to-please father (De Niro) who detests smokers and liars and idolizes her ex-fiancé.

When Focker, who goes by the nickname of Greg, decides to propose marriage, he needs Daddy's approval first. In a visit where he meets the parents, one outrageous disaster is followed by another, and Greg finds himself strapped to a polygraph machine answering questions from his future father-in-law, a former CIA psychological profiler.

Most men can relate to—or at least sympathize with—the stress of meeting the parents. Throughout the entire disastrous visit, Greg is only partly responsible for what happens, yet receives full blame for the unfortunate consequences. In addition to the nonstop humor (always at Greg's expense), his plight is revealed through metaphoric use of transportation.

He does nearly everything possible to ensure that his luggage is safe, yet the airline loses his bag and its precious contents. Greg remains equally helpless in the selection of his rental car, for which he is repeatedly ridiculed. Later in a comical drag race, he loses, not from a lack of will or skill but because as a visitor he is unfamiliar with the roads.

On his return flight, Greg encounters more problems from the same airline about the same piece of luggage. In the end, when he finally attempts to take control of the uncontrollable situation, he gets thrown off the plane. Can Greg regain control of his life and return to the Byrnes Family Circle of Trust?

Meet the Parents focuses on laughs more than romance, but the chemistry between Stiller and Polo is good and the overall casting excellent. Most of the comedy falls into the laugh-out-loud variety, even on repeated viewings. Listen for comic references to *Top Gun*, another great transportation-related date movie reviewed in this chapter.

For Stiller in another role as a hapless victim of love, see *There's Something About Mary* in Chapter 10. For more swimming scenes, see *Roman Holiday* in Chapter 3, *Titanic* in this chapter, *Bringing Up Baby* and *Dirty Dancing* in Chapter 5, *Children of a Lesser God* and *Shallow Hal* in Chapter 6, *All the Pretty Horses* and *Big Trouble in Little China* in Chapter 7, and *The African Queen*, *Romancing the Stone*, and *Six Days, Seven Nights* in Chapter 9.

Do Try This at Home: Bring a thoughtful gift when meeting the parents for the first time.

❥ Risky Business (1983)

Tom Cruise, Rebecca DeMornay, Joe Pantoliano, Curtis Armstrong
DIRECTED BY PAUL BRICKMAN
99 minutes; in color; R
Intimacy Comfort Level: Going Steady, Committed/Married
Make-Out Meter: ❙❙❙❙
Just for Her: An erotic train scene
Just for Him: Dream sequences

As Joel Goodsen, Cruise perfectly embodies the desires, needs, fears, and frustrations of a seventeen-year-old "good son" who longs to take a few risks while his rich parents are away on vacation. These risks include a dangerous chase driving his father's Porsche, sex with a pretty prostitute named Lana (DeMornay), confrontations with Guido the Killer Pimp (Pantoliano), a one-night "Future Enterprisers" experiment in his home, and missed final exams at school.

More of an in-depth exploration of teenage male sexual fantasies than an actual love story, *Risky Business* is a risk-free rental for date night, sure to satisfy male and female viewers. Not only will it leave you feeling romantic, but Brickman's screenplay may stimulate some interesting conversations as well.

Beneath the humor, eroticism, and drama lurk these intriguing questions: To what risks and what business does the title refer? Is Joel's entire adventure

Joel (Tom Cruise) and Lana (Rebecca DeMornay) find a train ride quite stimulating in *Risky Business*. (Copyright © 1983 Warner Bros., Inc.; courtesy of Photofest)

merely a dream? Do the frequent train scenes carry a Freudian connotation? Are Joel's wishes fulfilled or are his fears realized? Is it fair that Cruise went on to become one of the most powerful men in Hollywood while costar Armstrong went on to become "Booger" in the *Revenge of the Nerds* series?

The only obvious answer is to the last question. It's easy to see how this movie propelled Cruise to stardom. His fine acting, beautiful smile, and unforgettable "Old Time Rock & Roll" scene in his underwear reveal an actor willing to occasionally say "what the heck" and take a few risks.

Music by Tangerine Dream provides a sense of dream-like urgency with a distinctly locomotive sound. Layered characters, a clever script, and camera angles from alternating points of view create a rich, textured film worth watching several times.

For another movie with a rich-man, poor-prostitute theme, see *Pretty Woman* in Chapter 5.

Do Try This at Home: Don't restrict intimate encounters to the bedroom.

Chapter 4

❧ *Speed* (1994)

Keanu Reeves, Sandra Bullock, Dennis Hopper, Jeff Daniels
DIRECTED BY JAN DE BONT
115 minutes; in color; R
Intimacy Comfort Level: First Date, Going Steady, Committed/Married
Make-Out Meter: ❙❙
Just for Her: "Getting mushy" after the bus and train rescues
Just for Him: Speeding cars, buses, and trains; exploding bombs; a "wildcat"
 in handcuffs

For every *You've Got Mail* and *Crossing Delancey*—essentially chick flicks beefed up to entice male viewers—there is a *Speed* and *Top Gun* to do the exact opposite. In this testosterone-charged journey from one vehicle to another, two gum-chewing, speed-loving risk takers intend to find out whether relationships based on intense experiences can work.

Pumped up and always ready for action, Jack Traven (Reeves) is an LAPD SWAT team expert. His particular area of expertise involves swiftly taking control of a situation (with a gun) and acting on his impulses (with his muscles), while his partner Harry (Daniels) is a quick-thinking bomb diffuser who is clearly the brains of the operation.

When Jack thwarts a crazed bomber's plan to blow up a freight elevator filled with people, he finds himself the target of the bomber's next scheme. Suddenly he must call upon all his resources, both brawn and brain, to save the lives of innocent victims traveling on a city bus rigged to explode if it goes under fifty miles per hour. Charged with driving the bus (by default) is lead-footed Annie (Bullock), whose driver's license has been revoked for speeding.

The dynamic sound effects (which won an Academy Award), fast-moving story, and often dizzying camera action will keep you revved up throughout this exciting ride. Because the movie was really designed for men, *Speed* ranks low on the make-out meter, so you might want to transfer some of that tingling adrenaline rush you feel onto your partner.

Reeves looks great in this movie and really captures the spirit of a guy who's used to thinking with his body instead of his head. Bullock charms the bus riders—and the audience—with her spunky personality and questionable driving skills.

The sequel, *Speed 2: Cruise Control* with Bullock and Jason Patric, deals with a crisis on a cruise ship, but it lacks Reeves and the excitement of the original. You'll find more guys with guns in Chapter 7.

Do Try This at Home: Avoid being a backseat driver unless absolutely necessary.

Barrymore or Bullock?
3. **Did Drew Barrymore or Sandra Bullock win a Golden Globe award
for best actress in a miniseries or telefilm in 1993?**
Answer on page 205

The Sure Thing (1985)

John Cusack, Daphne Zuniga, Anthony Edwards, Nicolette Sheridan
DIRECTED BY ROB REINER
94 minutes; in color; PG-13
Intimacy Comfort Level: First Date, Going Steady
Make-Out Meter: ▮▮▮
Just for Her: Gib's final essay for class
Just for Him: The understanding semi driver; the dream sequence

Spanish novelist Miguel de Cervantes wrote in *Don Quixote* that "a bird in the hand is worth two in the bush." College freshman Walter "Gib" Gibson (Cusack) finds himself wondering if a "sure thing" now is worth a meaningful relationship that might develop into a sure thing later.

Gib is confronted with this dilemma as he journeys cross-country from New England during the Christmas break. He's headed for a college in Southern California where his best friend (Edwards) has arranged for him to spend an evening with a beautiful blonde stranger (Sheridan), who has guaranteed him a one-night stand with no questions, promises, or strings attached. During the long road trip, however, Gib becomes increasingly attracted to his irritating traveling companion, Alison (Zuniga), a brainy brunette classmate traveling to visit her fiancé at the same college.

For messy, casual, unstructured Gib, the main freshman-year objective is to find willing sexual partners. On the other hand, neat, uptight, organized Alison strives for straight A report cards and painstakingly accurate notes on every subject studied. Together these opposites argue, scream, taunt, banter, and eventually develop something deeper.

Their ill-fated road trip involves greasy diners, cheap motels, state troopers, cars, trucks, and (almost) a bus. As they explore the beautiful countryside during their travels, they also find time to explore their own not-so-beautiful behaviors and attitudes. Fantasy and dream sequences provide insight into Gib's adolescent development. Honest, funny, and well-acted, *The Sure Thing* is a sure thing for a great date film. (If you're in a long-term relationship, you also might enjoy this movie, especially if you met in college.)

For more mismatched couples who manage to get past their differences, see Chapter 5.

Do Try This at Home: Indulge yourselves with some bad-for-you food sometimes.

Carrey or Cusack?
1. Did Jim Carrey or John Cusack play a prep school student in his feature film debut?
Answer on page 205

❧ The Thomas Crown Affair (1999)

Pierce Brosnan, Rene Russo, Denis Leary, Frankie Faison
DIRECTED BY JOHN MCTIERNAN
111 minutes; in color; R
Intimacy Comfort Level: Going Steady, Committed/Married
Make-Out Meter: ▐▐▐▐▐
Just for Her: "Do you want to dance, or do you want to dance?"
Just for Him: Topless sunbathing; exotic transportation

New York billionaire Thomas Crown (Brosnan) has a problem. He's bored with crashing his $100,000 catamaran sailboat, flying his glider over the countryside, speeding through the city in his limousine, and driving his Shelby Cobra Mustang around the Caribbean when he visits his private getaway. Even secretly stealing a pricey Monet painting from the Metropolitan Museum of Art fails to excite him.

His amused therapist (Faye Dunaway, who starred in the 1968 original version) can't seem to help him overcome his intimacy and trust issues. The police ironically praise him for his cooperation as an eyewitness to the burglary. The museum board honors him for loaning one of his own paintings to replace the stolen masterpiece.

Poor Thomas. Maybe all this bad little playboy really needs is a little punishment.

Enter Catherine Banning (Russo), a confident insurance investigator who immediately poses a dangerous threat and an exciting challenge when she and Thomas play an alternating game of cat and mouse. They begin a strange affair that includes taunts, teases, suggestions, seductions, and, of course, traveling in his transportation menagerie.

But now that Thomas has met his match, Catherine needs to decide whether or not she has met hers. She wonders when and how their game will end and if there is a happily-ever-after for people like them.

If you, like Thomas and Catherine, crave action and romance, and despise boredom above all else, then this romantic thriller with its many surprises will keep you satisfied.

For a similarly themed movie that's also slick and stylish, see *Out of Sight* in Chapter 7. For more movies with characters discussing famous paintings, see *Notting Hill* and *Moonstruck* in Chapter 1.

Do Try This at Home: Stock your refrigerator with your partner's favorite beverage.

❧ *Titanic* (1997)

Leonardo DiCaprio, Kate Winslet, Billy Zane, Kathy Bates
DIRECTED BY JAMES CAMERON
194 minutes; in color; PG-13
Intimacy Comfort Level: Going Steady, Committed/Married
Make-Out Meter: ❙❙❙❙
Just for Her: Spitting lessons (you never know when you might need them)
Just for Him: Nude sketches; special effects; underwater action

In the blockbuster drama *Titanic*, beautiful socialite Rose Dewitt Bukater

(Winslet) and poor orphan Jack Dawson (DiCaprio) enjoy a passionate love affair much like the ocean liner itself—brand new, larger than life, dangerously fast, and doomed to fail. The two stars make an appealing couple, with Zane as Cal Hockley, her appropriately loathsome fiancé who will do anything to keep the lower-class lover from plucking his ripening Rose.

This tragic tale—based on factual events and Cameron's imagination as screenwriter and director—is a study of contrasts concerning modern and antiquated, young and old, rich and poor, bravery and cowardice, order and chaos, and ultimately, death and survival. The supposedly unsinkable ship of dreams turned into a nightmare for more than 2,000 people on board its maiden voyage to America in 1912. In this movie a high-tech crew is at the shipwreck site hoping to find and claim salvage rights to a missing 56-carat crown diamond pendant believed to be lost among the wreckage. The story is told in flashback by a survivor who is called to the site to identify the jewel.

Terrific for more established relationships, *Titanic* makes a poor choice for a first date because of its extreme length and emotional intensity. The dialogue sounds unnatural at times and the frequent use of the characters' names can be grating, so just allow yourself to get swept away in the cinematic current and you'll enjoy the trip.

Reportedly costing an incredible $285 million to make and containing 550 computer-animated shots, *Titanic* broke box office records that year and went on to win eleven Academy Awards including best picture, director, and cinematography. Cameron's acceptance speech included the famous quotation, "I'm the king of the world," which sounded far more innocuous when DiCaprio said the line.

For more star-crossed lovers see Chapter 5. For another romantic Rose involved in an onboard relationship, see *The African Queen* in Chapter 9.

Do Try This at Home: Revisit the place where you first met.

❧ *Top Gun* (1986)

Tom Cruise, Kelly McGillis, Val Kilmer, Anthony Edwards
DIRECTED BY TONY SCOTT
110 minutes; in color; PG
Intimacy Comfort Level: First Date, Going Steady, Committed/Married
Make-Out Meter: ▮▮▮

Just for Her: A sweaty, shirtless, rippling-muscle game of volleyball; locker
   room scenes
Just for Him: Aerial dogfights

Sure Pete Mitchell, a.k.a. Maverick (Cruise), looks good in his flight suit,
but if you went into battle would you want him with you? That's the question
facing the instructors and students at the Navy's special flight school for top
fighter pilots where Maverick attends classes. Known for creating turbulence
everywhere he goes, he struggles with his individual needs for showboating,
impulsive behavior, and proving himself in an atmosphere where teamwork is
valued above all else.

He also begins a clandestine affair with Charlie (McGillis), a civilian instructor at the school with a Ph.D. in astrophysics. She's older, better educated, and
in a position of power, but that doesn't stop Charlie from falling in love with the
cocky young pilot who takes unnecessary risks in the air such as flying inverted
to prove a point, and on the ground, such as speeding on his motorcycle without a helmet. In fact, Maverick's entire life is about breaking the rules of engagement.

The movie explores themes including discipline, individuality, responsibility,
and maturity through stunning aerial photography and manly banter on the
ground. The romantic subplot helps *Top Gun* glide right into the date movie category.

Without the romantic encounters at Charlie's house, corner bar serenades,
nearly naked locker room scenes, and gratuitous muscle flexing at the volleyball game, female viewers would likely lose interest in the unrelenting trials of
male bravado. While not quite a three-point landing, *Top Gun* satisfies overall,
and with any luck the onscreen sparks might lead to some afterburning offscreen.

The movie is filled with exciting music, including Berlin's Academy
Award–winning "Take My Breath Away." The attractive cast includes Meg Ryan
(in her pre–*When Harry Met Sally* days) in a small role as a pilot's wife.

For another hotshot fighter pilot fighting love see *An Officer and a Gentleman* in Chapter 5, and for more military action see *The English Patient* in Chapter 9. To see a lot more of Kelly McGillis try watching *Witness* in Chapter 7.

Do Try This at Home: Leave a romantic note on the pillow . . . afterward.

In *While You Were Sleeping*, Lucy (Sandra Bullock) is ready to come on board with Jack (Bill Pullman), the brother of her supposed comatose fiancé. (Michael P. Weinstein/Copyright © 1995 Hollywood Pictures Co.; courtesy of Photofest)

❧ *While You Were Sleeping* (1995)

Sandra Bullock, Bill Pullman, Peter Gallagher, Jack Warden
DIRECTED BY JON TURTELTAUB
103 minutes; in color; PG
Intimacy Comfort Level: First Date, Going Steady, Committed/Married
Make-Out Meter: ▮▮▮
Just for Her: An explanation of "leaning"
Just for Him: Brotherly love and one-upmanship

A lonely woman without a family, Lucy (Bullock) works in a dead-end job collecting tokens for the Chicago Train System. Lucy's stagnant personal and professional life make a sad contrast as she watches others on their daily commutes from her little tollbooth.

One day, a handsome lawyer, Peter (Gallagher), whom she has long admired from afar, is mugged at the train station and dumped unconscious onto the tracks. Lucy rescues him and is mistaken as his fiancée by the hospital staff and Peter's family. Suddenly she finds herself accepted into a warm, loving family by everyone except the comatose groom's brother, Jack (Pullman). He suspects foul play and therefore must spend countless hours with Lucy investigating her claims (and charms). Handsome and honorable (unlike his comatose brother, we learn), Jack also is going nowhere with his life. Carrying on the family business of estate buying, he longs to make wooden furniture by hand. Even though Lucy continues to pretend that she's engaged to Peter, she can't stop her growing feelings for Jack, prompting the transportation-related comment that she looks at him "like she'd just seen her first Trans Am."

A romantic comedy with a tinge of sadness, *While You Were Sleeping* uses the train as a symbol of Lucy's initial life as an outsider and eventual growth to an insider. When she opens her heart to love, she finally finds her life moving in the right direction.

For more lovers pretending to be something or someone that they're not, see Chapter 10. To see another woman who falls for the wrong brother first, see *Moonstruck* in Chapter 1. To see men falling for the wrong sister first, try *Ever After: A Cinderella Story* in Chapter 3 and *America's Sweethearts* in Chapter 6.

Do Try This at Home: Deliver important gifts (such as an engagement ring) in an unexpected place, time, or manner.

Barrymore or Bullock?
4. Did Drew Barrymore or Sandra Bullock star in a
short-lived television series?
Answer on page 205

For more transportation-related romance, see *Me, Myself & Irene*, *Raiders of the Lost Ark*, and *True Lies* in Chapter 7 and *The African Queen*, *The English Patient*, and *Six Days, Seven Nights* in Chapter 9.

Chapter 5

Opposites Attract (Then Repel, Then Attract Again)

Necessity is the mother of attraction.
Luke McKissack

STORIES ABOUT OPPOSITES generally follow a simple set of rules. First and foremost, because this is fantasy and not real life, the attracting opposites must be *attractive* opposites as well (like Richard Gere and Julia Roberts in *Pretty Woman*, for instance).

The opposites meet and initially hate each other or at least get off to an embarrassing or rocky start. They experience a growing attraction to each other until something or someone frustrates the characters or stifles them from expressing their true feelings. Just when the situation is resolved and a happy union seems inevitable, a seemingly insurmountable obstacle arises. The happy resolution requires that one or both of them make a sacrifice for love.

These sacrifices are not to be taken lightly. We have no reason to care about the characters if they have nothing to lose by falling in love. In *The American President*, widower Andrew Shepherd (Michael Douglas) has his presidential re-election at risk when he courts a spunky environmental lobbyist (Annette Bening). Liberal lawyer Glenda (Goldie Hawn) risks her marital stability by letting her unreliable ex-husband (Chevy Chase) back into her life in *Seems Like Old Times*. And reserved zoologist David (Cary Grant) is surely a gambling man at heart; he risks $1 million and his fiancée when he befriends a talkative socialite (Katharine Hepburn) in *Bringing Up Baby*.

The concept of attracting opposites is certainly nothing new. Some of the first magnets were stones discovered in ancient times in the country of Asia Minor called Magnesia. These stones were a type of iron ore called magnetite. Prescientific man had no explanation for why these stones attracted metal and therefore assumed that it must be magic.

In 1600, Dr. William Gilbert proved that the earth is one huge magnet and laid the groundwork for further study of magnetism, which would eventually create the law of poles (also conveniently the dogma of date movies): Like poles repel each other, and unlike poles attract each other. Furthermore, as all unattached people can sadly attest, any object that is attracted by a magnet becomes a magnet itself for as long as it remains in contact with the magnet. Hence, science can explain why it's easiest to get a date when you don't need one and hardest to get one when you do.

The ten selections in this chapter adhere strictly to the law of poles (and include a little of the ancient prescientific belief in magic, as well); however, these movies are not opposites. In fact, they have many traits in common. Although they highlight the opposite characteristics of two people, they also include emotional growth in one or both and a compromise in thought or action that accommodates the relationship.

Most of all, these movies rely on science. When you watch two opposites attract, there better be plenty of sexual chemistry involved—Julia Roberts and Richard Gere in *Pretty Woman* come to mind again.

The reason why most of the movies in this chapter are comedies is because opposites are funny. This incredibly strong attraction of opposites can force characters to do things they don't want to and that aren't necessarily good for them, achieving results that are often comical.

Dramas about opposites such as *Dirty Dancing, Jerry Maguire, An Officer and a Gentleman,* and *Say Anything* rely on a mixture of humor and seriousness. Sure, at times these characters are working through problems like unplanned pregnancies, unemployment, death, and embezzlement, but at other times they're still doing things they don't want to and that aren't necessarily good for them. These parallel subplots help put the romantic relationship in perspective.

As they struggle to overcome these obstacles, sexual tension mounts or else the audience loses interest. Their personalities may be incompatible, their jobs exotic or dangerous, their romance prohibited or secret, their barriers enormous, but their passion is inescapable and love cannot be denied because underneath it all, these opposites also have a few traits in common. The fun for us (and them) lies in figuring out which ones.

❧ *The American President* (1995)

Michael Douglas, Annette Bening, Martin Sheen, Michael J. Fox
DIRECTED BY ROB REINER
114 minutes; in color; PG-13
Intimacy Comfort Level: First Date, Going Steady, Committed/Married
Make-Out Meter: ▌▌▌
Just for Her: "The Slow-down Plan"
Just for Him: Advice to the wise: "Compliment her shoes"

It's hard enough getting friends and family to approve of your soul mate under normal circumstances. When you're a public figure, the task becomes even more difficult because of public scrutiny and speculation. When you're the most powerful man in the free world looking for love—a widowed United States President—the entire country wants to take a potshot at your newly appointed significant other.

At least that's what happens in *The American President*, when lonely-at-the-top Andrew Shepherd (Douglas) meets environmental lobbyist Sydney Ellen Wade (Bening). A widowed father for three years, Andrew is ready for a relationship. He's ready to rush into romance; she wants to take it slow. Hired by the Global Defense Council as a political strategist, she outspokenly talks her way into jobs, into the hearts of congressmen, and occasionally into trouble. Conversely, Andrew says little but commands great respect.

Most important, however, Andrew selfishly wants to pass whatever bill will get him reelected, while Sydney selflessly wants to pass bills that save the environment. Although the nosy press, interfering White House staff, and ruthless conservative opponent Robert Rumson (Richard Dreyfuss) try to disrupt the romance, the lovers' main conflict lies in their motives for pushing various bills through Congress. As with all attracting opposites, a compromise is necessary.

The colorful cast presents many delightful surprises. Bening is well suited to the role of a nervous, though gutsy lobbyist able to turn a president's eye. Douglas maintains the delicate balance of an active commander in chief ready to command a little action in the bedroom.

Supporting roles by Fox, Sheen, and David Paymer truly support the stars and the characters. Look for other familiar faces including Samantha Mathis, John Mahoney, and Wendie Malick. Television fans of *The West Wing* should enjoy the movie's screenplay by Aaron Sorkin, the force behind the popular television series.

For another politician in love see *Maid in Manhattan* in Chapter 10.

Do Try This at Home: Plan A: Get up and dance, even if you're the only couple on the floor. Plan B: Send flowers (or another token) when you break a date.

➤ *Annie Hall* (1977)

Woody Allen, Diane Keaton, Tony Roberts, Carol Kane
DIRECTED BY WOODY ALLEN
94 minutes; in color; PG
Intimacy Comfort Level: Going Steady, Committed/Married
Make-Out Meter: ▌▌▌
Just for Her: 3:00 A.M. arachnid emergency
Just for Him: A subtitled conversation so you really know what she's saying

Annie Hall (Keaton) is a Midwestern WASP who takes things at face value. A struggling singer, she has a mediocre voice, terrible driving record, and bizarre wardrobe. Alvy Singer (Allen) is an intellectual Jewish comedy writer obsessed with sex and death, who categorizes life into the horrible and the miserable. While he epitomizes New York City as a cold island, she is a warm, sunny day in Los Angeles.

These lovers are blissfully happy together—except when they are horrible and miserable.

The clever script was cowritten by Allen and Marshall Brickman and based largely on Keaton and Allen's earlier offscreen romance. The story includes flashbacks, split screens, comic monologues, and subtitles in a creative presentation of the pains and pleasures of an intimate relationship.

From the moment they meet, we can tell that these opposites are truly mismatched; in fact, all they really have in common is their neuroses. But psychotherapy and books about death aren't necessarily the strongest foundations on which to base a loving relationship.

Filled with appearances by current and future stars, *Annie Hall* won Academy Awards for best picture, best actress, best director, and best screenplay. Look for glimpses of Jeff Goldblum, Christopher Walken, Beverly D'Angelo, Sigourney Weaver, Colleen Dewhurst, Paul Simon, Shelley Duvall, and Dick Cavett.

Although many Woody Allen–directed films make good date movies, *Annie Hall* stands out among his early work because of its onscreen/offscreen parallels, classic one-liners, and influence on fashion and culture.

For other mismatched neurotic couples, see *Love & Sex* and *When Harry Met Sally,* both in Chapter 2. For more mixed-faith romances, see *Crossing Delancey* in Chapter 2, *Meet the Parents* in Chapter 4, and *Witness* in Chapter 7.

Do Try This at Home: Kiss early in the date to relieve tension and help digest food better.

CLASSIC DATE MOVIE SELECTION

❧ *Bringing Up Baby* (1938)

Katharine Hepburn, Cary Grant, Charles Ruggles, Walter Catlett
DIRECTED BY HOWARD HAWKS
102 minutes; in black and white; not rated, comparable to PG
Intimacy Comfort Level: First Date, Going Steady, Committed/Married
Make-Out Meter: ▮▮
Just for Her: A 1930s woman driving, stealing, smoking cigars, and going
   after what she wants
Just for Him: Big-game hunting; leopard mating calls

The pseudo-psychological premise of this original screwball comedy is that "the love impulse reveals itself through conflict." Nearly seventy years later, this remains a popular basis for romantic comedies.

Not surprisingly, there's lots of conflict in *Bringing Up Baby*, between the fast-talking, flamboyant socialite, Susan (Hepburn), and the quiet, reserved zoologist, David (Grant). He worries about everything; she worries about nothing. He's easily manipulated; she easily manipulates. Worst of all, David is engaged to be married; Susan falls in love with him instantly.

These attractive opposites with nothing in common continually cross paths because of one unmistakably important link: $1 million. David needs the money for his research at the museum, and Susan's aunt is the person making the donation.

Their misadventure begins on a golf course in New York and carries them to a jail cell in Connecticut. Along the way, they rip each other's clothes, chase two leopards on the loose, go digging for a dinosaur bone, fall in a creek, and fall in love. The frenetically paced action moves almost as fast as Hepburn's mouth, which never seems to be closed for more than a few seconds. Like a literary lady in love (see Chapter 2), Susan can't help herself from saying the wrong thing.

While much of the madcap comedy is still amusing today, contemporary audiences may find a man who won't speak up for himself and a woman who won't stop speaking for everyone else a little less endearing than 1930s audiences did. Concentrate on the time, place, and sentiment of the movie, and you'll enjoy this romantic comedy and appreciate its influence on today's films. If you still feel conflicted about whether or not to rent this particular romantic date movie, then remember that the love impulse reveals itself through conflict.

For recent examples of romantic screwball comedies, see *Blind Date* in Chapter 1, *Meet the Parents* in Chapter 4, *One Fine Day* and *Seems Like Old Times* in this chapter, *Bedazzled* in Chapter 8.

Do Try This at Home: Take an interest in your partner's pets.

❥ *Dirty Dancing* (1987)

Jennifer Grey, Patrick Swayze, Cynthia Rhodes, Jerry Orbach
DIRECTED BY EMILE ARDOLINO
105 minutes; in color; PG-13
Intimacy Comfort Level: Going Steady, Committed/Married
Make-Out Meter: ▌▌▌▌▌
Just for Her: Dirty dancing
Just for Him: Gratuitous fistfight

Aside from its tendencies toward manipulative melodrama, *Dirty Dancing* presents a timeless tale of two attracting opposites: An innocent seventeen-year-old girl from a wealthy family falls for an experienced older man, in this case a poor, uneducated dance instructor known for his good looks and smooth moves.

She's short; he's tall. She's an optimist; he's a pessimist. She wears white; he

In *Dirty Dancing*, an inexperienced rich girl (Jennifer Grey) prepares to get down and dirty with an impoverished dance instructor (Patrick Swayze) at a summer resort. (Courtesy of Photofest)

wears black. She's inhibited; he's the king of pelvic thrusts. She stands up; he backs down. She comes from affluent society; he comes from the streets. She plans for the future; he lives in the moment. She wants to join the Peace Corps and help underdeveloped countries; he wants to keep his job until at least the next payday. The list of opposite traits continues ad infinitum.

Grey (pre–nose job) and Swayze make a terrific team, whether on the dance floor or in the bedroom. She plays Baby, the younger daughter of a successful doctor and his wife who vacation in the Catskills where the sexy dance instructor (Swayze) works. The story takes place in 1963, which adds some colorful humor in terms of costume, dance, and music but also presents superficial subplots concerning class structure, abortion rights, and prejudice that detract and distract from the central romance.

The highlights of *Dirty Dancing* surround the dancing itself. Fun, flashy, and often erotic, the dance scenes alone could tell the story of their love's progression. Grey's cute little "spaghetti arms" wrapped around Swayze's finely muscled torso will embrace you and keep you following these romantic leads as they plod through the corny dialogue and then spring into the next dance scene.

The finale features the Academy Award–winning song, "(I've Had) the Time of My Life" in a triumphant scene that will surely have you sobbing. The dance scenes, musical interludes, and erotic encounters make *Dirty Dancing* a great date movie; if it weren't for that talking in between.

For more dancing (dirty and otherwise) that brings couples closer together, see *Emma, Four Weddings and a Funeral, The Wedding Planner,* and *The Wedding Singer* in Chapter 1; *When Harry Met Sally* in Chapter 2; *A Knight's Tale* in Chapter 3; *French Kiss* and *The Thomas Crown Affair* in Chapter 4; *The American President* in this chapter; *Children of a Lesser God* in Chapter 6; *All the Pretty Horses, True Lies,* and *Witness* in Chapter 7; *All of Me* and *The Mask* in Chapter 8; *George of the Jungle* and *Romancing the Stone* in Chapter 9; and *Coming to America, Maid in Manhattan, Shakespeare in Love,* and *The Mask of Zorro* in Chapter 10.

Do Try This at Home: Take a spontaneous swim fully clothed.

❧ *Jerry Maguire* (1996)

Tom Cruise, Renée Zellweger, Cuba Gooding Jr., Kelly Preston
DIRECTED BY CAMERON CROWE
139 minutes; in color; R
Intimacy Comfort Level: First Date, Going Steady, Committed/Married
Make-Out Meter: ▮▮▮
Just for Her: First-date kiss goodnight
Just for Him: Football action

Aggressive, smooth-talking sports agent Jerry Maguire (Cruise) has everything he needs in life—except a conscience. Engaged to a beautiful woman (Preston) and working at the powerful Sports Management International (SMI), he represents seventy-two clients and earns big bucks.

One day, the son of an injured client makes Jerry aware that along his climb to the top, he left his humanity behind. He worries about who he has become and hates his place in the world. After this late-night epiphany, he writes a lengthy idealistic mission statement that outlines what sports agents should be doing for their clients. Titled "The Things We Think But Do Not Say," the booklet is mailed to everyone at SMI, which immediately makes Jerry a folk legend . . . and unemployed . . . and unengaged.

One coworker, twenty-six-year-old Dorothy Boyd from the accounting department (Zellweger), is so impressed by his integrity that she quits the company to work for him. A widowed single mother, she and her son, Ray (Jonathan Lipnicki), become an integral part of Jerry's life. Meanwhile, Jerry has only one client left, Rod Tidwell (Gooding), a short, showboating football player far more concerned with fame and fortune than with sports.

Jerry "The King of House Calls" Maguire hates to be alone and is great at friendship, but has intimacy issues that ruin his relationships with women. Dorothy, on the other hand, loves totally and thrives on intimacy. Are the integrity and loyalty that she admired in Jerry's mission statement really just fleeting feelings embraced by the hard-nosed agent, perhaps inspired by an angry little boy and two slices of bad pizza?

Gooding received an Academy Award for his role and sparked a craze of "Show Me the Money" merchandising. Crowe wrote a thoughtful script that showcases the talents of stars Cruise and Zellweger. The R rating is based on a wild sex scene between Cruise and Preston, some rear nudity in the locker room, and profanity. A perfect blend of sentimentality and football action, *Jerry Maguire* really scores as a great date movie.

For other widowed spouses looking for love, see *Moonstruck* in Chapter 1, *Sleepless in Seattle* in Chapter 2, *The American President* in this chapter, and *Witness* in Chapter 7.

Do Try This at Home: Learn to say something romantic in another language.

❧ *An Officer and a Gentleman* (1982)

Richard Gere, Debra Winger, Louis Gossett Jr., David Keith
DIRECTED BY TAYLOR HACKFORD
126 minutes; in color; R
Intimacy Comfort Level: Going Steady, Committed/Married
Make-Out Meter: ▮▮▮▮
Just for Her: A determined female naval training candidate
Just for Him: Fistfights; tests of bravado; weekend romps with the "Puget Debs"

In this romantic drama set against the backdrop of a Naval Aviation Officer Candidate School in Washington near Puget Sound, Richard Gere plays a young, tattooed loser named Zack Mayo, who is neither an officer nor a gentleman when we meet him. Having grown up motherless on the streets of the Philippine Islands with only his alcoholic father (Robert Loggia) to look after him, Zack has no direction, no future, and no friends. What he does possess, however, are a love for his country and a strong desire to fly jets.

But these two attributes can take him only so far with his in-your-face drill sergeant (Gossett Jr. in his Academy Award–winning role). A stickler for rules and team reliance, Sergeant Foley takes an immediate dislike to Zack's disrespectful attitude, selfish actions, and violation of the codes of conduct. The thirteen-week training period becomes a proving ground for the two men: Will Zack become just another DOR (drop on request)?

The hardships of training soften a little when Zack meets Paula Pokrifki (Winger), a young local paper mill worker longing to be the wife of a navy pilot. While Zack's life lacks stability and a strong foundation, Paula's life is just the opposite. He needs to find a home and make some friends; she needs to leave her home and find different friends.

Like other girls dubbed Puget Debs by the cynical sergeant, Paula lives with her parents and siblings in a small town with few career opportunities and even fewer chances of meeting interesting men, other than the visiting naval candidates. Stuck in a dead-end job as an unskilled laborer, Paula is a low-class Emma Bovary, getting her views of the world from what she reads in *Cosmopolitan* magazine.

On the surface a simple story of love, lust, and self-discovery, *An Officer and a Gentleman* presents interesting interwoven subplots for those who find a good after-movie discussion as arousing as those hot scenes with Gere and Winger. The father–son relationship, never fully explored with his own father, comes into play when Zack meets Sergeant Foley. The romance between Zack and Paula is mirrored by another romance between their best friends. The friendship between the two men suffers, as does the friendship between the two women. And, finally, Zack's emotional obstacles to becoming a Navy pilot are contrasted with the physical obstacles faced by a determined female candidate.

For other men in (and out of their) uniform see *Top Gun* in Chapter 4 and *The English Patient* in Chapter 9.

Do Try This at Home: Make a surprise grand entrance to pick up your date; make an even grander exit.

Gere or Grant?
3. Did Richard Gere or Hugh Grant win a gymnastics scholarship to college?
Answer on page 206

❥ *One Fine Day* (1996)

Michelle Pfeiffer, George Clooney, Charles Durning, Mae Whitman
DIRECTED BY MICHAEL HOFFMAN
108 minutes; in color; PG
Intimacy Comfort Level: Going Steady, Committed/Married
Make-Out Meter: ▌▌
Just for Her: A tote bag that holds everything
Just for Him: "Superwoman" must admit she needs a "Superman"

Frantic architect and divorced mom Melanie Parker (Pfeiffer) and relaxed newspaper columnist and divorced dad Jack Taylor (Clooney) spend twenty-four hours trying to negotiate childcare for their two six-year-olds who miss the class field trip. Not only do the children dislike each other, but the newly introduced adults quickly develop a mutual repulsion/attraction.

Control freak Melanie regulates every movement of her son and got divorced because, as a freelance drummer who takes jobs when and where he can get them, her ex-husband could not be controlled.

Meanwhile, we learn that childish Jack has an angry ex-wife who left him because she was tired of being the adult all the time. On the surface, neither one of them seems like a great catch.

During the next twenty-four hours, the two opposites have repeated encounters, phone calls, and arguments. As they coordinate their work efforts and baby-sitting plans, they handle various crises with the two precocious children, including a nasty encounter with a red marble. Eventually Melanie and Jack reach a predictable (though no less satisfying) compromise.

The romance is light, with emphasis placed on the comedy instead. Young first daters may be turned off or feel left out by the frequent parents-of-small-children humor. Pfeiffer and Clooney look great and work well together, but the

One Fine Day together isn't quite enough for single parents (Michelle Pfeiffer and George Clooney), who also long for many stupendous nights. (Copyright © 1996 Twentieth Century-Fox; courtesy of Photofest)

mild story, cute characters, and romantic overtures will stay with you only about twenty-four hours, as well.

For more cute kids playing cupid, see *Sleepless in Seattle* in Chapter 2; *The American President* and *Jerry Maguire* in this chapter; *Kindergarten Cop, True Lies,* and *Witness* in Chapter 7; *The Birds* and *Chocolat* in Chapter 8; and *Maid in Manhattan* in Chapter 10.

Do Try This at Home: Take time to play in the puddles on a rainy day.

Paltrow or Pfeiffer?
3. Does Gwyneth Paltrow or Michelle Pfeiffer
have a sibling who also acts?
Answer on page 207

❧ *Pretty Woman* (1990)

Richard Gere, Julia Roberts, Jason Alexander, Hector Elizondo
DIRECTED BY GARRY MARSHALL
125 minutes; in color; R
Intimacy Comfort Level: Going Steady, Committed/Married
Make-Out Meter: ❚❚❚❚❚
Just for Her: Revenge on snooty sales clerks
Just for Him: A piano "duet"

In this cross between *My Fair Lady* and *Cinderella*, you have to use your imagination a little. What if Eliza Doolittle sold her body instead of flowers, and Henry Higgins had an obsession with fidgeting instead of phonetics? What if the fairy godmother were a Hispanic hotel manager and the pumpkin carriage a limousine? What if a vibrant soundtrack filled with chart-topping romantic hits accompanied this crossbred story? Well, you'd have something a lot like *Pretty Woman*.

A beautiful hooker named Vivian Ward (Roberts) hooks up with Edward Lewis (Gere), a lonely corporate type who's in Hollywood for a week on business. For a mere $3,000 she agrees to be his beck-and-call girl for six days and six nights in his fancy hotel penthouse in Beverly Hills. Not sure if he wants a prostitute, an escort, a girlfriend, or a confidante, Edward says he just doesn't want to be alone. Throughout the week, Vivian assumes all four roles at various times.

At first glance, they are total opposites. He's wealthy, cultured, meticulous, and jaded. He proudly boasts of going all the way through school. Vivian has gone all the way, too, but not in school. Dropping out in the eleventh grade, she moved to Hollywood in pursuit of her loser boyfriend and then drifted into

A streetwalking Cinderella (Julia Roberts) looks to an uptight business tycoon (Richard Gere) to be her knight in shining armor in *Pretty Woman*. (Copyright © 1989 Touchstone Pictures; courtesy of Photofest)

prostitution to pay the rent. She's poor, awkward, spontaneous, and naive. Plus there's that annoying fidgeting.

Luckily, she's a pretty woman and a sure thing—generally a good combination for a great date movie.

As the week progresses, however, we see that the unlikely couple has more in common than you'd expect. They both hustle for money without getting emotionally involved. And they both need each other. The problem becomes the degree of need. In keeping with the Eliza Doolittle–Cinderella-type tradition, Vivian wants it all. Nothing but the entire fairy tale will suffice. For someone who professes that "the bad stuff is easier to believe," Vivian seems more than willing to believe in her right to a fairy-tale ending.

Gere's career was already firmly established when the movie came out, but Roberts became a huge star because of this role (which includes an erotic bathtub scene), which earned her an Academy Award nomination. Supporting actor Alexander is the sleaziest of sleazy lawyers, and Elizondo is convincing as the tough hotel manager with a kind heart. Laura San Giacomo does a fine job as

Vivian's prostitute friend Kit. Marshall, Gere, Roberts, and Elizondo reteamed in 1999 for *Runaway Bride* (Chapter 1).

For more bathing scenes that range from the erotic to the chaotic, see *America's Sweethearts* in Chapter 6; *Out of Sight* and *Two Mules for Sister Sara* in Chapter 7; *The Bridges of Madison County*, *Crocodile Dundee*, *The English Patient*, and *Out of Africa* in Chapter 9; and *Coming to America* in Chapter 10.

Do Try This at Home: Play a board game by candlelight while sipping champagne and eating strawberries.

Gere or Grant?
4. Did Richard Gere or Hugh Grant get his first big break acting in the London production of the musical *Grease*?
Answer on page 206

❧ *Say Anything . . .* (1989)

John Cusack, Ione Skye, John Mahoney, Lili Taylor
DIRECTED BY CAMERON CROWE
100 minutes; in color; PG-13
Intimacy Comfort Level: First Date, Going Steady
Make-Out Meter: ▮▮▮
Just for Her: After-sex shaking
Just for Him: Guy talk and beer at the Gas 'N Sip

Surprisingly, the title of this movie does not refer to the adolescent lovers prominently featured in this film. Instead, the young woman, Diane Court (Skye), believes that she can say anything to her devoted single father (Mahoney) without fear of punishment or judgment. Throughout her blossoming romance with Lloyd Dobbler, a nice-guy kickboxing instructor portrayed by Cusack, she discovers that her father is not as understanding as she thought—nor is he particularly forthright in his own supposed soul baring.

We soon learn that Mr. Court has obtained his beautiful home and other possessions by ripping off the ailing inhabitants of the nursing home that he owns. As the brainy Diane contemplates her wayward father, her impending departure to England for college, and her growing intimacy with Lloyd, she is faced with more problems than even she (the class valedictorian) can handle.

Should she continue her relationship with this attractive opposite? No one can believe that they're actually dating. He was the popular class jock always surrounded by loyal friends, while she was the class brain who took college courses in high school and was too busy studying to develop any meaningful relationships. Can someone so "basic," as she calls him, be able to understand the depth and complexity of her situation?

Despite their romantic encounter on a deserted beach, Lloyd's beautiful love letter, and his famous shoulder-top boom box serenade of Peter Gabriel's "In Your Eyes," Diane decides to reduce their passionate coupling to "friends with potential" until she can straighten out her life.

The screenplay, written by director Crowe, is part drama, part comedy, and functions better on the latter level. The fine acting elevates the movie above typical adolescent romps. Look for cameos by Joan Cusack, Bebe Neuwirth, Eric Stoltz, and Jeremy Piven.

Although best suited for first dates or early dates, the likeable characters may appeal to some older committed/married couples in the mood to reminisce. See *The Sure Thing* in Chapter 4 for another teenage romance starring Cusack.

Do Try This at Home: Watch out for broken glass or other obstacles in the path of your loved one.

Carrey or Cusack?
**2. Did Jim Carrey or John Cusack star with Cameron Diaz
in a bizarre supernatural comedy?**
Answer on page 205

❧ *Seems Like Old Times* (1980)

Goldie Hawn, Chevy Chase, Charles Grodin, Harold Gould
DIRECTED BY JAY SANDRICH
102 minutes; in color; PG
Intimacy Comfort Level: First Date, Going Steady, Committed/Married
Make-Out Meter: ❙❙❙
Just for Her: Kitchen kissing
Just for Him: Kitchen knockouts

Written by Neil Simon and enhanced by the music of Marvin Hamlisch, this romantic comedy features the inspired silliness of Hawn and a barrage of one-liners by Chase. Their onscreen chemistry, also evident in the 1978 comedy *Foul Play*, predates the similar romantic rapport between Meg Ryan and Tom Hanks in their three films together (*Joe Versus the Volcano*, *Sleepless in Seattle*, and *You've Got Mail*).

In this story, author and Peter Pan Syndrome sufferer Nick Gardenia (Chase) gets kidnapped at gunpoint and forced to rob a bank. Without friends, resources, proof, or a clean shirt, he then shows up at his ex-wife's house for help. Glenda (Hawn) now works as a defense attorney comfortably married to a district attorney, Ira Parks (Grodin). Ira's new promotion to attorney general of the state of California means that Glenda must host fancy dinner parties for VIPs, including the governor. These parties take a comic turn when they're interrupted by her various pets, criminal employees, and fugitive ex-husband.

Glenda has a mixed reaction to this unexpected arrival. Although she finds contentment in her new marriage, Nick awakens familiar "quivers and shivers" in her, thus explaining the title of the movie.

An avid animal lover and defender of the guilty, Glenda's house remains filled with stray dogs and stray criminals with no place else to go. Nick is a lonely writer who lives and works by himself in an isolated cabin in the woods. While Glenda prides herself on being responsible, Nick playfully wallows in his boyish charm.

Poor Ira ranks high on integrity, loyalty, and responsibility, but bottoms out on Glenda's personal make-out meter—especially when Nick is around.

Many of the scenes are extremely funny, particularly the kitchen antics. Although the emphasis is on one-liners and situation comedy, the two leads make the romance work. From a cook who needs her feet scraped to a pack of wild dogs charging through the house, *Seems Like Old Times* keeps the good times coming.

Chevy Chase plays another wisecracking writer in *Fletch* in Chapter 10.

Do Try This at Home: Share pizza in the bathtub.

In one way or another, all romances concern the attraction of opposites and triumph over obstacles. Some just do it better than others.

For other particularly argumentative couples with nearly nothing in common see *Kate & Leopold* and *Runaway Bride* in Chapter 1; *Crossing Delancey* and *When Harry Met Sally* in Chapter 2; *Ever After: A Cinderella Story*, and *Roman Holiday* in Chapter 3; *French Kiss* and *The Sure Thing* in Chapter 4; *Breakfast at Tiffany's*, *Edward Scissorhands*, and *Rocky* in Chapter 6; *Out of Sight* and *Witness* in Chapter 7; *The Birds* and *Sleepy Hollow* in Chapter 8; *The African Queen* and *Six Days, Seven Nights* in Chapter 9; and *Coming to America* and *Maid in Manhattan* in Chapter 10.

Chapter 6

In the Eye of the Beholder

There are no ugly women; there are only women who
do not know how to look pretty.
Jean de La Bruyere

IN THE FARRELLY BROTHERS' comedy *Shallow Hal*, Mauricio (Jason Alexander), a friend of Hal's, confronts motivational speaker Tony Robbins (as himself) about how hypnotizing Hal to see only women's inner beauty has ruined his life. Mauricio complains that Hal has started dating physically unattractive women after spending his entire life chasing after "10s."

Not surprisingly, Robbins is disturbed by Mauricio's attitude, which is even slightly more shallow than Hal's. Robbins asks him, "Haven't you ever heard the phrase that beauty is in the eye of the beholder?"

Short, fat, bald (with an ill-fitting toupee), and suffering from a secret affliction, Mauricio replies, "Haven't you ever heard the song, 'Who Let the Dogs Out?'"

This superficial philosophy is the basis for the following ten movies, where people—both men and women—are unfairly judged by their appearances alone instead of by who they are and what they do. Thick glasses, big noses, bad hair, frumpy clothes, advanced age, facial scars, and an abundance of cellulite plague these inwardly beautiful people.

Take Gracie Hart, for instance. In *Miss Congeniality*, FBI agent Gracie (Sandra Bullock) established her reputation for toughness early in life by beating up boys on the school playground. Although little Gracie enjoyed the feelings of power and importance she received from whipping adolescent male butts, she failed to notice that some of the other boys were embarrassed and repulsed by her aggressive displays.

She grows into an ill-mannered slob who chews with her mouth open, snorts when she laughs, shoves her glasses up on her nose with an index finger, and uses her fists to enhance interpersonal communication.

Early in the movie, Miss Congeniality is anything but congenial.

But soon the FBI wants to crack a difficult case and needs a young woman with an attractive figure to pose undercover as a contestant in a beauty pageant. Gracie's well-toned abs and gluts—secretly lurking beneath her unisex clothing—help her qualify. A professional beauty consultant (Michael Caine) bleaches her dirty teeth, gives her two eyebrows again, and teaches her how to walk, eat, and talk. Soon Gracie becomes graceful: a beautiful, confident, poised young woman who always remembers her manners before using her fists to enhance interpersonal communication.

Other frumps include the passive, overweight, bespectacled Kiki (Julia Roberts) in *America's Sweethearts*, the 300-pound Rosemary (Gwyneth Paltrow) in *Shallow Hal*, and the frumpiest frump of all, poor Adrian (Talia Shire) in *Rocky*, an unstylish mouse in grandma's clothes and glasses who is too timid to even speak. Although not every frumpy Loretta turns into Cher (see *Moonstruck* in Chapter 1), all these women come to discover their inner beauty.

It's usually women who are judged solely by their appearances, but some men have fallen victim to the same fate: In *Sense and Sensibility*, an older, less-exciting man is insensitively passed over for a younger, more flamboyant one. In *Roxanne*, a big-nosed fire chief can't seem to light a fire in the woman he loves. In *Edward Scissorhands*, a scarred young man with scissors for hands can't cut it in the world of teenage romances. To make matters worse, these men have to deal face-to-face (or sometimes nose-to-nose) with their more handsome rivals, making our heroes' less-desirable looks even more obvious to the young ladies in question.

On the flip side are the beauties who are discriminated against because of their good looks (we should all be so lucky). College student Elle Woods (Reese Witherspoon) in *Legally Blonde* has an undergraduate degree in fashion design, created her own line of faux fur panties, wears sequined bikinis, displays perfectly painted nails and impeccably bleached blond hair, and coordinates her dog Bruiser's outfits to match her own.

Although her good grooming brings her personal satisfaction and an admiring bevy of sorority sisters, Elle's appearance also leads to problems. She gets lied to by sales clerks, dumped by her boyfriend, picked on by professors, ostracized by less-attractive students at Harvard, and propositioned by older men. "All people see when they look at me is blond hair and big boobs," she laments.

Actually, underneath Elle's outer beauty lies inner beauty as well. Although quick to point out those in need of a manicure, she honestly tries to befriend others and help with their problems, whatever their hair color or bust size. "First impressions are not always correct," she admonishes during a public address. Apart from her cloying perkiness, Elle is indeed smarter, deeper, and more caring than she first seems.

Similarly, party girl Holly Golightly (Audrey Hepburn) has lots of emotional baggage underneath her elegant facade in *Breakfast at Tiffany's*. Just as Elle seeks refuge in the nail salon to soothe her troubled mind, Holly heads for Tiffany's when the going gets tough. Despite appearing joyous and carefree, Holly is unable to go lightly through life. She, like other extremely attractive women, sometimes needs a little private time to contemplate the tremendous burden of beauty—or at least the irritation of being judged solely by her appearance.

The lovely Sarah Norman (Marlee Matlin) in *Children of a Lesser God* seeks solace in the swimming pool. A former wild child and promising student at a school for the deaf, Sarah now scrubs floors and cleans windows at the school in an effort to hide from the hearing world. Not to minimize Sarah's personal problems or disability, but she does wear very stylish and expensive clothes, has a terrific haircut, and maintains exceptionally good grooming for a school janitor. But to judge Sarah simply by the way she looks is a mistake.

As British poet and dramatist Oscar Wilde once said, "Crying is the refuge of plain women, but the ruin of pretty ones." Luckily for Elle, Holly, and Sarah, they don't have to do too much of it. Sure, it's not always easy being physically beautiful and judged accordingly, but how many times have you ever heard someone say, "Don't hate me because I'm beautiful . . . on the inside"?

An unstable actor (John Cusack) with a penchant for black leather has trouble choosing be-tween two beautiful sisters (Catherine Zeta-Jones and Julia Roberts) in *America's Sweethearts*. (Melinda Sue Gordon/Copyright © 2001 Revolution Studios; courtesy of Photofest)

❧ *America's Sweethearts* (2001)

Julia Roberts, John Cusack, Billy Crystal, Catherine Zeta-Jones
DIRECTED BY JOE ROTH
103 minutes; in color; PG-13
Intimacy Comfort Level: First Date, Going Steady, Committed/Married
Make-Out Meter: ▮▮
Just for Her: Forbidden bread sticks
Just for Him: An errant cactus

What does it take to make pretty woman Julia Roberts look unattractive? A fat suit, thick glasses, and Catherine Zeta-Jones. Ever since high school, over-weight (and naturally bespectacled) Kiki Harrison (Roberts) has played the role of personal assistant and social director for her beautiful movie star sister, Gwen (Zeta-Jones).

But that was sixty pounds ago. Now Kiki's trim appearance becomes a little threatening to the insecure actress, whose petty jealously is matched only by her selfish demands.

The situation most unacceptable to Gwen, however, is when her estranged actor husband, Eddie Thomas (Cusack), shows up at a press conference displaying more than a passing interest in his soon to be ex-sister-in-law. Although Gwen abandoned Eddie for a Spanish actor (Hank Azaria) she met during a recent movie shoot, she characteristically wants to have her flan and eat it, too.

Meanwhile Kiki loves Eddie, even though she knows he's still obsessed with Gwen. Eddie is so emotionally distraught he is unsure if he really loves anyone. Scheming press agent Lee Phillips (Crystal, who also wrote the screenplay and coproduced the movie) adores money, his job, and most of all generating publicity.

This love story involves lots of black leather jackets, comic breakups and makeups, and funny cameos by Larry King as himself and Alan Arkin as a greedy New Age guru. Christopher Walken plays an eccentric director who makes a shambles out of the carefully orchestrated press event. Romance plays a supporting role to satire, which leads the way to a Crystal-clear statement about idealized beauty.

For other movies with dramatic (and romantic) press conferences in their final scenes, see *Notting Hill* in Chapter 1 and *Maid in Manhattan* in Chapter 10.

Do Try This at Home: Butter your loved one's toast.

Roberts or Ryan?
5. Was Julia Roberts or Meg Ryan voted high school homecoming queen?
Answer on page 207

CLASSIC DATE MOVIE SELECTION

❥ *Breakfast at Tiffany's* (1961)

Audrey Hepburn, George Peppard, Patricia Neal, Buddy Ebsen
DIRECTED BY BLAKE EDWARDS
114 minutes; in color; not rated, comparable to PG
Intimacy Comfort Level: First Date, Going Steady, Committed/Married
Make-Out Meter: ❚❚
Just for Her: Diamonds and jewels
Just for Him: Taming the wild thing

You have to look like Audrey Hepburn to get away with such atrocious behavior. As the glamorous party girl Holly Golightly, she earns a living by dating and discarding rich suitors or "rats" (as Holly refers to them), rates her admirers by the earrings they give her, drinks and smokes excessively, disrupts her entire apartment building without remorse, steals from five-and-dime stores, consorts with convicted felons, and treats her friends and family callously.

Despite her eccentricities, Holly charms nearly everyone she meets in her New York City social circle, with the notable exception of her building superintendent, the diminutive photographer Mr. Yunioshi (Mickey Rooney as an embarrassing ethnic stereotype). And even he stops yelling at her and threatening to call the police when Holly bats her eyelashes and promises to pose for pictures some day. In fact, her beauty has attracted twenty-seven rats recently.

Yes, her appearance is impeccable, from the top of her expensive hat on her perfectly coiffed head (including designer earplugs) to the bottom of her expensive black alligator high heels. Breathtakingly beautiful and stylishly chic, Holly tries to hide her hillbilly past through her present-day sophistication, visiting Tiffany's to lift her spirits and charging her dates $50 so she can go to the powder room.

Her perfect—though perfectly phony—world comes crashing down around her when struggling writer Paul Varjak (Peppard) moves into the apartment below her. The sensitive bookish type, he immediately becomes smitten with the attractive opposite who lives upstairs. Although supported by a rich, female "patron of the arts" himself, Paul feels disgust at Holly's mercenary attitude toward men.

But the more he gets to know her, the more he sees the helpless little girl beneath the facade. As Paul becomes closer to Holly (his muse, of sorts), his writing becomes more prolific and inspired, which causes him to rethink his relationship with his older, married woman friend (Neal) who has supported him thus far. Winning Holly's heart isn't as easy as he thinks, however, because she thinks of herself as a fierce wildcat who refuses to be tamed or caged. Paul finds himself with a case of the "mean reds" (Holly's description of a depression worse than the blues) that is so severe even a visit to Tiffany's won't cure it.

Based on Truman Capote's novel, *Breakfast at Tiffany's* won an Academy Award for best song, Henry Mancini's "Moon River." Edwards really got his money's worth from this theme song by using it no fewer than eight times throughout the movie, even having Hepburn sing it on her window ledge and Peppard whistle it in the hallway.

A fun movie that's slightly dated by its party scene and demeaning portrayal of Asian Americans, *Breakfast at Tiffany's* is nonetheless a great way to get over the mean reds—cross my heart and kiss my elbow (as Holly would say).

For another classic date movie starring Audrey Hepburn, see *Roman Holiday* in Chapter 3. For another scribe suffering from writer's block, see *Shakespeare in Love* in Chapter 10.

Do Try This at Home: Spend the day together doing things that neither of you has ever done before.

❧ Children of a Lesser God (1986)

William Hurt, Marlee Matlin, Piper Laurie, Philip Bosco
DIRECTED BY RANDA HAINES
118 minutes; in color; R
Intimacy Comfort Level: Going Steady, Committed/Married
Make-Out Meter: ▮▮▮▮
Just for Her: The pool scene
Just for Him: Casual sex, loving sex, angry sex

Adapted by Mark Medoff from his stage play, *Children of a Lesser God* tells the story of James Leeds (Hurt), an iconoclastic speech teacher who comes to a small coastal town to work at a school for the deaf. He is immediately at odds with the school administrator (Bosco) because of his unorthodox teaching practices, history of job hopping, practice of cranking up the volume so that deaf students can feel the music, and courtship of Sarah Norman (Matlin), an attractive former student who now works as a janitor at the school.

As a speech teacher, James is focused on helping deaf and hearing-impaired students learn to speak and read lips (in addition to signing) in order to find better jobs and fit into society. When he spends personal and professional time with Sarah, he discovers that despite her high intelligence, she has no desire to speak or read lips—in essence she rejects the hearing world and all those who occupy it. As they begin to fall in love, James describes her as "the most mysterious, beautiful, angry person" he has ever met.

We soon learn why she's so angry. Sarah cleans toilets, empties trash cans, swims at the school pool, signs obscenities at coworkers, and dances through vibrations in her nose, but one thing she won't do is speak. As a child, she was ridiculed by people who said she looked ugly and sounded stupid when she tried to talk. Now she doesn't do anything that she doesn't do well.

Another thing Sarah does extremely well is sex. Her good looks and desire for acceptance made her an easy mark for the high school boys, who lined up to get their chance with the deaf girl. Years later, she still prides herself on being even better in bed than hearing girls. But at age twenty-five, her beauty and sexuality still define who she is; the real Sarah remains a mystery.

Although James doesn't complain about her nice appearance and skills in the bedroom, he does get a little irritated about her lack of self-awareness. In Sarah's case, her physical beauty has stunted her emotional development. But are a loving boyfriend, repentant mother (Laurie), and break from scrubbing toilets enough to bring about any real change?

Because much of the dialogue is translated from sign language, *Children of a Lesser God* doesn't waste words. Each line is important for explaining the story and characters. Hurt comes across as sensitive and loving—coming close, but never quite crossing over into sappy.

Strong acting and powerful drama led to Matlin receiving an Academy Award for best actress. Strong attraction and powerful sex scenes led to Matlin and Hurt continuing their onscreen romance offscreen for a while.

For other movies featuring sign language, see *Four Weddings and a Funeral* in Chapter 1 and *Jerry Maguire* in Chapter 5. For additional sensual swimming scenes, see *Roman Holiday* in Chapter 3, *Meet the Parents* and *Titanic* in Chapter 4, *Bringing Up Baby* and *Dirty Dancing* in Chapter 5, *Shallow Hal* in this chapter, *All the Pretty Horses* and *Big Trouble in Little China* in Chapter 7, and *The African Queen*, *Romancing the Stone*, and *Six Days, Seven Nights* in Chapter 9.

Do Try This at Home: Crawl under the covers and pretend you're in some romantic, distant place.

❧ *Edward Scissorhands* (1990)

Johnny Depp, Winona Ryder, Dianne Wiest, Anthony Michael Hall
DIRECTED BY TIM BURTON
105 minutes; in color; PG-13
Intimacy Comfort Level: First Date, Going Steady, Committed/Married
Make-Out Meter: ▮▮
Just for Her: "Hold me"
Just for Him: An introduction to "lemonade"

Created by an eccentric inventor (Vincent Price), Edward Scissorhands (Depp) is a compilation of high-tech robotics, pinking shears, black leather, and buckles. Edward is left with scissors for hands and a figurative hole in his sugar cookie heart when the inventor suddenly dies before completing his creation.

With chronically bad hair and a face full of scars, Edward lives alone in the inventor's mansion high on a hill inside a cul de sac. Trained in etiquette, poetry, and ethics, his only company is photographs cut out from magazines. One day, overzealous Avon lady Peg (Wiest) comes soliciting and meets Edward, a modern-day monster of Frankenstein—on the outside at least. Determined to improve his appearance, she takes him home with her. Despite using every concealing makeup product available through Avon, Peg is unable to make Edward look normal—that is, like everyone else in her rigid little pastel suburbia.

Although Edward laments that he has scissorhands because he's not finished yet, he seems more complete spiritually and intellectually than other characters in the movie. Peg wants to heal the world with a little beauty cream and concealer. Her pretty daughter Kim (Ryder) dates teenage thug Jim (Hall) and fears Edward because he looks different from everyone else. Other unfinished characters in this wretched neighborhood include a religious fanatic, town tramp, and gossip monger who conspire against Edward and eventually against Peg's family for befriending him.

Immediately smitten with Kim, Edward endures a variety of insults, indignities, and imbeciles in his quest to fit into the family and the town. He briefly ingratiates himself with the community by cutting lawns, styling hair, grooming dogs, and grilling shish kebabs.

The clueless Kim finally learns to see past the scissors and scars, but lots of physical and emotional damage is done in the process. Like angry villagers coming after Frankenstein's monster, the drab inhabitants in this particular Burton fable eventually come lusting after blood . . . and scissors.

Told in the context of a bedtime story, *Edward Scissorhands* explores our notions of beauty, monsters, and love. The morality lesson takes precedence over the romance, but scenes of Edward in a water bed, at a televised interview, and sculpting ice certainly have romantic appeal.

For another supernatural fable directed by Burton and starring Johnny Depp (without the scars) see *Sleepy Hollow* in Chapter 8.

Do Try This at Home: Turn your first meeting into a treasured story to be told and retold.

❧ *Legally Blonde* (2001)

Reese Witherspoon, Luke Wilson, Selma Blair, Matthew Davis
DIRECTED BY ROBERT LUKETIC
96 minutes; in color; PG-13
Intimacy Comfort Level: First Date, Going Steady, Committed/Married
Make-Out Meter: ❙❙
Just for Her: Refuge at the beauty salon and shopping mall
Just for Him: College admissions video; the "Bend and Snap"

The action starts immediately as immaculately groomed, perfectly coiffed, impeccably polite, blue-eyed blonde Elle Woods (Witherspoon) gets unexpectedly dumped by her longtime boyfriend (Davis). It seems that Warner Huntington III has plans to attend Harvard Law School, become a senator, and "marry a Jackie, not a Marilyn." Essentially, Warner breaks up with Elle because she is too blond.

Devastated by the breakup, she tries to lift her spirits at the sorority house through the usual means of chocolates and soap operas, plus frequent trips to

Elle (Reese Witherspoon) ventures to Harvard Law School to find love and to prove that she's no dumb blonde in *Legally Blonde*. (Tracy Bennett/Copyright © 2001 Metro-Goldwyn-Mayer; courtesy of Photofest)

the nail salon. When even these proven methods fail to bring comfort, Elle decides to show the world that she's not just a dumb blonde and enrolls as a Harvard Law School student with the hopes of winning Warner back. Based on her 4.0 grade point average, 179 on the LSAT, sorority-related accomplishments, and most of all her stylish admissions video, the all-male Harvard review board decides to let her attend.

Once there among the "boring, ugly, and serious," she is discriminated against because of her appearance and dismissed as a brainless Barbie doll. With help from a handsome young lawyer (Wilson), a motherly manicurist (Jennifer Coolidge), a harsh professor (Holland Taylor), and an abundance of girl power, Elle rises from the bottom to the top of her class.

For the first time in her life, she uses brains and beauty to get what she wants. Well, more accurately, she combines brains and beauty secrets to get what she wants. Elle confidently proclaims: "The rules of hair care are simple and finite." Not even the Supreme Court could argue with that.

Witherspoon is radiant as she struggles to find Elle's inner strength (and inner beauty, for that matter). When even her bible (*Cosmopolitan* magazine) provides no answers during her time of crisis, she learns to have faith in herself and others, forcing people to realize that first impressions are not always correct. The movie follows her transition from one relationship to another, and her growth from a sexist stereotype into a multileveled person.

What this story lacks in make-out meter heat, it more than makes up for in chocolate-like endorphins. *Legally Blonde* (and its sequel, *Legally Blonde 2: Red, White, and Blonde*) will make you feel good about life, love, and even blondes.

For other seemingly ditzy blondes, see *Seems Like Old Times* in Chapter 5, *Me, Myself & Irene* in Chapter 7, and *Some Like It Hot* and *Working Girl* in Chapter 10.

Do Try This at Home: Encourage your partner to achieve his or her personal best even when no one else does.

❧ *Miss Congeniality* (2000)

Sandra Bullock, Benjamin Bratt, Michael Caine, Candice Bergen
DIRECTED BY DONALD PETRIE
110 minutes; in color; PG-13
Intimacy Comfort Level: First Date, Going Steady, Committed/Married
Make-Out Meter: ❙❙❙
Just for Her: Emergency Makeover Unit
Just for Him: "Dress Up Sally" website

Here she is. She might be graceful in her heart, but style, poise, and manners never make it to the surface for Gracie Hart (Bullock), an awkward, unrefined FBI field agent who is forced to go undercover as a beauty queen when a mad bomber threatens the Miss United States Pageant.

Gracie is the kind of woman who snorts when she laughs, slumps when she walks, and pushes to the front of the Starbucks line flashing her FBI badge. She is the kind of woman who wrestles with men (and wins) and throws the rule book away when she wants to get the job done. Above all, she is the kind of woman who despises the objectification of other women through beauty pageants.

But when her FBI bosses discover that she's the only female undercover agent who looks good in a bathing suit, Gracie gets forced into an assignment to infiltrate the pageant and find the guilty party. Eric Matthews (Bratt) leads "Operation Thong" with one eye on the criminal investigation and the other eye on Gracie as she develops into a real beauty queen under the direction of Victor Melling (Caine), a Henry Higgins–type pageant consultant.

Gracie enters the pageant equipped with only her sarcasm and a gun. Under Victor's tutelage, however, she morphs from "Dirty Harriet" to "Mustang Sally." As Miss New Jersey Gracie Lou Freebush, she learns how to eat, speak, walk, dress, and apply makeup. Victor's hardest task becomes making her into a complete person who embraces her womanhood for the first time.

Bullock does a terrific job as Gracie, wringing laughs out of nearly every scene. Bratt is effective as the superficial handsome jock who learns something new about women in general and about Gracie in particular through the experience. As the pageant cohosts, Bergen and William Shatner are cartoonish buffoons who do little for the story other than provide some laughs. And speaking of Doolittle, although the crazed-bomber-lurking-among-the-beauty-contestants subplot is admittedly weak, the main storyline about Gracie becoming a fair lady is a winner.

For another movie about a female FBI agent, see *Out of Sight* in Chapter 7.

Do Try This at Home: Plan A: Notice and compliment any physical improvements in your partner. Plan B: Provide a pep talk when he or she needs it most.

Barrymore or Bullock?
5. Was Drew Barrymore or Sandra Bullock the sixth highest paid actress in Hollywood in 2002?
Answer on page 205

Two badly dressed misfits (Sylvester Stallone and Talia Shire) undergo physical and emotional makeovers in *Rocky*. (Copyright © 1976 United Artists Corporation; courtesy of Photofest)

❧ *Rocky* (1976)

Sylvester Stallone, Talia Shire, Burt Young, Carl Weathers
DIRECTED BY JOHN G. AVILDSEN
119 minutes; in color; PG
Intimacy Comfort Level: First Date, Going Steady, Committed/Married
Make-Out Meter: ▮▮▮
Just for Her: First kiss
Just for Him: Meat freezer training; big boxing match

Okay, so maybe "women weaken legs," but they sure can strengthen a man's self-esteem. Southpaw amateur boxer Rocky Balboa, a.k.a. The Italian Stallion (Stallone), makes forty bucks every two weeks boxing at his neighborhood gym in Philadelphia. He makes considerably more money threatening to break legs and crack heads for a local loan shark. A poor, uneducated, self-described bum, the big-hearted Rocky fancies Adrian (Shire), a painfully shy pet store clerk with outdated glasses and a thrift-store wardrobe.

Although Adrian's brother Paulie (Young), a friend of Rocky's, calls his sister a loser and a freak and the loan shark's driver calls her "retarded," Rocky insists that she's just shy. Indeed, one date with Rocky—followed by a memorable visit to his apartment—is all Adrian needs to overcome her shyness.

They both change as a result of this new relationship: Adrian's eyesight miraculously improves and she no longer needs glasses. She discards her frumpy attire for some form-fitting clothes and perky little berets. Likewise, Rocky cleans up his act, donning some fancy sweaters and a little self-confidence.

These two misfits clearly need each other in order to fit into society. He confides that his father told him that he wasn't born with much of a brain so he better develop his body. Adrian reveals that her mother had told her the opposite: that she wasn't born with much of a body so she better develop her brain.

Finding love is only part of the story, of course. Rocky tells the tale of an underdog's triumph in the bedroom, in his own mind, in the boxing arena, and in the eyes of the world as he experiences the rags-to-riches American dream.

The heavyweight boxing champion of the world, Apollo Creed (Weathers), a character much like Muhammad Ali, challenges Rocky to a bicentennial bout on January 1, 1976, as a novelty act because he thinks Rocky's nickname, The Italian Stallion, would look great on a marquee. Fighting with sheer will (and a little training from his cranky old manager Mickey [Burgess Meredith]), Rocky may just surprise everyone with his staying power.

Stallone wrote the screenplay and choreographed the boxing scenes for *Rocky*, which won Academy Awards for best picture, director, and film editing. Look for Stallone's father, Frank, as a timekeeper, his brother, Frank Jr., as a street singer, and his dog, Butkus, playing himself. Can a movie with so much fighting, violence, and testosterone make a great date movie? Absolutely.

Four *Rocky* sequels line the shelves at your favorite video store. The original is by far the most romantic, but if you just can't get enough of The Italian Stallion, knock yourself out and rent all five. (For further proof of Stallone's well-developed body, you might want to rent the 1970 X-rated movie *The Italian Stallion*, in which Stallone plays Stud, a very festive and enthusiastic party host. Originally titled *A Party at Kitty and Stud's*, the movie was renamed and rereleased in 1985 to capitalize on Stallone's fame. Then again, you might not.)

Do Try This at Home: Fill each other's gaps.

❧ *Roxanne* (1987)

Steve Martin, Daryl Hannah, Shelley Duvall, Rick Rossovich
DIRECTED BY FRED SCHEPISI
107 minutes; in color; PG
Intimacy Comfort Level: First Date, Going Steady, Committed/Married
Make-Out Meter: ▮▮▮
Just for Her: A man who knows how to express his feelings
Just for Him: Tennis-racket revenge; X-rated nose jokes

An updated *Cyrano de Bergerac*, *Roxanne* has sparkling performances and the crisp, witty dialogue at which Martin excels. Not so coincidentally, Martin also wrote and executive produced the movie. In addition to the wonderful screenplay, *Roxanne* boasts inspired performances from a colorful cast of characters.

For example, instead of Cyrano de Bergerac, there's C.D. Bales (Martin), a big-nosed, well-read fire chief who lives in a small town. He is friends with Dixie (Duvall), the owner of the most popular restaurant in town. C.D. has fun sniffing out fires, talking with Dixie, making up tall tales for the little old ladies who happen to cross his path, and challenging Bozos who unwisely comment on the size of his nose. It's a happy, if lonely, existence.

C.D. wants to settle down with a woman, but he's afraid it would be just the three of them: her, him, and his nose. Deathly allergic to anesthetics and afraid of the word rhinoplasty, C.D. finds himself stuck with his hellacious honker.

The town gets shaken up a bit with two new arrivals: Roxanne (Hannah), a beautiful astronomer who rents a house that provides an unobstructed view of the sky as she searches for a new comet, and Chris (Rossovich), a hunky fire expert brought on to help the pathetic group of volunteers who currently make up the fire department.

Chris and Roxanne develop an immediate physical attraction to each other. At the same time, C.D. develops a sincere respect, admiration, and love for the brainy scientist, who accidentally locks herself out of the house while naked and winds up at his firehouse for assistance. (See *Splash* in Chapter 3 for more naked encounters with Daryl Hannah. And for that matter, *Summer Lovers* [1982], *Reckless* [1984], and *At Play in the Fields of the Lord* [1991]), if you're into that kind of thing.)

Although Roxanne considers herself to be a deep person above superficialities, she nonetheless falls instantly for the terminally dim-witted Chris, who can barely string enough words together for a sentence. Roxanne comes to C.D. for help in catching Chris, while at the same time Chris comes to C.D. for help communicating with Roxanne. C.D. finds himself expressing his most profound sentiments and heartfelt desire in love letters and speeches delivered by someone else to the woman he loves.

Moving, tender, romantic, and funny, *Roxanne* concerns itself with beauty and its relationship to love through the eyes of every character in the movie.

For more star-gazing and constellation-naming, see *Shrek* in Chapter 3 and *Serendipity* in Chapter 8.

Do Try This at Home: Write a heartfelt love letter.

❧ *Sense and Sensibility* (1995)

Emma Thompson, Alan Rickman, Kate Winslet, Hugh Grant
DIRECTED BY ANG LEE
136 minutes; in color; PG
Intimacy Comfort Level: First Date, Going Steady, Committed/Married
Make-Out Meter: ▮▮▮
Just for Her: Cheek pinching
Just for Him: The good guys win

Okay, there's not much action here. Just an Academy Award–winning screenplay by Emma Thompson, an ensemble cast of talented British actors, beautiful scenery, memorable moments, clever plot twists, interesting characters with secret pasts, and a classic tale of finding love the hard way.

Mrs. Dashwood (Gemma Jones) and her three lovely daughters, Elinor (Thompson), Marianne (Winslet), and eleven-year-old Margaret are suddenly forced out of their home and into a country cottage when Mr. Dashwood (Tom Wilkinson) dies leaving all his possessions to his greedy son (from an earlier marriage) and daughter-in-law, in accordance with early-nineteenth-century English laws.

Marrying for money rather than love was also in accordance with the social customs of the time. Therefore, the highly eligible Elinor and her younger sisters become suddenly undesirable. Sensible Elinor realizes her chances of finding a suitor diminish by the day, but she still secretly holds out hope that Edward Ferrars (Grant), the brother of her stepsister by marriage, might return her feelings of esteem and admiration, even though it would mean forfeiting his financial security.

Fresh-faced Marianne, however, makes no secret that she gives in to her romantic sensibilities, proclaiming, "To love is to burn, to be on fire." She adores the dashing young John Willoughby (Greg Wise), a handsome playboy with much to hide. Also courting Marianne is Colonel Brandon (Rickman), a middle-aged neighbor who represents the antithesis of Willoughby. Brandon possesses patience, integrity, strength, and grace but lacks the flamboyant charm and good looks of the younger suitor.

So the question remains for the two sisters: Is it better to love with your head or with your heart? Perhaps with a little luck they can both find love that lies somewhere between burning fire and "polite affections."

For other movies based on Jane Austen novels, see *Emma* in Chapter 1 and *Bridget Jones's Diary* in Chapter 2. For another Ang Lee–directed romance, see *Crouching Tiger, Hidden Dragon* in Chapter 3.

Do Try This at Home: Bring flowers when your loved one is sick.

Gere or Grant?
5. Was Richard Gere or Hugh Grant involved in a long-term, offscreen romantic relationship with a beautiful supermodel?
Answer on page 206

❧ *Shallow Hal* (2001)

Gwyneth Paltrow, Jack Black, Jason Alexander, Joe Viterelli
DIRECTED BY BOBBY FARRELLY AND PETER FARRELLY
113 minutes; in color; PG-13
Intimacy Comfort Level: First Date, Going Steady, Committed/Married
Make-Out Meter: ▮▮▮
Just for Her: A man who can see a woman's inner beauty
Just for Him: A pipeline to the big boss

An otherwise great guy, Hal (Black) has a deep-seated, all-encompassing psychological disturbance concerning beauty. Therefore, the average-looking Hal is doomed to failure because he always chases extraordinarily beautiful women who are out of his league. Unless a woman possesses physical qualities usually associated with international pop stars under the age of twenty-five, Hal isn't interested in dating them. Although he's often cruel in his superficial judgments of women, his best friend, Mauricio (Alexander), is even more shallow—not to mention thoughtless and vulgar—and breaks up with a generous, loving woman (who is extremely attractive by anyone's standards) because her second toe is longer than the first.

One day, Hal gets stuck on an elevator with motivational guru Tony Robbins (as himself), who performs a mind-altering hypnosis that frees Hal from his superficiality by allowing him to see only a person's inner beauty. According to the logic of this particular movie, Hal can see beyond exterior attributes of men and women, children and adults, but only of new people whom he hasn't seen before he was hypnotized.

With this new outlook (or more accurately "inlook") on life, he finds that beautiful women are funny, smart, and nice—four traits that usually don't go together. He becomes oblivious to obesity, blind to bad teeth, and unaware of ugliness. So when Hal meets 300-pound Rosemary—coincidentally the boss's daughter—he instead sees lovely Gwyneth Paltrow. Although his constant compliments about her beauty (as he perceives it) make her uncomfortable at first, Rosemary does enjoy being with him.

Hal responds to her upbeat attitude and quick wit, and they quickly form a romantic relationship. Paltrow donned a fat suit for certain scenes; other times, body doubles were used to portray unsightly "cankles" and produce a more authentic jiggle factor. In most scenes, however, Rosemary is shown as the beautiful blond Paltrow, tall and thin with lovely, delicate features.

Meanwhile, Mauricio finds Hal's transformation disturbing and complains that his friend has undergone "beer goggle laser surgery" so that even obese, frizzy-haired women with buckteeth and decidedly indelicate features look like supermodels to him. When Hal seeks his friend's approval of Rosemary, Mauricio berates him with a slew of crude one-liners such as "She doesn't just take the cake, she takes the whole bakery."

For her part, Rosemary remains skeptical that Hal finds her so lovely. Her inner beauty abounds, however: she has a good sense of humor, keen intellect, a soft spot for sick children, and a desire to help others. Paltrow retains the vulnerable quality of the physically unattractive in all her scenes—whether looking like herself in a bathing suit or as Rosemary in the fat suit. Her confidence grows throughout the movie, until of course the inevitable plummet when Hal discovers what she really looks like.

When the hypnotic spell is broken, the question remains: "Did this experience give Shallow Hal any more depth?"

To explore more of the Farrelly brothers' obsession with physical deformities and abnormalities, see *Me, Myself & Irene* in Chapter 7 and *There's Something About Mary* in Chapter 10, where the glamorous stars share screen time with an assortment of unusual characters with real and feigned afflictions.

Do Try This at Home: Share a large milkshake at a 1950s-style diner.

Paltrow or Pfeiffer?
**4. Did Gwyneth Paltrow or Michelle Pfeiffer star
in a rendition of a Shakespearean tale?**
Answer on page 207

For more great romantic date movies about ugly ducklings turning into swans see *Moonstruck* in Chapter 1, *Shrek* in Chapter 3, *True Lies* in Chapter 7, and *Romancing the Stone* in Chapter 9.

Chapter 7

Is That a Pistol/Knife/Nunchak in Your Pocket?

*A doctor could make a million dollars if he could figure out a way to
bring a boy into the world without a trigger finger.*
Arthur Miller

TEXAS COWBOY John Grady Cole (Matt Damon) in *All the Pretty Horses* encounters many challenges to his moral code during his ill-fated adventure in Mexico. The easygoing ranch hand known for his integrity is forced into several split-second life-or-death decisions, and finds that his violent actions (or lack of violent actions) nag his conscience. Whether justifiably killing a man in self-defense or failing to save a life out of self-preservation, John Grady concludes, "That don't make it right."

The men in the following ten movies are forced to confront their relationship to violence: The sensitive guys find their inner toughness, and the tough guys find their inner sensitivity. Nowhere is the transition more obvious than in the Farrelly brothers' gross-out comedy *Me, Myself & Irene*. Rhode Island state trooper Charlie Baileygates (Jim Carrey) passively accepts his mistreatment by others with a nonconfrontational "you betcha." Despite the gun hanging from his belt, people aren't threatened by the repressed cop who, unbeknownst to him, is the town joke.

On one particularly humiliating day, Charlie has a mental breakdown and a second personality emerges. Hank Evans (Carrey) aggressively rejects any mistreatment of himself, his companion/prisoner Irene (Renée Zellweger), the state laws, the environment, and especially the ozone layer. Hank doesn't need the threat of a gun around his waist, he's got his fists for hands-on confrontations.

When a careless softball player tosses his cigarette butt on the ground in a parking lot, Charlie launches a full-scale attack. "Hey man, take it easy. It's just a cigarette," the softball player says. But Hank's in no mood for excuses. "Oh yeah. Well, this is just a fist, but when I start throwing it around it can leave one hell of a mess."

American spy T.R. Devlin (Cary Grant) in *Notorious* uses his intellect, charm, and survival instincts to dodge dangerous situations. Only when he needs to infiltrate enemy territory does he stuff a pistol in his pocket.

Likewise, Jack Foley (George Clooney) in *Out of Sight* is a sweet, sensitive career bank robber who has cleaned out more than 200 vaults across the country without ever using a weapon. "You'd be surprised what you can get if you just ask for it in the right way," he says.

The other male characters in this chapter, however, shoot/stab/hit first and ask questions later. Tough guys becoming more sensitive is the more common theme.

In *Witness*, Harrison Ford plays John Book, a hardened police detective working to save an Amish widow, Rachel Lapp (Kelly McGillis), and her son from the corrupt assassins who work with him on the Philadelphia police force. Hiding in her home for a while, he tries to blend in with the community by dressing and behaving according to peaceful, modest, and gentle Amish customs. First and foremost, he must give up his gun to Rachel, who promptly hides it in the kitchen cupboard and stashes the bullets in the flour bin.

Despite his best efforts to squelch his violent tendencies in their presence, he and Rachel realize that he's a little more proficient at shooting guns than milking cows. "I just don't like my son spending all his time with a man who carries a gun and goes around whacking people," she complains.

Although John takes issue with the "whacking" allegation, he is later forced to admit that violence is indeed his way of getting results. Along the way, however, he does become a more peaceful, modest, and gentle hardened police detective.

Other tough guys also soften their stance because of love. Independent trucker Jack Burton (Kurt Russell) in *Big Trouble in Little China* learns to value one particular woman's life as much (well *almost* as much) as his prized eighteen-wheeler. Muscle-bound undercover officer John Kimball (Arnold Schwarzenegger) in *Kindergarten Cop* finds that a beautiful woman and her son can penetrate his heart more effectively than a bullet. American spy Harry Tasker learns that it takes only one man (as long as he's Arnold Schwarzenegger) to defeat a well-armed group of angry terrorists, but it takes two to tango in *True Lies*. In *Two Mules for Sister Sara*, Hogan (Clint Eastwood), a lone mercenary, discovers something better than money. And adventurer Indiana Jones (Harrison Ford) gets the treasure, the prize, and the booty in *Raiders of the Lost Ark*.

There is a downside to carrying a weapon, however. Sometimes these men get hurt. When tough guys get physically hurt they become much more sympathetic to viewers. When they also suffer from emotional wounds inflicted by the women they love, their plight becomes even more engrossing. John Grady gets unjustly imprisoned, knifed, and shot. Jack Burton gets captured, blindfolded, tied to a wheelchair, and beat up repeatedly. John Kimball gets shot. Charlie Baileygates gets beat up, drop-kicked, sodomized, and shot. Jack Foley gets shot. Indiana Jones gets beat up and shot. Harry Tasker gets pumped full of truth serum, punched a few times, shot at, and his shirt ripped open to reveal his muscled torso. Hogan gets shot with an arrow. John Book gets shot. With so many bullets (and that arrow) flying, it's easy to see why these men need a woman's tender loving care.

The only man who doesn't take a beating or a bullet is T.R. Devlin, but his female spy counterpart doesn't exactly fare too well as a captive of escaped Nazi war criminals.

In general, these movies tend to be faster paced than most of the other date movies in this book—although *All the Pretty Horses*, *Two Mules for Sister Sara*, and *Witness* take the time to enjoy the scenery between the violence. Overtly aimed at male audiences (and covertly directed at women), they also have rougher language than, say, *How to Lose a Guy in 10 Days* (Chapter 2), where the word "penis" is used a couple of times in the dialogue to elicit embarrassed tittering throughout the audience. While often brutal, these ten movies have something to say about man's primitive instinct toward violence and something even more important to say about love.

These handsome heroes with sensitive sides also have strong romantic feelings because their cravings for violence and sex go hand in hand. While on the surface, these movies are aimed exclusively at male audiences, the added romantic element engages women and makes the bone-crunching, mind-numbing violence a necessary evil until the next kissing scene.

Let's hope that John Grady (Matt Damon) removed his pistol from his pocket before slow dancing with Alejandra (Penelope Cruz) in *All the Pretty Horses*. (Van Redin/Copyright © 2000; courtesy of Photofest)

❧ *All the Pretty Horses* (2000)

Matt Damon, Penelope Cruz, Henry Thomas, Lucas Black
DIRECTED BY BILLY BOB THORNTON
116 minutes; in color; PG-13
Intimacy Comfort Level: First Date, Going Steady, Committed/Married
Make-Out Meter: ▮▮▮
Just for Her: A cowboy with integrity
Just for Him: Taming wild horses and a wild woman

It's almost inevitable that when an immensely popular and critically acclaimed book is made into a movie, there will be some naysayers (or in this case, neighsayers). Cormac McCarthy's National Book Critics Circle Award–

winning novel *All the Pretty Horses* is retooled for translation to the big screen and restyled by director Thornton to update the traditional Western drama with an artful, tightly edited retelling that includes slow motion, freeze frames, jump cuts, and dream sequences.

Purists who like their Westerns dusty and dirty, their heroes ill-mannered and stubble-faced, and their stories simple and straightforward are out of luck. Under Thornton's direction and with a screenplay by Ted Telly, this particular Western has beautiful rolling countrysides and sparkling clear rivers, clean-shaven cowboys who rarely spit or curse, and a narrative told more through implication than explanation.

It's a Western for people who don't like Westerns.

Set in 1949, the film focuses on John Grady Cole (Damon), a Texas ranch hand who ventures to Mexico with his friend Lacey Rawlins (Thomas) to see what it's like to be a real cowboy. Along the way, they meet Jimmy Blevins (Black), a spunky adolescent with a stolen horse who has run away from his abusive stepfather. Although John Grady feels a responsibility to take care of the boy, Lacey senses trouble from the beginning and cautions repeatedly against helping the young thief.

Once in Mexico, Jimmy loses his horse, gun, and clothes, which sets in motion a complicated series of events—some pleasant, some less so.

Among the most pleasant is when John Grady and Lacey get jobs breaking in horses on a beautiful ranch, and Jimmy goes out on his own. They earn the respect of the other ranch hands, and John Grady meets the owner's beautiful daughter, Alejandra de la Rocha (Cruz). They have an immediate attraction, and it isn't long before she's sneaking into his bunk at night.

Unfortunately for John Grady, despite his integrity and good intentions, their intimate relationship will ruin her reputation, which is all she has, according to her old-maid aunt Senorita Alfonsa (Miriam Colon). In addition, Jimmy has been arrested for stealing his horse back from the Mexican who took it and shooting him dead in the process.

With so much working against them, the two gringos soon get arrested themselves and wind up in a brutal penitentiary where Lacey is continually beat up and John Grady is forced to fight to the death. This rude foray into the world of violence causes John Grady to have lots of flashbacks and dream sequences, where he relives his happier and less-violent times back on the ranch, breaking in horses and, of course, romancing Alejandra.

Damon, Thomas, and Black provide strong likeable performances, and Cruz is sufficiently beautiful and exotic to make us understand why John Grady would take such dangerous risks to pursue this forbidden love.

For another Western love story, see *Two Mules for Sister Sara* in this chapter.

Do Try This at Home: Go for a midnight swim (bathing suits optional).

❧ *Big Trouble in Little China* (1986)

Kurt Russell, Kim Cattrall, Dennis Dun, James Hong
DIRECTED BY JOHN CARPENTER
99 minutes; in color; PG-13
Intimacy Comfort Level: First Date, Going Steady, Committed/Married
Make-Out Meter: ❚❚
Just for Her: Lipstick stains
Just for Him: Magical martial arts

Pistols, knives, and nunchaks bulge from the pockets of nearly every man in *Big Trouble in Little China*, a tongue-in-cheek martial arts action/fantasy/romance. Rough-and-ready San Francisco trucker Jack Burton (Russell) gets himself in a little trouble when his beloved truck, "The Pork Chop Express," gets stolen. His best friend Wang Chi (Dun) gets himself in big trouble when his beautiful green-eyed fiancée, Miao Yim (Suzee Pai), gets kidnapped by some Asian thugs from Little China who work for Lo Pan (Hong), an evil spirit who longs to become human again.

Jack and Wang attempt a daring rescue in the bowels of Chinatown, along with help from cute lawyer Gracie Law (Cattrall), a wily old tour guide and nemesis of Lo Pan (Victor Wong), and a newspaper reporter (Kate Burton). To their horror, they discover that Lo Pan plans to conduct some ancient Chinese black magic rituals with Miao, then marry her in order to transform from spirit to flesh. Because his magic only works with green-eyed women, he figures "What the heck?" and doubles his chances for success by also kidnapping Gracie so he can have a double wedding ceremony.

The story and acting are outrageously unbelievable, but the fight scenes are supernaturally sensational with the characters "Thunder," "Rain," and "Lightening" presenting a dazzling display of martial arts, special effects, and powers from beyond. Best of all, there are three separate romances going on simultaneously—and that's not even counting Lo Pan's green-eyed bigamy plan.

Men will enjoy the martial arts action and special effects, while women should find Jack's swashbuckling heroism a nice change from the usual guy with a gun. He stays cool whether fighting ancient evil spirits, hideous monsters from the sewers beneath the city, warriors with unusual weapons and abilities, or his own warm, fuzzy feelings for Gracie.

Although Jack admits that sooner or later he rubs everybody the wrong way, Gracie probably wouldn't agree.

For more date movies where ethnicity plays a role in the romance, see *Moonstruck* in Chapter 1, *Crossing Delancey* in Chapter 2, *Crouching Tiger, Hidden Dragon* in Chapter 3, *Meet the Parents* in Chapter 4, *Annie Hall* in Chapter 5, *Rocky* in Chapter 6, *Witness* in this chapter, and *Coming to America* and *Maid in Manhattan* in Chapter 10. Also see Chapter 8 for more stories outside the realm of reality.

Do Try This at Home: Kiss on an elevator (moderate intensity somewhere between air kissing and shaking the pillars of heaven).

❧ *Kindergarten Cop* (1990)

Arnold Schwarzenegger, Penelope Ann Miller, Pamela Reed, Linda Hunt
DIRECTED BY IVAN REITMAN
111 minutes; in color; PG-13
Intimacy Comfort Level: First Date, Going Steady, Committed/Married
Make-Out Meter: ▮▮
Just for Her: Milk mustache
Just for Him: Punches; baseball bats; bullets to the deserving

Although the next listed movie in this chapter, *Me, Myself & Irene,* concerns a paranoid schizophrenic, *Kindergarten Cop* has something of a split personality itself. The violent beginning looks like the start of other mindless action Schwarzenegger movies such as *Commando, Eraser,* or *Raw Deal.* But after John Kimball's (Schwarzenegger) hardened Los Angeles cop status is established, the story takes on a lighter tone. You could call it dual personalities or merely a sensitive movie getting in touch with its masculine and feminine sides.

Fiercely independent Kimball is forced to take on a female partner, the delightfully droll Phoebe O'Hara (Reed), who will work undercover as a kindergarten teacher at Astoria Elementary School in Oregon to find the ex-wife

(Miller) and child (Joseph Cousins and Christian Cousins) of Crisp (Richard Tyson), a brutal thug whom Kimball has been tracking for years. The day of the big assignment, Phoebe develops a bad case of stomach flu and John must take her place. She informs John that he already possesses the skills for teaching: "If you show fear, you're dead—like any police situation."

But lacking any experience with children or teaching, John finds that without his gun or other forms of intimidation, he is overwhelmed by two dozen screaming six-year-olds. A divorced father who barely even knows his son, John gets a crash course in parenting and teaching. He soon finds that kindergarten is much like the ocean: you never turn your back on it. The children are predictably precious and ultimately teach John about love, family, and human anatomy. Along the way, he does meet Crisp's ex-wife and manages to fall in love with her, which isn't really that surprising since he and Crisp have parallel personalities and lives.

After some comical classroom scenes, a tender dinner by firelight, and some heartfelt confessions, the action shifts back to the traditional macho movie you'd expect from Schwarzenegger with a deadly shootout inside the elementary school. The violence is sometimes graphic and extreme, although the humor and romance have an equally strong presence.

Hunt plays feisty school principal Mrs. Schlowski, and Tyson makes a sufficiently sleazy villain out of Crisp, a character made somewhat sympathetic by his manipulative mama.

For another undercover officer out of his element, see *Witness* in this chapter. For another romantic Schwarzenegger movie, see *True Lies*, also in this chapter.

Do Try This at Home: Enter the three-legged race at the fair.

❧ *Me, Myself & Irene* (2000)

Jim Carrey, Renée Zellweger, Chris Cooper, Robert Forster
DIRECTED BY BOBBY FARRELLY AND PETER FARRELLY
116 minutes; in color; R
Intimacy Comfort Level: Going Steady, Committed/Married
Make-Out Meter: ▮▮▮
Just for Her: Racing for the train
Just for Him: Front-yard revenge; "morning after" bathroom scene

Can a heartbroken Rhode Island state trooper suffering from advanced delusionary schizophrenia with involuntary narcissistic rage find happiness with a ditzy, blond golf-course groundskeeper fleeing her former boss and the corrupt police and FBI agents on his payroll? That's the question posed by *Me, Myself & Irene*, another crude, rude, and lewd comic installment by the Farrelly brothers.

There's lots of other stuff occurring besides the love story, which is by far the most entertaining aspect of the movie due to the considerable talent and on-screen chemistry between Carrey and Zellweger. Subplots range from lame to strong, respectively: the complicated and contrived Cedar Creek Country Club Golf Course conspiracy; three illegitimate, foul-mouthed, black genius triplets that Charlie Baileygates (Carrey) has raised as his own sons; Whitey, a lonely albino boy (Michael Bowman) whom Irene Waters (Zellweger) and Charlie befriend; and Charlie's mental disintegration and reconstruction.

Just as Charlie's personality and the story itself are multilayered, the humor comes fast and furious on several levels throughout the entire movie. Written by the Farrelly brothers and Mike Cerrone (note the softball jerseys in the cigarette butt/gas station scene), the movie uses physical comedy, sight gags, slapstick, hyperbole, understatement, metaphor, irony, double entendre, non sequitur, gross-out humor, and even Hitchcockian camera angles and techniques to get laughs.

Narrated by Rex Allen Jr., the story begins eighteen years earlier when Charlie marries Layla (Traylor Howard), the smartest and prettiest girl in town. On their arrival home from the wedding, she falls in love with Shonte (Tony Cox), the limousine driver who brought them back; he's a dwarf African American with a bad attitude, membership in Mensa, and big set of . . . nunchaks.

When Layla soon gives birth to high-IQ black triplets and names them Shonte Jr., Lee Harvey, and Jamaal, Charlie still refuses to acknowledge that his wife is cheating on him. When she eventually leaves him for her lover, Layla abandons the three boys—who grow into obese high-IQ black triplets—with poor, forlorn Charlie.

The naturally modest and nonconfrontational Charlie spends the next several years "trapped behind a wall of politeness" until the day his short-fused, violent alter ego emerges as Hank Evans (Carrey). Diagnosed with schizophrenia, Charlie is prescribed a strong antipsychotic. When he's on the medication, he feels fine; when he doesn't take it, he starts to "feel . . . funny."

As Charlie, Hank, and Irene begin a long road trip together, they also begin the journey toward regaining Charlie's mental health. Mostly tacky, occasionally touching, *Me, Myself & Irene* showcases the comedic skills of the two leads, who carried their onscreen romance offscreen for a while.

Cooper is wasted as a crooked lieutenant, and Forster has a forgettable role as an ineffective colonel. Bowman made his debut performance in the movie, and reportedly used his own high-powered glasses, complete with attached telescope, in his role as the mysterious albino.

For another showcase of Carrey's repressed dark side, see *The Mask* in Chapter 8. For another movie about two people sharing one body, see *All of Me*, also in Chapter 8. And for a kinder, gentler romantic road trip, see *The Sure Thing* in Chapter 4.

Do Try This at Home: Make love on a train.

Carrey or Cusack?
3. Did Jim Carrey or John Cusack attend New York University?
Answer on page 205

CLASSIC DATE MOVIE SELECTION

❧ *Notorious* (1946)

Cary Grant, Ingrid Bergman, Claude Rains, Louis Calhern
DIRECTED BY ALFRED HITCHCOCK
101 minutes; in black and white; not rated, comparable to PG
Intimacy Comfort Level: First Date, Going Steady, Committed/Married
Make-Out Meter: ▍▍▍
Just for Her: Beautiful gowns and jewelry
Just for Him: Intrigue and espionage

After her father is convicted of treason for aiding Germany during World War II, Miami's resident playgirl Alicia Huberman (Bergman) drowns her shame

In *Notorious*, two spies (Cary Grant and Ingrid Bergman) make a dangerous discovery in the wine cellar. (Copyright © 1954; courtesy of Photofest)

through liquor and wild parties. Proud to be the daughter of an American mother, Alicia feels her father's betrayal of his country as if it were her own disloyalty. Her downward spiral is interrupted by suave American agent T.R. Devlin (Grant), who enlists her help in spying on Nazi war criminals living in Brazil.

In an effort to clear the Huberman name—or at least her own name—she agrees to get up close and personal with some of the most important German refugees in Rio de Janeiro. In particular, she will be required to spy on Alexander Sebastian (Rains), a close friend of her father. Though considerably older and shorter than she, Alex has always desired the beautiful party girl. She soon finds that his jealousy leads to an especially unpleasant level of closeness in order to maintain her cover.

What makes her situation even more dangerous and suspenseful is the budding romance between herself and Devlin, which was cut short by the assignment. Their famous kissing scene (just before she receives her unfortunate assignment) was choreographed by Hitchcock to prolong the eroticism while complying with the Hollywood censorship code, which limited kisses to a mere three seconds. Hitchcock chose an exciting alternative that makes their feelings for each other abundantly clear.

And with those kinds of feelings, how long can Devlin stand having her live in the same house and share the same bed with Alex? By the way, even though Devlin is a self-admitted "fat-headed guy full of pain," eventually he *does* have a pistol in his pocket *and* is happy to see her.

The acting is terrific, especially Leopoldine Konstantin as Alex's glacial Nazi mom and Rains as her sniveling mama's boy, a relationship that foreshadows the creepy duo at the Bates Motel in Hitchock's later film *Psycho*. Rains won an Academy Award for best supporting actor, and writer Ben Hecht won for his screenplay inspired by the short story "The Song of the Dragon" by John Taintor Foote. Look for unusual camera angles, dramatic framing, and special effects—all quite uniquely Hitchcockian.

For another romantic thriller directed by Hitchcock, see *The Birds* in Chapter 8. For more movies about spies and secret agents, see *Miss Congeniality* in Chapter 6 and *True Lies* in this chapter.

Do Try This at Home: High-Budget Plan A: Take a trip to Rio de Janeiro together. Low-Budget Plan B: Share a vintage bottle of wine.

❧ *Out of Sight* (1998)

Jennifer Lopez, George Clooney, Ving Rhames, Don Cheadle
DIRECTED BY STEVEN SODERBERGH
123 minutes; in color; R
Intimacy Comfort Level: Going Steady, Committed/Married
Make-Out Meter: ▮▮▮▮
Just for Her: Karen's dream
Just for Him: Boxing; violence; pretending that it's you locked in the trunk and spooning with Jennifer Lopez

Out of Sight tells the story of two attracting opposites: Jack Foley (Clooney) is a smooth, prolific career criminal who robs banks without using weapons; and Karen Sisco (Lopez) is a federal marshal and weapons aficionado who upholds the law at any cost. Unlike the opposites in Chapter 5, however, these two would-be lovers are brought together and kept apart by something other than misunderstandings about love and lust. Weapons, violence, criminals, and the law interfere with the happy union of this particular couple.

Jack briefly takes Karen hostage during a prison break, but he's careful to keep her safe, comfortable, and entertained during her captivity. When he's not imprisoned and required to fight for his life against ruthless murderers, Jack is basically a nice, polite, well-mannered bank robber (with more than 200 robberies on his resume) who compliments the tellers for their cooperation and tells them to have a nice day after each "transaction." Even his ex-wife (Catherine Keener) refers to him as "very considerate, lights on or off." Although her job is to bring the fugitive back to Glades Correctional Institute, Karen finds herself wondering (and dreaming) about what Jack would be like with the lights off.

The complicated plot shifts back and forth through time, using freeze frames to focus your attention and quick editing to keep things moving. Early scenes may be confusing, but they become clear later as the story progresses and character traits become more distinct and important. Soderbergh provides a slick flick filled with dark humor in this adaptation of the Elmore Leonard novel.

As the story moves from sunny Miami to snowy Detroit, the whole movie becomes a bit darker with increased violence and gentleman Jack's eventual adoption of weaponry. Though not the happiest of movies, *Out of Sight* presents a sexy, cerebral, stylish look at crime. Look for Albert Brooks in a supporting role as a crooked business tycoon and Steve Zahn as a dim-witted pothead, plus cameos by Michael Keaton, Nancy Allen, and Samuel L. Jackson.

For another fast-paced date movie in which the good girl pursues the bad boy see *The Thomas Crown Affair* in Chapter 4. For more of Lopez, see *The Wedding Planner* in Chapter 1 and *Maid in Manhattan* in Chapter 10. For more of Clooney, see *One Fine Day* in Chapter 5.

Do Try This at Home: Role-play foreplay.

❧ *Raiders of the Lost Ark* (1981)

Harrison Ford, Karen Allen, Paul Freeman, Ronald Lacey
DIRECTED BY STEVEN SPIELBERG
115 minutes; in color; PG
Intimacy Comfort Level: First Date, Going Steady, Committed/Married
Make-Out Meter: ▮▮
Just for Her: Classroom crushes; nautical nursing
Just for Him: Action; violence; pyrotechnics; special effects

In 1936, American archeology professor, adventurer, and occult expert Dr. Indiana Jones (Ford) studies the life and cultures of past civilizations through the excavation of ancient cities and artifacts. He regularly travels around the world to acquire precious relics for a museum of antiquities, using his extensive knowledge to decipher hidden messages and his physical prowess (not to mention a whip and gun) to dodge other treasure seekers and deadly booby traps.

Strong, brave, charming, handsome, and intelligent, Indiana has three weaknesses: He fears snakes; loathes Nazis; and dreads romantic commitment.

When American sources intercept a message from the Nazis claiming to have found the resting place of the lost Ark of the Covenant, Indy is asked to surreptitiously visit their archeological dig outside Cairo and find the prize himself. Unfortunately for Indy, this assignment proves to be his greatest challenge ever when his weaknesses are tested simultaneously. He must enlist the aid of embittered former girlfriend Marion Ravenwood (Allen), battle sadistic Nazi soldiers, and survive entrapment in a tomb full of snakes.

Though he can't charm snakes, Indy knows exactly how to charm the ladies—in the classroom and in the bedroom. His earlier fling with Marion caused her father, a fellow archeologist who mentored Indy, to distance himself from the brash young adventurer who takes what he wants. Now, ten years later, the tough-talking Marion runs a dilapidated saloon in Nepal where she hosts (and participates in) nightly drinking contests.

Before his death, Dr. Ravenwood gave his daughter a prized medallion that coincidentally serves as the headpiece on a staff that points the way to the lost Ark of the Covenant. This ensures that not only Indy but scores of nasty Nazis and a frisky Frenchman are after Marion as well.

Beyond the amazing stunts, pyrotechnics, and special effects (which earned four Academy Awards), *Raiders of the Lost Ark* presents entertaining characters involved in their own personal struggles for power, fame, riches, and love. Indy's high IQ and sharp shooting don't help him much when it comes to controlling the supernatural power emanating from the Ark or from the irresistible power of love.

Unlike most sequels, which present dreary rehashings of the originals, *Indiana Jones and the Temple of Doom* (1984) and *Indiana Jones and the Last Crusade* (1989) stand alone as excellent films. *The Temple of Doom* includes some exciting chemistry between Ford and Kate Capshaw as a cranky lounge singer (qualifying it as a great date movie), but *The Last Crusade* focuses more on the father–son relationship and comedic sexual exploits than on romance.

For more movies with Harrison Ford, see *Witness* in this chapter, *Six Days, Seven Nights* in Chapter 9 and *Working Girl* in Chapter 10.

Do Try This at Home: Kiss it and make it better.

Ford or Fraser?
1. Did Harrison Ford or Brendan Fraser portray a crazed
artist in a 1994 drama?
Answer on page 206

True Lies (1994)

Arnold Schwarzenegger, Jamie Lee Curtis, Tom Arnold, Bill Paxton
DIRECTED BY JAMES CAMERON
114 minutes; in color; R
Intimacy Comfort Level: Going Steady, Committed/Married
Make-Out Meter: ‖‖
Just for Her: The tango
Just for Him: Striptease; Arnold versus terrorists; Harrier jet

Written and directed by James Cameron, *True Lies* has much in common with his 1997 blockbuster *Titanic* (see Chapter 4). This movie has incredible special effects, lots of action and destruction of people and property, a love story within the larger story, a sexist (and sexy) take on romance, unexpected humor, and corny, unrealistic dialogue.

Boring computer salesman Harry Tasker (Schwarzenegger) lives with his equally boring wife, Helen (Curtis), a mousy, bespectacled office worker. Married for fifteen boring years, they have a rebellious fourteen-year-old daughter.

Unbeknownst to Helen, Harry works as one of America's top secret agents investigating Middle Eastern terrorists smuggling nuclear arms inside of priceless artifacts. One day Helen is approached by sleazy used-car salesman Simon (Paxton), who poses as a spy to get women into bed with him. Needing to feel needed and desiring to feel desired, Helen agrees to help Simon in his supposed plan to save the country.

It isn't long before one of America's top secret agents investigating Middle Eastern terrorists smuggling nuclear arms inside of priceless artifacts learns of the phony spy trying to seduce his wife. He uses his ample supply of secret agent resources to teach the unsuspecting Simon and Helen a lesson.

Part of Helen's lesson involves performing a striptease in a darkened hotel room for a suspected bad guy (actually Harry hiding in the shadows using a tape-recorded voice). She delivers a jaw-dropping dance that is alternately clumsy (she's never done this before) and sexy (remember she's been holding back all these years).

Men will love the action; explosions, special effects, and graphic violence get much more screen time than the love story. But there's something very romantic about a married couple falling in love with each other again after fifteen years. The film's ending shows that the next fifteen years will be anything but boring for Harry and Helen.

Watch for Tom Arnold in the role he was born to play, Harry's wisecracking, divorced partner Gib, who alternately respects and resents his married coworker. Tia Carrere appears as a corrupt antiquities buyer who likes to flaunt her body; and Charlton Heston (whose appearance is so brief he doesn't have time to flaunt anything) shows up as the big boss.

For other mousy women who suddenly develop curves, style, and perfect vision, see Chapter 6. For more high-flying action, see *The Thomas Crown Affair* and *Top Gun* in Chapter 4 and *Six Days, Seven Nights* in Chapter 9. For more couples who keep secrets from each other, see Chapter 10.

Do Try This at Home: Perform a private dance for your lover.

Sister Sara (Shirley MacLaine) makes it a habit to tease and torment the lanky gunslinger (Clint Eastwood) who comes to her rescue in *Two Mules for Sister Sara*. (Courtesy of Photofest)

❧ *Two Mules for Sister Sara* (1969)

Clint Eastwood, Shirley MacLaine, Manolo Fabregas, Alberto Morin
DIRECTED BY DON SIEGEL
105 minutes; in color; PG
Intimacy Comfort Level: First Date, Going Steady, Committed/Married
Make-Out Meter: ❚❚❚
Just for Her: A not-so-frank discussion of "those feelings" in women
Just for Him: A violent attack on a fort

Released in 1969, back in the days of the GP rating (today it would surely earn a PG-13 for its brief but extreme violence), *Two Mules for Sister Sara* is not quite old enough to find in most classic sections, nor is it recent enough to find in the popular rental section of most video stores. Although hard to locate, it's worth the effort.

MacLaine shines as Sister Sara, a cigar-smoking, liquor-guzzling, profanity-spewing nun who helps Hogan (Eastwood), an American mercenary in nineteenth-century Mexico fighting against the French occupation. After Hogan saves her from would-be rapists, he finds himself stuck with Sara's company on his journey to take over an enemy fort. He finds Sara's good deeds as tiresome as her good looks are frustrating.

Loyal to no army and no woman, Hogan values his freedom to smoke, drink, gamble, and spend money. He considers himself an independent thinker, but Sara believes him to be as stubborn as her mule. Most of the time, they irritate each other and argue about accidents versus miracles. But sometimes in quiet moments he confesses his barely restrained lust for her, and sometimes she flirts with him in a most un-nunlike fashion.

The chemistry between Eastwood and MacLaine is as explosive as the dynamite he casually throws at people or uses to blow up trains. Living in such a hostile environment—they are attacked by Indians and threatened by a rattlesnake—brings out the tougher side of Sara. Hooking up with the naughty nun whose favorite excuse is "in times like this, the church grants dispensations" helps bring out the softer side of the rugged adventurer. After much waiting and anticipation, the satisfying conclusion proves that cleanliness is indeed next to godliness.

For Clint Eastwood in another outdoor adventure, see The *Bridges of Madison County* in Chapter 9. For another Western romance, see *All the Pretty Horses* in this chapter. For other characters hiding their true identities, see Chapter 10.

Do Try This at Home: Take things slowly at first. Allow some time for the attraction to grow and sexual tension to build.

❧ *Witness* (1985)

Harrison Ford, Kelly McGillis, Lukas Haas, Danny Glover
DIRECTED BY PETER WEIR
112 minutes; in color; R
Intimacy Comfort Level: Going Steady, Committed/Married
Make-Out Meter: ▮▮▮▮
Just for Her: Barn dancing and nursemaiding
Just for Him: Barn raising and sponge bathing

Unlike many romantic date movies in this category where action is added to offset the romance (e.g., *Me, Myself & Irene*) or romance is added to offset the action (e.g., *Big Trouble in Little China*), *Witness* contains a delicate balance of both. This artsy drama is a combination of forbidden love, corruption within the Philadelphia police department, and two cultures colliding.

After the recent death of her husband, an Amish woman, Rachel Lapp (McGillis), and her young son, Samuel (Haas), leave their rural Lancaster County home to visit relatives in Baltimore. At the train station in Philadelphia, Samuel witnesses the murder of a policeman in the men's restroom. Internal Affairs Detective John Book (Ford) is assigned to the case and soon learns that fellow officer McFee (Glover) was the trigger man.

This discovery makes John, Samuel, and Rachel the targets of several assassins working within the Philadelphia Police Department. After taking a bullet in the torso, John decides they'd all be safer hiding out in Amish territory until he regains his health and decides what to do about the interdepartmental corruption.

The plainclothes officer soon gets a lesson in the true meaning of plain clothes when he dons Amish garb to blend in among Rachel's community. But, as you might have guessed, putting these two appealing costars in drab clothes just makes their physical attractiveness that much more noticeable.

As in *Kindergarten Cop*, in which undercover officer John Kimball (Arnold Schwarzenegger) unwittingly brings violence into an incongruous setting (a small-town elementary school), in this case an undercover officer unwittingly brings modern-age violence into a quaint rural town of Amish pacifists. Although the contrasts in *Kindergarten Cop* are mostly for laughs, the visual contrasts in *Witness* serve as a comment on the role of artificial violence in a natural setting.

138

For example, when bullies torment a group of Amish people traveling down the road by horse-drawn buggies, John springs into action while the others stare in amazement. Old Eli Sapp (Josef Summer) cautions him not to react, "It's not our way." "But it's my way," John replies before whacking away.

The movie's strengths lie in its strong visual appeal, sexual tension between John and Rachel, and unexpectedly funny dialogue. *Witness* won Academy Awards for best original screenplay and film editing. Especially memorable moments include when Samuel first recognizes the killer, when the Amish community comes together to build a barn for newlyweds, when Rachel and John dance in the barn, and Rachel's topless sponge bath scene.

An altogether wonderful date movie for both sexes, *Witness* is full of interesting parallels and stylish touches by Australian director Weir, known for his equally artful work on films including *Picnic at Hanging Rock* (1975), *The Year of Living Dangerously* (1982), and *The Mosquito Coast* (1986).

For more love in Philadelphia, see *Mannequin* in Chapter 3 and *Rocky* in Chapter 6. For more dancing that brings couples closer together, see *Emma*, *Four Weddings and a Funeral*, *The Wedding Planner*, and *The Wedding Singer* in Chapter 1; *When Harry Met Sally* in Chapter 2; *A Knight's Tale* in Chapter 3; *French Kiss* and *The Thomas Crown Affair* in Chapter 4; *The American President* and *Dirty Dancing* in Chapter 5; *Children of a Lesser God* in Chapter 6; *All the Pretty Horses* and *True Lies* in this chapter; *All of Me* and *The Mask* in Chapter 8; *George of the Jungle* and *Romancing the Stone* in Chapter 9; and *Coming to America*, *Maid in Manhattan*, *Shakespeare in Love*, and *The Mask of Zorro* in Chapter 10.

Do Try This at Home: Try some long, lustful glances to communicate your feelings.

Ford or Fraser?
2. Was Harrison Ford or Brendan Fraser voted one of *People* magazine's top ten best-dressed celebrities and most beautiful people in the world in 1997?
Answer on page 206

For yet another movie in which Harrison Ford gets shot, see *Six Days, Seven Nights* in Chapter 9. For more men with guns, see *Speed* in Chapter 4, *Miss Congeniality* in Chapter 6, *The Mask* in Chapter 8, and most of the movies in Chapter 9.

Chapter 8

Love Is a Supernatural Thing

At times there is nothing so unnatural as nature.
Carolyn Wells

SUPERNATURAL STORYTELLING derives its effectiveness from centuries-old superstitions that still lie hidden deep in the dark cracks and corners of today's scientific minds. Despite their education or background, most people find reassurance in hearing stories and myths about love, death, nature, and other mysteries that cannot be explained through the science of the day. Inventing stories about supernatural beings with the power to control nature often has a soothing effect on people when nature proves especially frightening.

Legends and superstitions have existed since the beginning of civilization; it's only the stories themselves and the method of delivery that have changed. Many ancient people believed that the gods delivered messages through nightly dreams; today, many of us believe that if the information comes by e-mail, it must be true (see *You've Got Mail* in Chapter 2). Ancient superstition or modern urban legends: It's really just a question of semantics.

But how do natural and supernatural love compare? Actually it's not the love that's different, but our heightened reaction to the supernatural elements. In order to accept a situation that reaches beyond the realm of natural possibility, we need to shut off the logical left side of the brain and enable the emotional, artistic, intuitive right side to come out and play. These dark, seductive storytelling shadow zones explore magical elements that tap into our deep-seated desires, fears, and beliefs. And when we allow ourselves to believe, we allow ourselves to feel.

Filmmakers tap into these primeval feelings in the following ten movies. *Chocolat*, *The Mask*, *Serendipity*, and *What Women Want* peek into our secret desires about love, such as magically knowing what someone wants, changing form to be more desirable, trusting fate, and reading the minds of members of the opposite sex. *Bedazzled*, *Ghost*, and *Sleepy Hollow* unearth our fear of the unknown aspects of death, hell, and life after death. *The Birds* pecks away at our simple explanations about our natural environment, *All of Me* delves into love and death, and *Groundhog Day* endlessly explores all three.

Trapped in an unexplained time loop, big-city weatherman Phil Conners (Bill Murray) in *Groundhog Day* must endure the same loveless relationships with his colleagues, a dreadfully boring—though immortal—existence in a small town, and a devastating blizzard each day until he manages to get things right. Orchestrated by an unknown supernatural power for an unknown reason, this time loop affects Phil (and us) in every aspect of his life, forcing him to re-evaluate how he wants to spend his time on earth, assuming all his time is confined to one repeated day.

Coupled with our temporary willingness to suspend disbelief, these supernatural situations become more real and more important because of weaknesses within the characters. In *Bedazzled*, Elliot (Brendan Fraser) lacks style, wit, charm, grace, and, not surprisingly, friends. Because of his ineptitude at everything, the devil has more power over him. In *Ghost*, Sam (Patrick Swayze) has a preoccupation with dying young and carries lucky charms, which unfortunately fail to save him. In *Sleepy Hollow*, Ichabod (Johnny Depp) endures a childhood trauma involving his mother's persecution for witchcraft that haunts him in his dreams. And in *Serendipity*, television news producer Jonathan (John Cusack) believes only what he can see; he has no faith in faith.

Brought together naturally, the lovers in these movies stay together because of supernatural occurrences. If it weren't for killer birds, Melanie (Tippi Hedren) surely would have made an early migration out of boring Bodega Bay in *The Birds*. It's doubtful that the beautiful Tina (Cameron Diaz) would have developed an initial interest in nerdy banker Stanley (Jim Carrey) without his supernatural abilities as The Mask. And sharing a room with Edwina (Lily Tomlin) is too close for comfort until Roger (Steve Martin) also has to share his body with her in *All of Me*.

More than other types of movies—except perhaps fairy-tale romances—supernatural love stories force the audience to abandon logic and reason for a while and rely upon faith and emotion instead. So get in touch with centuries-old superstitions as these supernatural lovers get in touch with each other.

❧ *All of Me* (1984)

Steve Martin, Lily Tomlin, Victoria Tennant, Madolyn Smith
DIRECTED BY CARL REINER
93 minutes; in color; PG-13
Intimacy Comfort Level: Going Steady, Committed/Married
Make-Out Meter: ▮▮▮
Just for Her: Edwina acting like a man
Just for Him: Bathroom assistance; tingles

Roger Cobb's thirty-eighth birthday isn't going very well. A by-the-rules attorney by day and improvising jazz musician by night, Roger (Martin) already has something of a split personality. He hates his job but loves his hobby. He dates the boss's daughter, but they have nothing in common.

Worst of all, he is forced into handling the most undesirable cases in order to prove himself worthy of becoming a partner at the law office. In particular, he must handle the affairs of prudish heiress Edwina Cutwater (Tomlin), who has been on her deathbed since her childhood. And after years of false alarms that she's dying, this time she might actually mean it.

Aided by the incomprehensible Prahka Lasa (Richard Libertini), a non–English-speaking swami from Tibet, Roger accidentally becomes the unwilling recipient of the transmigrated soul of Edwina and literally becomes two different people. The soul of the spinster takes control of the right side of his body, while he maintains control of the left side. In addition to sharing the body, they share each other's thoughts and, much to his dismay, fantasies.

Complicating the already complicated situation is his floundering career, broken relationship with the boss's daughter (Smith), and midlife crisis. Poor Edwina must face the fact not only that she has physically died and no one attended her funeral, but also that Terry (Tennant), the beautiful daughter of her stable man, who was the intended recipient of her soul, has tricked her out of

Roger (Steve Martin) doesn't want to share his body—at least not all of it—with the transmigrated soul of a dead heiress (Lily Tomlin) in *All of Me*. (Greg Gorman/Copyright © 1984 Universal City Studios, Inc.; courtesy of Photofest)

her fortune. Terry fully intends to hold on to her body and soul. (Although Roger isn't much interested in Terry's soul, he's quite agreeable to holding on to her body.)

Meanwhile Prahka Lasa is wandering around with his magic bowl seeking Edwina's essence for a retransmigration into the correct body. Roger keeps him (and his bowl) nearby at all times in case they get another chance to transmigrate Edwina's soul into the conniving Terry. While Roger moves from crisis to crisis, he forms a surprisingly close bond with Edwina's spirit.

At times sentimental, at other times crass, *All of Me* relies on Martin's considerable physical comedy and Tomlin's snappy delivery to get it through the rough spots. Based on the novel *Me Too* by Ed Davis, the story of souls traveling from body to bowl to body may be less inspired than the acting.

For another onscreen romance between former offscreen spouses Martin and

Tennant, see *L.A. Story* in Chapter 2, and for a less supernatural, more psychological case of split personality see *Me, Myself & Irene* in Chapter 7.

Do Try This at Home: Work together as a team whenever possible.

❧ *Bedazzled* (2000)

Brendan Fraser, Elizabeth Hurley, Frances O'Conner, Miriam Shor
DIRECTED BY HAROLD RAMIS
93 minutes; in color; PG-13
Intimacy Comfort Level: First Date, Going Steady, Committed/Married
Make-Out Meter: ▮▮▮
Just for Her: Elliot's attempts to be the perfect man
Just for Him: The devil's many disguises

An obnoxious outsider without any friends, Elliot Richards (Fraser) cries himself to sleep each night. He longs for love and respect, but continually sabotages his chances for either. Then one night he plays pool with a beautiful woman (Hurley) who promises that she can help him get Allison (O'Conner), the woman of his dreams, to fall in love with him.

Elliot acknowledges that his attractive newfound friend is hot, but he has no idea exactly how hot until she confides a little secret: She's the devil.

Prepared to grant him seven wishes in exchange for the eternal damnation of his soul, the devil in a red dress (and a collection of other sinfully sexy clothes) shows Elliot a video of how happy he could be with Allison. Assured that the devil is a full-service provider with offices in purgatory, hell, and Los Angeles, he finally agrees to sign on the dotted line.

Just in case anything goes wrong with his wishes, the devil gives Elliot a bright red pager that will release him from the wish when the numbers 666 are entered. Naturally, when you're dealing with the devil, a lot can go wrong. Elliot goes through a series of encounters with Allison in which he changes his appearance, personality, intelligence, and financial status to win her over. But will he be able to get with magic what he can't get on his own?

Ramis has plenty of fun answering this question as he puts Elliot through various torments. Fraser changes teeth, hair, and noses for each version of himself, often with amusing results. Girl-next-door O'Conner has her work cut out for her with supermodel Hurley stealing scenes with one fabulous costume after another. Laughs supercede romance here, but the concept of loving oneself before being able to love others is central to the movie's theme.

For another Harold Ramis–directed comedy, see *Groundhog Day* in this chapter. For more characters altering their identities for romantic pursuits, see Chapter 10.

Do Try This at Home: Enjoy each other's company so much that you can ignore the rest of the world when you're together.

Ford or Fraser?
3. Is Harrison Ford or Brendan Fraser mentioned in
two different pop songs?
Answer on page 206

CLASSIC DATE MOVIE SELECTION

❧ The Birds (1963)

Rod Taylor, Tippi Hedren, Suzanne Pleshette, Jessica Tandy
DIRECTED BY ALFRED HITCHCOCK
120 minutes; in color; PG-13
Intimacy Comfort Level: First Date, Going Steady, Committed/Married
Make-Out Meter: ▌▌
Just for Her: Perfectly manicured fingernails and clean, pressed dress
   throughout two days of boating, face slapping, running, and dodging
   bird attacks
Just for Him: The horrific bird attacks may make your companion need
   physical comfort

Why would hundreds of birds of a different feather join together in viciously attacking the peaceful inhabitants of a quaint little city by the bay? Did the beautiful Melanie Daniels (Hedren) prompt this supernatural event with her unexpected arrival? Did the appearance of two seemingly innocent lovebirds—ironically the only birds in Bodega Bay that are unaffected—somehow start the war between birds and humans? Or were the feathered friends just really offended by Melanie's politically incorrect and ecologically insensitive fur coat?

These are the questions people want answered when rich playgirl Melanie Daniels comes roaring into town in her sports car in pursuit of handsome criminal lawyer Mitch Brenner (Taylor). Her penchant for practical jokes is a factor in their first two meetings; however, the sophisticated prankster finds no humor in the supernatural avian attacks.

In her debut performance, Hedren delivers a cool, crisp portrayal of the icy blonde who steals the heart of handsome, everyman Mitch. Much to the dismay of his neurotic mom (Tandy) and dumped girlfriend (Pleshette), the couple becomes closer as the ordeal worsens.

This movie depicts a truly horrifying supernatural phenomenon that figuratively cages two unlikely lovebirds in a house with two literal lovebirds while flocks of hateful birds attack from outside. Perfect for snuggling and holding hands, *The Birds* shocks and terrifies with no predictable resolutions or simple explanations.

No music was used throughout the entire movie; only bird noises, electronic sounds, and that creepy schoolhouse song punctuate the action. Although most of the birds are real, you can see a few fakes in some of the attack scenes, and watch for superimpositions when the children flee the schoolhouse. Hitchcock's trademark cameo comes early in the movie as he walks his dogs near the pet store. Based on a story by Daphne du Maurier, *The Birds* provides thrills, romance, and an occasional laugh. Hitchcock was the designated master of suspense, but he mastered the date film, as well.

You're pretty safe (in a manner of speaking) with any of his films, or see Chapter 7 for a description of his 1946 thriller *Notorious*.

Do Try This at Home: Find time for a peck on the cheek even in the midst of a crisis (supernatural or otherwise).

❥ *Chocolat* (2000)

Juliette Binoche, Johnny Depp, Judi Dench, Alfred Molina
DIRECTED BY LASSE HALLSTROM
121 minutes; in color; PG-13
Intimacy Comfort Level: First Date, Going Steady, Committed/Married
Make-Out Meter: ❘❘❘
Just for Her: A man who fixes things, plays the guitar, and looks like Johnny
    Depp
Just for Him: Candy as an aphrodisiac

Part fairy tale, part love story, part comedy, part drama, *Chocolat* (not to be confused with the 1988 French film of the same name) is a delicious blend of the finest quality ingredients: a good story (based on the novel by Joanne Harris), beautiful cinematography, interesting characters, and a wonderful cast. (For an interactive effect, try watching this one as you nibble or sip something chocolate.)

A beautiful single mother, Vianne (Binoche) blows into a traditional French rural town with a sly wind from the north. Amid the monochromatic wardrobe of the locals, her red high heels and exotic collection of capes, shawls, and dresses stand out as different, radical, and threatening. Moreover, she disturbs the tranquility of the rule-abiding village by avoiding the church and opening her decadent little chocolate shop (Chocolaterie Maya) during Lent.

Everyone has a secret in this repressed environment. Vianne and her magical mix of chocolate confections expose what lies deep within. In a story within a story, she tells her daughter about the mysterious medical properties of chocolate—how cocoa can unlock hidden yearnings and reveal destinies.

Described by Comte de Reynaud, the hypocritical mayor (Molina), as "Satan's Helper," Vianne remains a free spirit dedicated to love, lust, living, and chocolate. Her magic spreads to an abused wife (Lena Olin), an aged widow (Leslie Caron), a cold mother (Carrie-Anne Moss), a sick grandmother (Dench), and Roux, a handsome river rat gypsy (Depp). Vianne offers temptation, cures the impotent, and encourages others to live life to the fullest by relishing sensual pleasures. The textured characters ultimately reveal their secrets as they begin to enjoy the sensual pleasure Vianne introduces to the town.

Her romance with Roux serves as icing on the cake, representing only one of her many mysterious transformations. He carries his home with him as he travels; she travels from place to place seeking a home. Together, they are no longer outsiders, feeling safe, warm, and at home in each other's arms. Depp's late arrival in the film and relatively small role are much like a craving for chocolate; a small scrumptious taste leaves you longing for more.

For full portions of Depp, see *Don Juan DeMarco* in Chapter 3, *Edward Scissorhands* in Chapter 6, and *Sleepy Hollow* in this chapter.

Do Try This at Home: Study your lover well enough to guess his or her favorites.

Ghost (1990)

Patrick Swayze, Demi Moore, Whoopi Goldberg, Tony Goldwin
DIRECTED BY JERRY ZUCKER
127 minutes; in color; PG-13
Intimacy Comfort Level: Going Steady, Committed/Married
Make-Out Meter: ▌▌▌▌
Just for Her: The sculpting scene
Just for Him: Ghostly revenge

You can promise yourself not to cry. You can tell yourself that it's only a movie. But good luck making it through *Ghost* dry-eyed.

The theme of luck weaves itself throughout the movie with lucky pennies, a charmed life, and a superstitious fear that the bubble will burst. As you might have guessed, this particular happy little bubble of love and luck bursts just a few minutes into the film.

The story begins with banker Sam (Swayze) and sculptor Molly (Moore) moving in together. Within minutes, a sculpture of an angel ascends to the sky as Molly pulls it through her apartment window. Then Sam talks about his superstitious fear of sudden death. It's very clear that something bad will happen soon to someone good. Sure enough, Sam gets murdered in the street, and his ghost carries on in limbo because he can't go to heaven until justice is served.

Meanwhile, Sam's coworker (Goldwin) starts making moves on the grieving girlfriend, while Sam desperately enlists the aid of phony psychic reader Oda Mae Brown (Goldberg), who surprises herself by actually talking to the dead for the first time in her so-called career. Together they attempt to communicate with Molly about Sam's murder. Goldberg (who received an Academy Award for best supporting actress) provides unexpected, though certainly welcome, comic relief to this romantic tearjerker.

Dazzling special effects reveal Sam's exploration of his supernatural powers as a ghost. Swayze's physical grace (as evidenced in *Dirty Dancing*, see Chapter 5) serves him well as an energy force without a corporeal home.

A mixture of suspense, action, comedy, and of course, romance, *Ghost* became one of the top-grossing films of 1990 and took home another Oscar for best original screenplay by Bruce Joel Rubin. In addition to its onscreen supernatural themes, *Ghost* has a magical offscreen effect, too. Although it has an infinitely sad premise, the story somehow manages to leave you feeling infinitely romantic.

For a considerably lighter look at ghosts, see *All of Me* in this chapter.

Do Try This at Home: Let your partner keep his or her favorite chair, even if it's ugly.

❧ *Groundhog Day* (1993)

Bill Murray, Andie MacDowell, Chris Elliot, Brian Doyle-Murray
DIRECTED BY HAROLD RAMIS
103 minutes; in color; PG
Intimacy Comfort Level: First Date, Going Steady, Committed/Married
Make-Out Meter: ❚❚
Just for Her: Rita's description of the perfect man
Just for Him: Guy's night out at the bowling alley

Bored Pittsburgh weatherman Phil Conners (Murray) hates his job and most especially his required annual trip to Punxsutawney, Pennsylvania, for live coverage of Groundhog Day festivities. Accompanying him on this particular trip are his two upbeat coworkers, a newly hired producer named Rita (MacDowell) and his longtime cameraman (Elliot).

An unexpected blizzard traps them in Punxsutawney. But when Phil awakens the next morning, he finds that he is reliving the same day over again. No one else is aware of this supernatural time loop except for him. As days go by (or, actually, *don't* go by), he uses his advantage to seduce women, eat rich foods, hurt himself, learn to play the piano, sculpt ice, and eventually help others besides himself.

Written by Ramis and Daniel F. Rubin, the clever screenplay never grows tiresome, unlike the situation faced by our unlikely hero. Yet, despite the humor and light romance between Phil and Rita, there's something cold about this movie—besides the blizzard and early February chill, that is. The characters themselves come across as a little frosty. Rita remains distant and detached throughout the seemingly endless repetition of February 2, and Phil is not particularly likeable until he gradually transforms his personality because of the time loop.

The best part about *Groundhog Day* is wondering what you would do if you were stuck in the same supernatural situation. What would you say and do to win someone's heart if you knew that tomorrow would be exactly like today unless you did something to change it. Just for fun, come up with your own theories as to why a supernatural time loop allows a sarcastic, egocentric, loner repeated chances to make amends when so many other people are more deserving.

For another supernatural tale of a lovestruck weatherman, see *L.A. Story* in Chapter 2. For more ice sculpture incidents, see *My Best Friend's Wedding* in Chapter 2 and *Edward Scissorhands* in Chapter 6.

Do Try This at Home: Read romantic poetry in bed together.

❧ *The Mask* (1994)

Jim Carrey, Cameron Diaz, Peter Greene, Peter Riegert
DIRECTED BY CHUCK RUSSELL
100 minutes; in color; PG-13
Intimacy Comfort Level: First Date, Going Steady, Committed/Married
Make-Out Meter: ❚❚
Just for Her: Tina's jailhouse visit
Just for Him: Shoot-outs; long-overdue revenge

Repressed bank clerk Stanley Ipkiss (Carrey) gets abused by his landlady, his boss, car mechanics, and just about everyone else in the cartoonish little town known as Edge City. Tina, a sexy singer from the Coco Bongo Club (Diaz in her debut role), visits his bank one day to case the joint for her criminal boyfriend, and poor out-of-his-league Stanley feels more frustrated than ever by their interaction.

Just when things couldn't get any worse for him, Stanley finds a primitive mask in the river which gives the wearer supernatural powers. Out of curiosity, he puts on the mask one night and winds up attacking the landlady, robbing his bank, violating the car mechanics, and making quite an impression on Tina.

He comes to understand this behavior after talking to an expert on literal and figurative masks and learning that the wooden face on this particular mask represents the Norse night god of mischief. Wearing the mask brings the innermost desires of the wearer to life, or, in the case of someone so repressed, makes them larger than life.

When he wears the mask, it alters his physical form and allows him to change matter and accelerate time at will. With help from the mask, Stanley's dark side emerges: a playful, though dangerous, child with no fears or inhibitions, just an insatiable appetite for sex and violence. Riegert (terribly miscast) plays the police detective intent on criticizing Stanley's choice of pajamas and arresting him for committing crimes in his masked persona.

Sometimes frightening, sometimes humorous, Stanley's secret identity does things like transform him into a cartoon wolf, turn balloon sculpture into working ammunition, and romance Tina with the line "Our love is like a red, red rose and I am a little thorny."

Aided by his newfound confidence, Stanley dances with Tina at the Coco Bongo and arranges an evening rendezvous with her at Landfill Park. Tina—like everyone else in Edge City—praises Stanley for being a nice guy, but longs for the confident masked character who dazzled her at the club. When she discovers the dual identity of the nerdy banker, she decides to break up with her evil boyfriend, Dorian (Greene), and establish a new relationship with Stanley—just as soon as he gets out of jail.

The Mask features amazing special effects, a cute dog that certainly must have aced every test at obedience school, and a voluptuous, well-rounded Diaz several pounds heavier than she appears in later movies, including *My Best Friend's Wedding* (Chapter 2) and *There's Something About Mary* (Chapter 10). Taken as a supernatural tale of love, this enjoyable date movie makes for great entertainment despite its relatively low ranking on the make-out meter.

For another movie in which Carrey's character struggles against his dark side, see *Me, Myself & Irene* in Chapter 7. For more men behind masks, see *The Princess Bride* and *Don Juan DeMarco*, both in Chapter 3, and *The Mask of Zorro* in Chapter 10. To see Riegert in a far better role, see *Crossing Delancey* in Chapter 2.

Do Try This at Home: Throw away your mask when you fall in love.

Carrey or Cusack?
4. Did Jim Carrey or John Cusack have an early role as a
virgin who is stalked by a female vampire?
Answer on page 205

❥ *Serendipity* (2001)

John Cusack, Kate Beckinsale, Molly Shannon, Jeremy Piven
DIRECTED BY PETER CHELSOM
91 minutes; in color; PG-13
Intimacy Comfort Level: First Date, Going Steady, Committed/Married
Make-Out Meter: ❚❚❚
Just for Her: "Favorite New York moment"
Just for Him: Explanations of *Cool Hand Luke* and *The Godfather* series

Although most romantic date movies lean toward Freudian psychology (if they lean toward any school of psychological thought, that is), this supernatural love story adopts a Jungian philosophy instead. For Freudian concepts such as repression, wish fulfillment dreams, and penis envy there are *French Kiss*, *Bringing Up Baby*, *Risky Business*, *Titanic*, and *The Mask*. For the woefully neglected theory set forth by psychiatrist Carl Jung of a synchronous universe where everything is connected, there's *Serendipity*.

The twisted, tangled tale begins in New York five days before Christmas when Jonathan (Cusack) and Sara (Beckinsale) both want the last pair of black gloves at a department store. They decide to share the gloves—with each taking one as a memento of their meeting—and share the evening together. Romantically involved with other people, they can't deny an attraction to each other, which leads them to an outdoor skating rink where they talk, laugh, and look at the night sky. Later they visit a fancy hotel and a little restaurant named Serendipity.

Sara is convinced that they must part as strangers, without even giving each other their names. At her suggestion, he writes his name and phone number on a five-dollar bill and she writes her name inside a book called *Love in the Time of Cholera*—a novel in which long-separated lovers are fatefully united. She immediately spends his five dollars and promises to sell the book to a used bookstore the following day. Sara assures the skeptical Jonathan that if the book and bill return to them at some point, then they were meant to be together.

The scene then shifts to a few years later. Jonathan works in New York as a television producer for ESPN and is engaged to be married, yet he still checks every used bookstore for a copy of *Love in the Time of Cholera*. Sara has moved to California where she works as a therapist and is engaged to a self-absorbed new-age musician (John Corbett). She checks every five-dollar bill for a name and address in red ink.

As their wedding dates draw nearer, both feel the need to explore the possibilities of their "chance" encounter years before. That's when the story gets very funny, very complicated, and very serendipitous.

Beckinsale is lovely as the superstitious young Brit who seems afraid to trust her feelings. Cusack plays his usual likeable character, with the exception of sticking his chewed gum behind a bench for Sara to find later. Oh, and there is that little thing about searching for another woman on the day of his wedding. But somehow we can't really blame Jonathan for following his destiny—after all, it was written in the stars.

For another bicoastal romance in which the man lives in New York and the woman moves to Los Angeles, see *Annie Hall* in Chapter 5. For other supernatural stories about love and destiny see *Kate & Leopold* in Chapter 1 and *Splash* in Chapter 3.

Serendipity bears an amazing (dare we say serendipitous) resemblance to *Splash*. For example, a couple's two chance meetings seem like pieces of an elaborate jigsaw puzzle, the setting for the story is New York, years pass between the scenes, the lovers skate outside on a snowy evening, and Eugene Levy plays a comic supporting character. The two films share a common message: Believe in destiny, magic, and serendipity, but still work hard at your relationship.

Do Try This at Home: Look at the stars together.

Carrey or Cusack?
5. Did Jim Carrey or John Cusack have a small supporting role
in the 1987 comedy *Broadcast News*?
Answer on page 205

❧ *Sleepy Hollow* (1999)

Johnny Depp, Christina Ricci, Miranda Richardson, Casper Van Dien
DIRECTED BY TIM BURTON
105 minutes; in color; R
Intimacy Comfort Level: Going Steady, Committed/Married
Make-Out Meter: ❘❘
Just for Her: Despite blood, guts, decapitations, and gruesome special
      effects, the two lovers still managing to meet cute
Just for Him: Blood, guts, decapitations, and gruesome special effects

It's 1799 in the state of New York, and religious superstition is substituted
for justice in and outside the courtroom. However, Ichabod Crane (Depp), an
eccentric man of science, is determined that books, experiments, and analysis
can solve crimes better than current methods. Based on Washington Irving's
story "The Legend of Sleepy Hollow," this horror film uses the romantic element to lighten an otherwise dark supernatural tale.

Disliked by the legal community in New York City, Crane is sent upstate on
a doomed mission to Sleepy Hollow, an isolated farming community that has
endured a rash of decapitation murders by a rumored headless horseman.
Armed with his self-designed medical instruments and scientific books, the
squeamish inspector heads off (so to speak) to find the murderer.

He unexpectedly finds a lovely young lady as well. Katrina Van Tassel
(Ricci), the mysterious daughter of one of the town leaders, seems nice enough
but also practices a little witchcraft in her spare time. Through a series of three
dream sequences, we learn that Ichabod's own mother had been murdered by

If only she weren't blindfolded, it would be love at first sight for Christina Ricci and Johnny Depp in *Sleepy Hollow*. (Clive Coote/Copyright © 1999 Paramount Pictures; courtesy of Photofest)

her husband because she was a suspected witch. Ichabod, who says he lost all faith at age seven when she died, describes his late mother as a child of nature.

Whether a child of nature or an offspring of the supernatural, Katrina does bewitch Ichabod to the extent that he can hardly do his job. Apart from the romance, the story weaves intricately around the suspicious group of town elders and can get confusing at times. In typical Burton fashion, grotesque makeup and horrifying special effects combine with beautiful set design, romance, action, and drama in a story that's difficult to categorize. (Be prepared to hold someone's hand throughout the entire movie.)

For another Burton-directed date movie starring Depp, see *Edward Scissorhands* in Chapter 6.

Do Try This at Home: Show your lover the house where you grew up.

❥ *What Women Want* (2000)

Mel Gibson, Helen Hunt, Marisa Tomei, Alan Alda
DIRECTED BY NANCY MEYERS
126 minutes; in color; PG-13
Intimacy Comfort Level: Going Steady, Committed/Married
Make-Out Meter: **▮▮▮**
Just for Her: Leg waxing
Just for Him: A better explanation of penis envy

There's obviously something about supernatural occurrences that brings out the sensitive side of men. In *Shallow Hal* (see Chapter 6), superficial womanizer Hal (Jack Black) is hypnotized into seeing women's inner beauty as an exterior manifestation. In *Groundhog Day*, egocentric weatherman Phil Conners (Bill Murray) gets magically trapped in a time loop and eventually decides to spend his time helping other people. In *Spider-Man* (Chapter 10), after a radioactive spider bites clueless Peter Parker (Tobey Maguire), suddenly his "spider sense" tingles at the slightest hint of danger (or the entrance of Mary Jane).

Likewise, in *What Women Want*, man's man Nick Marshall (Gibson), a smooth-talking hound who describes women as babes and broads, turns into Mr. Sensitivity after a freak electrical accident. Perhaps because he was experimenting with women's products when the accident occurred or perhaps because he was so deficient in this area, somehow the accident enables him to hear women's thoughts and thereby know what women want.

This comes in handy with his job as a copywriter at one of Chicago's largest advertising agencies, an agency that coincidentally plans to go after more women's product accounts. He's passed up for a promotion to creative director when the agency's head (Alda) hires an outsider. Darcy McGuire (Hunt) assumes the job, and Nick immediately plans to use his new power to get her fired. However, he never dreamed that her beauty and aggression were matched by her sincerity and generosity.

The title refers to Sigmund Freud's dying lament that despite all his knowledge, he still didn't know what women want. Nick's supernatural power to read women's minds provides him with this long-sought-after knowledge. And once this womanizer knows what women want, he fully intends to give it to them.

In addition to this main story, some intriguing subplots serve as wake-up calls to Nick. Shortly after he acquires the ability to read women's minds, he cal-

Through a freak accident that causes him to be able to read women's minds, Nick (Mel Gibson) learns how to apply makeup and bikini wax, squeeze into pantyhose, and contort into a cobra position in *What Women Want*. (Andrew Cooper/Copyright © 2000 Paramount Pictures; courtesy of Photofest)

lously uses a vulnerable coffee shop waitress (Tomei) to enhance his sexual prowess, with disastrous results. His fifteen-year-old daughter endures a fate similar to the waitress. Nick also overhears the suicidal thoughts of a lonely coworker and feels compelled to help. All these problems come crashing down on him in full force the moment he loses his mind-reading ability in another bizarre accident. Watch for Bette Midler as the therapist who convinces him that his power is a blessing not a curse, Lauren Holly as his ex-wife, and Delta Burke as an adoring coworker at the agency.

What Women Want is recommended for established couples going steady or in committed relationships. After all, on first dates men are probably much better off not knowing what women are really thinking about them.

For other insensitive clods getting in touch with their feminine sides, see *All of Me* in this chapter and *Tootsie* in Chapter 10.

Do Try This at Home: Take turns being the rescuer and the rescuee.

In some date movies, the supernatural elements are secondary to other elements such as comedy, special effects, and action. For more love stories that extend the laws of nature just a little too far for believability, see *Kate & Leopold* in Chapter 1; *L.A. Story* in Chapter 2; *Crouching Tiger, Hidden Dragon, Ladyhawke, Mannequin,* and *Splash* in Chapter 3; *Shallow Hal* in Chapter 6; *Raiders of the Lost Ark* in Chapter 7; *The Mummy* in Chapter 9; and *Spider-Man* in Chapter 10.

Chapter 9

Watch Out for That Tree!

In each human heart are a tiger, a pig, an ass, and a nightingale;
diversity of character is due to their unequal activity.
Ambrose Bierce

RETURNING TO NATURE in romantic date movies takes characters one step closer to their animal instincts, reliance on the senses for information, and deep-rooted psychological needs to transform the environment in order to survive. (You can always spot the villain in these movies as the person determined to conquer nature rather than merely transform what is necessary for survival.)

Even in cases where outdoor adventurers encounter supernatural elements along the way, Rick O'Connell (Brendan Fraser) in *The Mummy* for instance, the characters use their natural abilities to conquer the supernatural. This scenario sharply contrasts with most of the movies in Chapter 8, in which characters often use supernatural abilities to deal with natural situations (or in cases such as *The Birds*, where the supernatural element overshadows the story and dictates the romance).

In the 1951 classic date movie *The African Queen*, a scruffy steamer captain (Humphrey Bogart) reluctantly gives a ride to Rose, an uptight, stranded missionary (Katharine Hepburn) who needs safe passage away from the African village where she is working. During their voyage, they struggle against the weather, the water, animals and insects, foreign enemies, and each other. He drunkenly insults her with a cutting remark that deeply hurts the prim young missionary. The captain—accustomed to braving the elements—works with nature whenever possible, resorting to transforming his environment only when necessary . . . or incessantly prodded by Rose.

In the 1998 romantic comedy *Six Days, Seven Nights*, simplicity-loving charter pilot Quinn Harris (Harrison Ford) crash lands on a remote island with complicated editor Robin Monroe (Anne Heche). As assistant editor of New York's *Dazzle* magazine, she gives orders, makes lots of money, and chooses each word carefully. Yet, on the island, she foolishly ignores Quinn's practical advice, demands her flight money back, and scoffs at his dreams. He tells her that she talks too much, has too many opinions, and is stubborn, sarcastic, and stuck-up. While she's naively trying to get her cell phone to function, he works with nature to secure shelter and food. Eventually they team up to use the natural elements of the island for survival because Quinn warns they might be stuck there for a very l-o-n-g time. Their escape requires moderately transforming their natural environment—and severely transforming the pirate ship threatening them.

In addition to changing their surroundings, characters in outdoor adventures face inner changes, too. The theme of war—and choosing sides—occurs in *The African Queen*, *The English Patient*, *The Last of the Mohicans*, and *Out of Africa*. The characters face the threat of death and the destruction of land and property by warring factions. This intrusion of man-made conflicts complicates the existing struggle against nature and the battle of the sexes. These conflicts tend to darken the story and slow the pace, with all four of the above movies taking time (and sometimes a little too much of it) to include tragic incidents caused by man's intrusion upon nature.

And if the men in these movies tend to be strong, independent fortune hunters (*The Mummy*, *Out of Africa*, and *Romancing the Stone*), the women are usually bookworms. Literate ladies appear in six of these adventures—*Crocodile Dundee* (newspaper reporter), *The English Patient* (storyteller and artist), *The Mummy* (librarian), *Out of Africa* (author), *Romancing the Stone* (novelist), and *Six Days, Seven Nights* (magazine editor)—perhaps because the sedentary, cerebral life of a bookworm is such a nice contrast to the life of an adventurer. It's worth noting that these outdoorsy men become accustomed to the quietude of nature, only to have noisy, talkative—and, alas, sometimes screaming—women enter their territory.

These adventurers, bookworms, and other inhabitants of environmentally themed date movies get in touch with their primitive instincts when they get in touch with nature. For others, such as Ursula (Leslie Mann) in *George of the Jungle*, Robert (Clint Eastwood) in *The Bridges of Madison County*, and Jack (Michael Douglas) in *Romancing the Stone*, the great outdoors represents a salvation from the daily stresses of life and pressure to conform. Hiding aggressive urges during everyday life in the big city makes the untamed wilderness—in which natural urges are not only acceptable but also desirable—lush with intrigue, allure, and, most important, romance.

CLASSIC DATE MOVIE SELECTION

❧ *The African Queen* (1951)

Humphrey Bogart, Katharine Hepburn, Robert Morley, Peter Bull
DIRECTED BY JOHN HUSTON
105 minutes; in color; not rated, comparable to PG
Intimacy Comfort Level: First Date, Going Steady, Committed/Married
Make-Out Meter: ▌▌
Just for Her: Onboard bathing and sleeping arrangements
Just for Him: Breaking the boat and fixing it

A scruffy, gin-guzzling steamer captain named Charlie Allnut (Bogart) rescues a prudish missionary (Hepburn) in Africa when her brother dies and her village is destroyed after an invasion by German soldiers in the early days of World War I. Without a moment's hesitation, Charlie offers Rose safe passage on his thirty-year-old boat named *African Queen* and thereby ends his long and not-very-profitable career of being his own boss.

The unlikely pair shares a mutual dislike for each other based on their obvious differences and unfortunate circumstances. In a drunken fit he calls her a "crazy, psalm-singing, skinny old maid." In return, she dumps his ample stash of gin overboard.

As if fighting each other weren't enough of a challenge, they also attempt to ward off German soldiers, storms, heat, white water rapids, swarming insects, leeches, and their own animal instincts. While Charlie says he's a slave to hu-

Riverboat captain Charlie (Humphrey Bogart) finds out from Rose (Katharine Hepburn) who is really queen of the jungle in *The African Queen*. (Courtesy of Photofest)

man nature, Rose says nature is "what we are put on earth to rise above."

Their hazardous trip down the river is indeed a struggle with nature. As their close quarters force him to rise above his usual base existence, she learns to enjoy the rapids and the closeness of a man, which stimulate her for the first time in her life. (Previously, only a good sermon or hymn could arouse her passion.)

Their river journey is a metaphor for romantic love, and the closer they get to their ultimate destination, the more perilous and painful the trip becomes. Charlie warns against going downriver, but Rose insists upon taking the most dangerous course of action.

Based on a novel by C. S. Forester, *The African Queen* was shot mainly on location in Africa, with Hepburn suffering from dysentery most of the time in the stifling jungle heat. In 1987, Hepburn wrote *The Making of The African Queen*, a book about her experiences in the jungle and in the London studios where some of the water shots were filmed.

Bogart won his only Academy Award for his role as the filthy, cigar-smoking captain who suffers from gastrointestinal distress. The movie contains a steady stream of light humor and romance, while the exciting struggles against nature (human and otherwise) rise and fall like the ever-changing current.

For another Rose on a boat, see *Titanic* in Chapter 4.

Do Try This at Home: Take a long exotic cruise together (monsoons, leeches, and insects optional).

❧ *The Bridges of Madison County* (1995)

Clint Eastwood, Meryl Streep, Victor Slezak, Annie Corley
DIRECTED BY CLINT EASTWOOD
135 minutes; in color; PG-13
Intimacy Comfort Level: Going Steady, Committed/Married
Make-Out Meter: ▋▋▋▋
Just for Her: "Poisonous" flowers
Just for Him: A role model for tough-guy romanticism

Let's get something straight right from the beginning: Clint Eastwood doesn't do chick flicks. That said, *The Bridges of Madison County* may not satisfy some men who normally look to Eastwood's earlier movies for violent spaghetti Westerns and *Dirty Harry* sequels. As Robert Kincaid, Eastwood plays a divorced, middle-aged nature photographer on assignment from *National Geographic* to photograph the covered bridges of Madison County, Iowa. Highly attuned to his senses, Robert *makes* pictures rather than takes them.

He gets lost and winds up at the farmhouse of Francesca Johnson (Streep), an Italian housewife whose husband and two children are away for four days at the state fair. There's an instant attraction between the world-traveling loner with no roots or responsibilities and the bored farm wife who fills her life with family details to keep herself safely rooted to one spot. She finds him exciting, while he finds her comforting.

Robert talks about how within the laws of nature everything changes. Things change drastically during the next four days, as Francesca guides the

An outdoor photographer (Clint Eastwood) spends some quality indoor time with a lonely farm wife (Meryl Streep) in *The Bridges of Madison County*. (Ken Regan/Camera 5/Copyright © 1995 Warner Bros.; courtesy of Photofest)

lonely photographer to the bridges of Madison County . . . and her bedroom. The bedroom scenes and candlelit dining and bathing are truly romantic and erotic, without being graphic.

Their connection goes far deeper than a physical attraction, however. Robert evaluates places by how they affect his senses. He loves the air of Africa and its "cohabitation of man and beasts with no imposed morality." He loves the land of Madison County because of its natural beauty and rich, earthy smell. Indeed his love for Francesca can be evaluated similarly; without makeup, fancy clothes, or even shoes, she emanates a mother earth quality that the nature photographer cannot resist. Beyond the "imposed morality" of her small, judgmental farming community, their love, though quickly established, lasts eternally.

Based on the bestselling novel by Robert James Waller, *The Bridges of Madison County* is a drama within a drama. Told within the framework of Francesca's adult children reviewing her will, the story is presented in flashback as her son and daughter alternate reading from her journals. As they reflect upon the woman they loved but barely knew, they are forced to reflect upon their own floundering marriages.

If there were any justice in the movie business, "This kind of certainty comes but just once in a lifetime" would be just as famous a line as "Go ahead: Make my day."

For Eastwood in a more traditionally Eastwood role, see *Two Mules for Sister Sara* in Chapter 7.

Do Try This at Home: Exchange treasured pieces of jewelry with each other.

❧ *Crocodile Dundee* (1986)

Paul Hogan, Linda Kozlowski, Mark Blum, John Meillon
DIRECTED BY PETER FAIMAN
97 minutes/102 minutes; in color; PG-13
Intimacy Comfort Level: First Date, Going Steady, Committed/Married
Make-Out Meter: ▮▮▮
Just for Her: Aussie Mick trying to fit into the New York scene
Just for Him: New Yorker Sue trying to act tough in the Outback

Reporter Sue Charlton (Kozlowski in her debut performance) writes for *Newsday*, which is conveniently owned by her wealthy father and edited by her obnoxious boyfriend (Blum). She travels to the Australian Outback to interview legendary crocodile hunter Michael J. "Crocodile" Dundee, otherwise known as Mick (Hogan), a larger-than-life adventurer. For personal and professional reasons, Sue asks him to come back to New York with her for a while after her interviews and research are completed.

The first half of the movie follows Sue, the overly confident New Yorker, floundering around in her attempts to negotiate Walkabout Creek and conquer the wilds of Australia. After a few unfortunate encounters with crocodiles, snakes, and Aborigines, she becomes a little more humble about her survival skills. Her Victoria's Secret–style underclothes are especially inappropriate in the Outback, though most male viewers probably won't mind.

The second half of *Crocodile Dundee* takes place in New York, exemplifying the old jungle-to-jungle scenario found in *George of the Jungle*, *Romancing the Stone* (both in this chapter), and *Coming to America* (Chapter 10) as well. Mick fares slightly better than Sue does when taken out of his natural element. The naive Aussie endures some eating dilemmas, an encounter with a bidet, an embarrassing intrusion upon his bath, and attacks by native animals, but still manages to enjoy his adventure.

It's obvious from the start that Mick and Sue belong together. But where? She soon learns that the Outback is "no place for a city girl." He, on the other hand, was raised by Aborigines, people who don't own the land but belong to it. How can two people so attached to their respective jungles find a place to be happy together? That question gets answered in the 1988 sequel *Crocodile Dundee 2*, a slightly less inspired effort that's still lots of fun. By the time the lame third installment limped into theaters in 2001, the Crocodile had lost its bite.

Hogan cowrote the script with John Cornell and Ken Shadie. *Crocodile Dundee* was a surprise hit in 1986, and featured an offscreen surprise as well: The married Aussie Hogan and single New Yorker Kozlowski had a highly publicized love affair, which resulted in marriage.

For more bathing scenes that range from the erotic to the chaotic, see *Pretty Woman* in Chapter 5; *America's Sweethearts* in Chapter 6; *Out of Sight* in Chapter 7; *The Bridges of Madison County*, *The English Patient*, and *Out of Africa* in this chapter; and *Coming to America* in Chapter 10.

Do Try This at Home: Camp out in sleeping bags.

❧ *The English Patient* (1996)

Ralph Fiennes, Kristen Scott Thomas, Juliette Binoche, Willem Dafoe
DIRECTED BY ANTHONY MINGHELLA
162 minutes; in color; R
Intimacy Comfort Level: Going Steady, Committed/Married
Make-Out Meter: ▮▮▮▮
Just for Her: Bodice ripping and bodice sewing
Just for Him: Two beautiful women in various stages of undressing and bathing

Like *The Bridges of Madison County* and *Out of Africa*, *The English Patient* takes us on a long (nearly three-hour, in this case), beautiful, romantic, outdoor journey through time and place. And like the other two movies, *The English Patient* has a sensual depiction of forbidden love, flashbacks aplenty, fine acting, great locations, and insightful direction, yet still won't appeal to everyone. Its leisurely pace may be welcome during the erotic encounters, but you may not be patient enough (English or otherwise) to wait out the long intervals between action.

Winner of nine Academy Awards including best picture, best director, and best supporting actress (Binoche), this movie tells the story of people haunted by ghosts from the past following World War II. And what better place to be haunted by these metaphoric ghosts than in an abandoned monastery in Tuscany filled with hidden explosives set by the Germans?

A nurse named Hana (Binoche), her dying patient Almasy (Fiennes), and a mysterious stranger who calls himself Caravaggio (Dafoe) deal with their own emotional land mines as they recount the events of Almasy's life through his journal. Flashbacks and memories intertwine with the present and future of the three characters.

As the story of his past is slowly revealed, we learn that Almasy was a writer and cartographer with the Royal Geographical Society on an expedition to map the North African desert a few years before when he became romantically involved with Katharine (Scott Thomas), an associate's wife who accompanied them. Almasy wrote in his journal that "the heart is an organ of fire," and he is living (well, technically dying) proof of this. He literally crashes and burns in matters of the heart, for he is dying from burns sustained in an airplane collision. Almasy needs to piece together the story of his life for some attempt at closure. His story goes beyond his own immediate needs, however. Hana needs to hear his story so she can learn how to love, and Caravaggio needs to learn how not to hate.

A gripping movie that takes its own sweet time in the telling, *The English Patient* should be enjoyed on a long, lazy afternoon.

For other wartime dramas see *Casablanca* in Chapter 4; *Notorious, Raiders of the Lost Ark*, and *Two Mules for Sister Sara* in Chapter 7: *The African Queen, The Last of the Mohicans*, and *Out of Africa* in this chapter; and *The Mask of Zorro* in Chapter 10.

Do Try This at Home: Plan A: Set up a trail of candles. Plan B: Claim favorite body parts as your own.

❥ *George of the Jungle* (1997)

Brendan Fraser, Leslie Mann, Thomas Hayden Church, John Cleese (voice
   of Ape)
DIRECTED BY SAM WEISMAN
91 minutes; in color; PG
Intimacy Comfort Level: First Date, Going Steady, Committed/Married
Make-Out Meter: ❘
Just for Her: George's "sensual intelligence"; the leopard-skin loincloth
Just for Him: Mating rituals from an ape

Some nights all you need is chilled wine, mellow cheese, and sweet fruit to
accompany a sophisticated film such as *Emma*, *Sense and Sensibility*, or *Shakespeare in Love*. Other times, what you really want is cold beer, hot pizza, and a
Farrelly brothers movie. *George of the Jungle* presents another option for those
beer and pizza nights. Featuring PG crudeness instead of R-rated raunchiness,
this Disney Studios film contains running gags involving a talking flatulent ape,
a friendly elephant with a full bladder, unfortunate George (Fraser) enduring
full-frontal crashes into trees, and many chances for you to practice your Tarzan
yell.

The narrated story begins with lovely urban heiress Ursula (Mann) video-
taping herself in the jungles of Africa during a well-funded adventure. A city
woman, she survives the jungle by using her charm, good looks, and a large
supply of moist towelettes. Having experienced most of what the area has to offer, she becomes intrigued when the natives tell her about a legendary seven-
foot white ape that roams through the jungle. When her obnoxious fiancé, Lyle
(Church), unexpectedly shows up to take her back home to San Francisco, she
refuses to leave until she gets a glimpse of this mysterious creature.

So Ursula and Lyle venture into the jungle without the guides in pursuit of
the white ape. On the verge of being attacked by a lion, Ursula (and notably not
Lyle) is whisked away by George as he swings by to rescue her. Having never
seen a woman before, George finds himself intrigued and takes her to his plush
tree house.

Soon Lyle come looking for Ursula, and shoot George in process. Ursula
then bring jungle man to big city for medical attention. Once in San Francisco,
George become fish out of water like Ursula in Africa. Before long, George eat
coffee grounds, offend Ursula's parents, and swing off Golden Gate Bridge.

Throughout movie, George continue to talk like this. George become slightly annoying, but still look good in loincloth.

Based on a late 1960s animated television series, *George of the Jungle* is like Tarzan with a sense of humor. Weisman never misses the chance for a knee (or tree)-to-the-crotch. He's also quite fond of scatological humor. The story has few surprises and the characters are shallow stereotypes, but there's something quite endearing about Ursula's genuine goodness and George's social and sexual awakening. Even so, silliness surpasses sensuality here.

George craves a mate; Ursula craves an adventure. When you're craving wild fun with a tame romance, *George of the Jungle* really hits the spot . . . and the tree.

For Frasier with more clothes and better lines, see *Bedazzled* in Chapter 8 or *The Mummy* in this chapter. For another "swinger," see *Spider-Man* in Chapter 10.

Do Try This at Home: Celebrate a special occasion (traditionally held inside) outside in a garden/tropical/jungle setting.

Ford or Fraser?
4. Did Harrison Ford or Brendan Fraser play a supporting
role early in his career in a movie set in the 1960s
about a Vietnam soldier?
Answer on page 206

❧ *The Last of the Mohicans* (1992)

Daniel Day-Lewis, Madeleine Stowe, Jodhi May, Russell Means
DIRECTED BY MICHAEL MANN
114 minutes; in color; R
Intimacy Comfort Level: First Date, Going Steady, Committed/Married
Make-Out Meter: ❙❙
Just for Her: A strong, outspoken woman in a time when women were not
    known for being strong or outspoken
Just for Him: Not much talking; lots of action

That long brown hair blowing in the breeze. Those delicate features and ex-
quisite bone structure. That graceful figure running swiftly through the wilderness. Yes, it's hard to decide who's more beautiful in this movie, Daniel Day-
Lewis or Madeleine Stowe.

As Nathaniel "Hawkeye" Bumpo, Day-Lewis plays a white frontiersman
raised by Mohicans after his family dies, loyal to no one but his new Mohican
trapper family and friends. The English and French are battling over American
colonies, while native Indian tribes are bribed or coerced into choosing sides.

Meanwhile, Cora Munro (Stowe), daughter of a British officer, finds her persistent suitor entirely unsuitable but keeps her eye on Hawkeye after his daring
rescue of her traveling party. Although he had previously claimed no allegiance
to any side, Hawkeye finds his loyalties change when he meets the lovely outspoken Brit in the striped skirt.

Her father betrays him despite his rescue efforts on their behalf, and Hawkeye soon finds himself imprisoned for sedition with a death sentence hanging
over his head. Cora stands up in his defense but cannot budge her father from
his position—only the much larger French army can do that.

In addition to the characters, the scenery plays a large part in this movie.
Forests, waterfalls, and wilderness reveal the untamed country—the soon-to-
be-lost frontier—before man pushed forward in the name of progress.

Based on the James Fenimore Cooper novel, *The Last of the Mohicans* includes in-fighting among Cora's family and among each warring group, in addition to the large-scale war overshadowing the drama. The R rating is for violent
depiction of these fights rather than for sexual explicitness. Sometimes grisly
and graphic, the violence seems justified considering the context. The romance

is less necessary, but certainly welcome as a means of personalizing a bit of American history.

For other movies with more weapons than actors, see Chapter 7.

Do Try This at Home: Make a seemingly impossible promise and keep it.

❧ *The Mummy* (1999)

Brendan Fraser, Rachel Weisz, Arnold Vosloo, John Hannah
DIRECTED BY STEPHEN SOMMERS
124 minutes; in color; PG-13
Intimacy Comfort Level: First Date, Going Steady, Committed/Married
Make-Out Meter: ❙❙
Just for Her: Strong men; a drunken librarian
Just for Him: Gun battles; special effects; open-jaw scream; flesh-eating
    scarabs; bug-chomping mummy

Adventurer Rick O'Connell (Fraser) seeks excitement and riches wherever they lead him. Rick takes risks in life and love but never with his money. This time, he winds up in Egypt, where he meets Evelyn (Weisz), a cute librarian who longs to prove herself a book scholar, and her integrity-challenged brother, Jonathan (Hannah), who longs for anything except regaining his integrity.

The trio holds various beliefs. Rick believes that evil lies out in the desert waiting to be reawakened. Evelyn discounts fairy tales, legends, and curses but believes in books and treasure. For his part, Jonathan believes in stealing anything that isn't nailed down.

Together they seek an ancient treasure until Evelyn accidentally unleashes ten horrible plagues and unlocks the tomb of Imhotep (Vosloo), an ancient mummy intent upon regenerating himself and his girlfriend and killing everyone who crosses his path. Within minutes of reading from the ancient "Book of the Dead," they all share Rick's belief that evil can and does reside in the tombs beneath the sands.

Apart from ancient curses, grisly special effects, a hideous regenerating mummy, and flesh-eating scarabs, *The Mummy* is actually a fun little love story that doesn't take itself too seriously. Fraser's broad humor and sturdy build are perfect for the role. Weisz's fragile character is like a little girl trapped inside a woman's body; she desperately needs to be protected and Rick's just the man to do it.

Considering he's tasked with rescuing a damsel in distress, killing an immortal being, and saving the world, Rick takes things pretty lightly. Even with these enormous responsibilities, he's never too busy to sneak a kiss from Evelyn or punch someone in the face. Big on action and light on romance, *The Mummy* features comedy, adventure, drama, horror, and effects in a jaw-dropping display of date movie madness.

The back story surrounding Imhotep's "naughty" deeds and bizarre burial explain that despite the monster he appears to be now, his ancient actions were done out of love. In fact, his love affair is compared and contrasted with the Rick–Evelyn relationship throughout *The Mummy* and *The Mummy Returns*, the equally good sequel to the first installment.

Look for John Hannah in another fun supporting role in *Four Weddings and a Funeral* in Chapter 1.

Do Try This at Home: Go for a long, leisurely camel ride together—try horses if you don't happen to be in Egypt.

❥ *Out of Africa* (1985)

Robert Redford, Meryl Streep, Klaus Maria Brandauer, Michael Kitchen
DIRECTED BY SYDNEY POLLACK
153 minutes; in color; PG
Intimacy Comfort Level: First Date, Going Steady, Committed/Married
Make-Out Meter: ▮▮▮
Just for Her: A stunning hat collection
Just for Him: Lion stalking; lion whipping; lion shooting

Based on the true story of a Danish woman who ran a coffee plantation in Kenya, Africa, *Out of Africa* is set in 1913, when European settlers came to East Africa for a new life. Baroness Karen Blixon (Streep) marries her lover's brother, Bror (Brandauer), because she needs his title and he needs her money. As you might imagine, his constant harping on her promiscuous past and her frequent reminders that it's her money funding the farm don't do much to keep the home fires burning.

Their loveless union quickly deteriorates even further by Bror's lengthy trips, flagrant infidelity, and lack of interest in plantation work. After one particularly embarrassing incident in the city, Karen tells him to move out of the house.

But a wealthy white woman with a pretty face and huge hat collection needn't stay lonely for long in early-twentieth-century Africa. A handsome, fiercely independent big-game hunter named Denys (Redford) soon fills the void in Karen's life. He likes her long-winded stories, and she likes his thoughtful gifts. Her estranged husband doesn't like either one of them very much, as we observe in a pithy exchange between the two men when Bror wanders home one afternoon.

Although the characters are not perfectly suited for each other, the actors are perfectly suited for their roles. Redford conveys the occasional detachment of a rugged adventurer unwillingly submitting to love. As a displaced Danish woman, Streep works hard at maintaining an authentic accent throughout the film; furthermore, she puts up with frequent costume changes and an incredible assortment of hats, despite the uncomfortable heat.

There's not really much talking in *Out of Africa* (except for Karen's stories); therefore, what is spoken contains much meaning. The scenery and wildlife tell most of story. (In fact, of the hundreds of African extras used during location filming, very few of them even spoke English.) And men may be disappointed to learn there's not much action either. The winner of seven Academy Awards including best picture, best director, best cinematography, and best adapted screenplay, this movie does offer beautiful scenery, a forbidden romance, top-notch actors, and an epic tale based on real experiences. Especially good for nature lovers, *Out of Africa* is an exotic journey for all lovers who want to share unusual experiences and "speak of nothing ordinary" when together.

For other African-themed romances, see *The African Queen* and *George of the Jungle* in this chapter and *Coming to America* in Chapter 10.

Do Try This at Home: Wash each other's hair.

❧ *Romancing the Stone* (1984)

Michael Douglas, Kathleen Turner, Danny DeVito, Alfonso Arau
DIRECTED BY ROBERT ZEMECKIS
106 minutes; in color; PG
Intimacy Comfort Level: First Date, Going Steady, Committed/Married
Make-Out Meter: ▌▌▌▌▌
Just for Her: Pre-Colombian Joan vs. Post-Colombian Joan
Just for Him: Guns; car chases; mudslide

What could be sadder than a bestselling romance novelist with no romance in her life? Neurotic New York novelist Joan Wilder (Turner) overcomes her travel anxiety long enough to make a trip to Colombia in order to save her kidnapped sister's life. In her possession are Italian leather shoes, lots of beige clothes, a few airline liquor bottles, and a treasure map sent by her late brother-in-law.

All goes well until she takes the wrong bus and gets stranded in the jungle with a corrupt cop (Manuel Ojeda), a sleazy thug (DeVito), and a rugged American fortune hunter, Jack T. Colton (Douglas). For $375, Jack reluctantly agrees to help guide her back to civilization so she can rescue her sister in Cartagena. Their simple arrangement soon becomes complicated when it's revealed that each of them is hiding important secrets from the other.

Along the way, Joan's real-life adventures in the rainforest start to resemble the exciting scenarios described in her romance novels. She flees drug runners, narrowly escapes being drowned, shot, and eaten by crocodiles, and digs for buried treasure with a handsome adventurer. When she and Jack find the priceless jewel—*El Corazón* (The Heart)—her situation becomes even more dangerous. If she and her sister can make it out of Colombia alive, Joan will have lots of inspiration for writing her romantic thrillers. For the first time in her life, she can rely on memory rather than imagination for a story idea.

Douglas, who also produced the movie, is well cast as the less-than-heroic American fortune hunter seeking less-than-legal shortcuts in Colombia. Turner presents a delightful transition from hopeless romantic to hopeful romantic. There's plenty of action, comedy, and romance in this wild ride through the jungle.

Turner and Douglas make a terrific onscreen couple with sidekick DeVito;

Digging for buried treasure means a great time for a mousy romance novelist (Kathleen Turner) and a selfish adventurer (Michael Douglas) in *Romancing the Stone*. (Copyright © 1984 Twentieth Century-Fox; courtesy of Photofest)

all three reprise their roles in the uninspired 1985 sequel *The Jewel of the Nile* and reteam in different roles in the 1989 DeVito-directed dark comedy *The War of the Roses*.

Do Try This at Home: Enjoy another culture's celebration together.

❥ *Six Days, Seven Nights* (1998)

Harrison Ford, Anne Heche, David Schwimmer, Temuera Morrison
DIRECTED BY IVAN REITMAN
102 minutes; in color; PG-13
Intimacy Comfort Level: First Date, Going Steady, Committed/Married
Make-Out Meter: **▮▮▮▮**
Just for Her: One hundred and two minutes of pretending that it's you
    trapped on a remote island with Harrison Ford
Just for Him: Flying, crashing, and fixing an airplane; fighting with pirates;
    grabbing a snake that crawls inside Heche's shorts

A self-assured assistant magazine editor, Robin Monroe (Heche) finally stops working long enough to travel with her weak-willed fiancé (Schwimmer) to a tropical island. Immediately called away to Tahiti for a photo shoot, she leaves the island with crusty charter pilot Quinn Harris (Ford) in his well-used plane. Despite the age of his equipment, it still looks good and functions fine, Quinn assures her with a smile.

Nonetheless, an unexpected storm causes them to crash-land on a remote island. Thus begins a fight against nature and against themselves. Although quite mechanical (he's shown working on the plane earlier in the movie), Quinn makes it clear that he's not the sort of guy who can go into the wilderness with a "pocket knife and Q-tip" and build a shopping mall. Robin is especially ill equipped to deal with their situation; without her morning coffee, cell phone, and Xanax, she can hardly make it through the day.

The age difference and personality clash—not to mention the ever-present engagement ring on her finger—cause lots of friction between them. The mismatched pair starts the adventure at each other's throats and ends up with their tongues down each other's throats. Quinn claims that she deserves someone "fresher." Watch these two together and decide for yourself.

Heche and Ford have great chemistry, whether arguing about lifestyles, rebuilding the plane, battling natural elements, running from pirates, or snuggling on the beach. Ford's intentionally unglamorous appearance does nothing to lessen his considerable sex appeal; likewise Heche's widely publicized off-screen affair with Ellen Degeneres at the time doesn't detract from her obvious charms. Schwimmer as the spineless boyfriend and Morrison as Quinn's buxom playmate of the month add to the fun. Ford's real-life experience as a pilot makes a nice inside joke. In fact, this entire romantic comedy is packed with tropical punch—snappy comebacks and quick wit, plus lots of outdoor action/adventure for him and comedy/romance for her.

See Chapter 2 for more writers who misuse words and readers who can't read signs of love, and Chapter 4 for more transportation-related love stories.

Do Try This at Home: Roll around in the surf together.

Ford or Fraser?
5. Did Harrison Ford or Brendan Fraser receive the
Cecil B. DeMille Award in 2002?
Answer on page 206

For other great date movies that have characters watching out for trees and other objects, see *Crouching Tiger, Hidden Dragon* in Chapter 3 and *Raiders of the Lost Ark* in Chapter 7.

Love in Disguise

*I do not paint a portrait to look like the subject; rather does the person
grow to look like his portrait.*
Salvador Dali

EVEN IN PREHISTORIC TIMES, people might have had ulterior motives for the costumes (i.e., animal skins) they wore. Based on early cave drawings, it is theorized that early men might have worn these skins to show off their hunting prowess or in the belief that they would adopt the characteristics of the animal they had slain.

Like actors on the stage, disguised characters adopt other personas based on costumes, masks, props, or all of the above. The strutting cave man gave way to loincloths, tunics, and robes worn in ancient times and onstage in Greek drama where the addition of full head masks completely obscured the actors' identities.

The characters in the following ten movies understand the manipulative power of a disguise, but fail to grasp that the less of a man (or woman) the character is, the more is required of the clothes.

In *The Mask of Zorro*, the hero wears two different disguises that alter his appearance. In *Coming to America*, *Maid in Manhattan*, and *Working Girl*, the characters wear clothing and hairstyles that change their social status. In *Fletch*, *Shakespeare in Love*, *Some Like It Hot*, *Spider-Man*, *Tootsie*, and *There's Something About Mary*, people completely change identities using everything from false teeth to facial hair.

The degree of disguises varies. Hotel maid Marisa Ventura (Jennifer Lopez) merely "borrows" a $5,000 suit from a guest in *Maid in Manhattan* to impress a handsome politician (Ralph Fiennes). However, actor Michael Dorsey (Dustin Hoffman) in *Tootsie* really gets into his disguise by shaving his body hair, wearing padding, applying makeup, and buying women's clothes. In *There's Something About Mary*, the actual physical disguises are a little less pronounced—though still crass—and are based more on lies and misrepresentation than elaborate costumes.

The one thing all ten movies have in common, besides romance, of course, is that characters use these masks, costumes, and props to deceive others. Most of the time, they're also deceiving themselves because they already possess most of the traits of the assumed personality even without the disguise.

Their reasons for deception are as varied as the disguises themselves. Prince Akeem (Eddie Murphy) in *Coming to America* hides his true identity to find a bride who loves him for himself rather than for his title. In *Fletch*, Irwin Fletcher (Chevy Chase) dons a variety of comic disguises and accents to perform better in his job as an investigative reporter for a major newspaper. In *Shakespeare in Love*, Lady Viola (Gwyneth Paltrow) disguises herself as a young male actor so she can have an adventure before she is forced into marriage. In *Some Like It Hot*, two male musicians pretend to be women in a traveling band to hide from Chicago gangsters.

The most noble reason for donning a disguise, however, goes to newspaper photographer Peter Parker (Tobey Maguire), who hides his everyday appearance beneath the Spider-Man costume in order to keep the city safe from supernatural psychos. Unfortunately, Peter also seems to suffer more than any other disguised character. As he says, his gift is his curse. While others can extricate themselves from their tangled web of lies spun while hiding incognito, Spider-Man cannot. When he openly loves people, such as his uncle and aunt, he puts their lives in danger. He has far more at risk than, say, Tess McGill (Melanie Griffith) in *Working Girl*, a secretary who pretends to be a high-powered businesswoman. She may lose the account, her job, or her boyfriend, but she isn't likely to find herself engaging in hand-to-hand combat with the Green Goblin when she reveals her true identity. Therefore, Peter, the lonely superhero, is forced to hide his feelings, his body, and his face, while Tess can (and does) flaunt all three.

Psychiatrist Carl Jung wrote in his book *Modern Man in Search of a Soul* that "there appears to be a conscience in mankind which severely punishes the man who does not somehow and at sometime, at whatever cost to his pride, cease to defend and assert himself, and instead confess himself fallible and human." In short, people eventually demand that every disguise be removed. Perhaps this is why people are so fickle in their devotion to masked men and caped crusaders, and the crowd one day heralds Spider-Man a hero and the next day a villain.

But what happens when the masks and costumes do come off and the truth comes out? Well, there's usually lots of angry shouting at first and, because these are great date movies, lots of passionate kissing later.

❧ Coming to America (1988)

Eddie Murphy, Shari Headley, Arsenio Hall, James Earl Jones
DIRECTED BY JOHN LANDIS
116 minutes; in color; R
Intimacy Comfort Level: First Date, Going Steady, Committed/Married
Make-Out Meter: ▎▎▎
Just for Her: A dance by the jukebox
Just for Him: Royal bathers; the bar scene

Oh, what a feeling to be loved. And what better place for an African prince to find his bride than in Queens, New York? At least, that's what Prince Akeem of Zamunda (Murphy) thinks when he awakens on his twenty-first birthday to the prospect of an arranged marriage to a stranger. Although his father (Jones) believes that Akeem wants to travel to America to "sow his royal oats," the defiant prince actually hopes to find true love—or at the very least, "a woman that's going to arouse my intellect as well as my loins."

Pretending to be a poor African student and former goat herder, Akeem comes to America with his sidekick Semmi (Hall), a servant and friend who displays all the pampered, superficial qualities that Akeem is able to rise above. After he cuts his hair, changes into street clothes, and rents a filthy apartment, Akeem takes Semmi to visit the bars in search of a bride. Instead, they encounter a stable of women with severe emotional problems and eventually wind up at a Black Awareness Rally, where the prince finally finds a woman of interest: the lovely Lisa McDowell (Headley), the daughter of a conniving fast-food restaurant owner (John Amos).

The two men continue their charade as poor African students by obtaining jobs as sanitation workers at McDowell's Restaurant so that Akeem can get to know Lisa better. Aiding their efforts is a chubby coworker (Louie Anderson) striving for a management job, and thwarting their efforts is Lisa's current boyfriend, Darryl (Eriq La Salle), a vain, greasy-headed heir to a hair-care-products fortune.

Further complications in Akeem's quest for love include Lisa's lusty younger sister, Patrice (Allison Dean), Semmi's inability to live frugally, Mr. McDowell's preference for Darryl, and ultimately the king's intervention.

Although *Coming to America* aims for laughs (especially through costume and makeup that allow Murphy and Hall to assume other roles in the movie), the romance feels genuine. Lisa possesses intellectual, emotional, and physical traits that make her rise above others in an almost regal way. Her own exceptional qualities allow her to recognize those same qualities in Akeem (with or without a crown), unlike anyone else living in Queens or Zamunda.

The largely black cast is exceptionally attractive and full of surprising cameos (such as a very young Cuba Gooding Jr.), and the universal themes of independence, freedom, and love relate to everyone. The ethnicity comes out mostly in the terrific Nile Rodgers soundtrack and the attempts at humor, which though laced with profanity, are very frequent and very funny. A lawsuit resulted in newspaper columnist Art Buchwald being credited for the story (instead of Murphy), but don't let that little unpleasantness get in the way of your enjoying this fun date movie.

For another case of royalty going slumming, see *Roman Holiday* in Chapter 3. For other African-themed romances, see *The African Queen*, *George of the Jungle*, and *Out of Africa* in Chapter 9.

Do Try This at Home: Play (or just relax) on the swings together.

❥ *Fletch* (1985)

Chevy Chase, Dana Wheeler-Nicholson, Joe Don Baker, Tim Matheson
DIRECTED BY MICHAEL RITCHIE
98 minutes; in color; PG
Intimacy Comfort Level: First Date, Going Steady, Committed/Married
Make-Out Meter: ❚❚
Just for Her: Revenge on a very naughty husband
Just for Him: Car chase; basketball fantasy; "Moon River"

Irwin M. Fletcher, a.k.a. Fletch (Chase), works as an investigative reporter who goes undercover to write his "Jane Doe" expose column for a Los Angeles newspaper. While researching an article about a drug ring on the beach, he stumbles onto an even bigger story when Alan Stanwyck (Matheson), an eccentric businessman, hires him to commit a murder. Claiming to be dying of bone cancer, Alan promises Fletch a large stack of cash for killing him so his wife can get more insurance money.

You don't have to be an investigative reporter to be suspicious of this scenario. Fletch immediately begins a background check on Alan and his independently wealthy wife, Gail (Wheeler-Nicholson). In order to properly conduct his research, he adopts a variety of ridiculous disguises using costumes, wigs, voices, and false teeth. In Fletch's line of work, deception—bolstered by sarcasm—gains him access to the truth.

Hiding behind a protective facade of indifference on the job and off, Fletch eventually drops the act, lowers his defenses, and tells Gail the truth about what Alan has been doing . . . and suggests they go on a date to a Lakers game once the whole mess is finished. Complicating the dangerous situation with Stanwyck are a homicidal police chief (Baker), Fletch's stickler-for-deadlines boss (Richard Libertini), a persistent attorney seeking alimony payments, some bloodthirsty dogs, and a doctor who's a little too eager with the rubber gloves and KY Jelly.

In the role he plays so well, Chase portrays a wisecracking cynic who needs a good woman to soften his outlook on life. Look for Geena Davis in a supporting role as Fletch's assistant and Kareem Abdul-Jabbar in a cameo during a basketball dream sequence.

In *Fletch*, the pairing of the betrayed undercover reporter who hides behind disguises and the betrayed socialite who hides behind polite country club rituals seems perfectly natural. Once they lower their respective masks, you know they'll be happy together on a private little island getaway or at a crowded Lakers game.

Based on Gregory McDonald's novel, *Fletch* shoots mainly for laughs but also scores on romance. The dreary 1989 sequel, *Fletch Lives*, starring Chase and Julianne Phillips, misses both by a long shot.

For more Los Angeles stories, see *L.A. Story* in Chapter 2, *Speed* in Chapter 4, *Pretty Woman* in Chapter 5, and *Kindergarten Cop* in Chapter 7.

Do Try This at Home: Order something extravagant from room service.

❧ *Maid in Manhattan* (2002)

Jennifer Lopez, Ralph Fiennes, Natasha Richardson, Stanley Tucci
DIRECTED BY WAYNE WANG
100 minutes; in color; PG-13
Intimacy Comfort Level: First Date, Going Steady, Committed/Married
Make-Out Meter: ▮▮▮
Just for Her: Loyal friends and coworkers pooling their resources to get "Cinderella" ready for the ball
Just for Him: An outspoken female lead who inspires respect and lust

The imposed credo of every maid working at a posh Manhattan hotel is to "strive to be invisible." However, a drab uniform isn't enough to make Jennifer Lopez fade into the background. Her lovely face, beautiful skin, and ample curves make her stand out from the rest of the lavatory scrubbers and pillow fluffers. And if the maid is disguised in a $5,000 designer suit and the finest gowns and jewels the hotel shops have to offer, then this particular Cinderella has a shapely leg up on finding her handsome prince.

Instead of a wicked stepmother holding her back and a magic fairy godmother egging her on, housekeeper Marisa Ventura (Lopez) has a working-class Hispanic mother who scoffs at her daughter's desire for upward mobility and a cherubic, gifted son (Tyler Garcia Posey) who plays matchmaker for his mom.

The "prince" in *Maid in Manhattan* remains something of a mystery and an anomaly: Christopher Marshall (Fiennes) is a handsome state senator who loves children, dogs, and the truth, yet hates public speaking and politics. Campaigning for his late father's seat in the U.S. Senate, Chris seems far less interested in his career than does his overzealous campaign manager, Jerry Siegel (Tucci).

What does interest Chris is the feisty hotel guest he knows as Caroline, who is actually Marisa the maid in disguise. Several hotel service personnel aid Marisa in her little charade, most notably Lionel, a kindly British butler (Bob Hoskins). On the flip side, there's the real Caroline (Richardson), a spoiled socialite who's recently been dumped by her boyfriend and decides to snag an aspiring U.S. senator for her next beau.

Maid in Manhattan is a satisfying date movie compilation of similar films that preceded it. The hotel backdrop brings back images of *Pretty Woman* (Chapter 5). The unreliable ex-husband calling to cancel a commitment to the child is reminiscent of *One Fine Day* (Chapter 5). The hourly worker disguised as a woman of affluence also is the subject of *Working Girl* (this chapter). Marisa's difficulty breathing as she departs for the "ball" echoes a beautifully depicted scene in *Ever After: A Cinderella Story* (Chapter 3). And the final dramatic press conference also is used effectively in *Notting Hill* (Chapter 1) and *America's Sweethearts* (Chapter 6).

The one element that the other movies lack is Marisa. Charming, beautiful, sweet, enchanting, creative, she is unlike the brittle female characters in some of the above movies, partly because she is Hispanic, and partly because her original intention was not to find love or success through deceit and disguise.

For another politician in love see *The American President* in Chapter 5.

Do Try This at Home: Give a small gift at your second meeting that relates back to the first.

In *The Mask of Zorro,* underneath the mask, Alejandro (Antonio Banderas) is really just like any other prospective suitor trying to impress his girlfriend's father (Anthony Hopkins). (Rico Torres/Copyright © 1997 TriStar Pictures; courtesy of Photofest)

❥ *The Mask of Zorro* (1998)

Antonio Banderas, Catherine Zeta-Jones, Anthony Hopkins, Stuart Wilson
DIRECTED BY MARTIN CAMPBELL
137 minutes; in color; PG-13
Intimacy Comfort Level: First Date, Going Steady, Committed/Married
Make-Out Meter: ❙❙❙
Just for Her: The confessional
Just for Him: Action; violence; sword fights

What better face to find beneath a mask than that of Antonio Banderas? In fact, with or without a mask, his deep voice, dangerous lifestyle, and barely contained lust attract the sheltered Elena (Zeta-Jones). As the horse thief Alejandro, a.k.a. Zorro, Banderas displays the flashy bravado that makes women swoon and crowds cheer. Unfortunately, it also makes people like the sadistic

Captain Harrison Love (Matt Letscher) that much more determined to dispatch the flamboyant do-gooder and display his remains in a gruesome collection.

Through a series of coincidences over twenty years, Alejandro is chosen by an aging Zorro, actually Don Diego de la Vega (Hopkins), to replace him as the Mexican freedom fighter and folk hero. During a difficult training period in which the unkempt horse thief is taught the subtleties of swordplay, he also gets lessons in hygiene and etiquette.

Training a new Zorro has several benefits for de la Vega. He wants someone else to carry on the tradition of fighting for the underdog. He seeks revenge on Don Raphael Montero (Wilson), an evil governor who murdered de la Vega's wife, stole his daughter Elena, and schemes to establish an independent republic of California using stolen gold. Zorro also wants to properly train Alejandro so the younger man can seek his own vengeance for his brother's murder without getting killed in the process.

For sweet, confused Elena, everyone is in disguise. She has grown up not knowing her real mother and father. Montero, the man she thinks is her father, is actually a murderer and liar. He real father, de la Vega, is the former Zorro, now disguised as a servant. Her love interest, Alejandro, appears in two disguises, causing her to wonder whom she can trust or love.

The romantic interludes between Alejandro and Elena don't happen often, but occur with vigor—much vigor—when they do. Banderas goes from a dirty, disheveled bandit to a suave, sexy swordsman. Zeta-Jones looks gorgeous throughout the entire movie. As the central prize that all the men fight over, she is a spirited beauty with nothing to hide.

For other sexy men in masks, see *Don Juan DeMarco* and *The Princess Bride*, both in Chapter 3.

Do Try This at Home: Get in good with the father.

❧ *Shakespeare in Love* (1998)

Gwyneth Paltrow, Joseph Fiennes, Colin Firth, Ben Affleck
DIRECTED BY JOHN MADDEN
122 minutes; in color; R
Intimacy Comfort Level: Going Steady, Committed/Married
Make-Out Meter: ▮▮▮▮▮
Just for Her: Wars with words; stage kisses
Just for Him: Battles with swords; backstage sex

Welcome to London in 1593—a time when raw sewage is thrown out of windows, entire cities can be wiped out by the plague, marriages are arranged by parents, and women are not allowed to act on stage because of decency laws. It is also a time when two rival theaters, The Rose and The Curtain, vie for writers, actors, audiences, and royal acceptance.

The story is intricate and ironic, much like a Shakespearean play. Nearly bankrupt, The Rose has scheduled a performance of Will Shakepeare's (Fiennes) newest play, a rough, sketchy version of what will become *Romeo and Juliet*. Besides the time pressure, Will's biggest obstacle is a staggering case of writer's block. He has lost his muse and with it his ability to release any "creative juices."

Desperate for inspiration wherever he can find it, the bard can't keep his pen in his own ink pot. He steals ideas from his everyday life and the stories of others and similarly has no qualms stealing women from their other lovers. When he first meets the lovely Lady Viola (Paltrow), she is disguised in men's clothes in order to audition for the part of Romeo in his play. Impressed by her performance, but confused by her refusal to take off her hat, Will follows this "boy" home to learn more about "him."

Viola comes from a wealthy family and finds herself forced into constantly doing what's expected of her, such as becoming engaged to the detestable Lord Wessex (Firth). Despite her duties, she longs for poetry, adventure, and love in her life. Will, who pretends to be the writer Christopher Marlowe on occasion, respects the young man on stage and loves the young woman in her bedroom.

The outstanding acting, costumes, and screenplay helped *Shakespeare in Love* win seven Academy Awards, including best picture, best actress, best costumes, and best screenplay. The love scenes with Paltrow and Fiennes are tempestuous, topless, and totally in keeping with Will's description that his love "is like a sickness and a cure together."

Look for Affleck as a pompous actor, Geoffrey Rush as the poverty-stricken theater owner, Judi Dench in her Oscar-winning role for best supporting actress, and Rupert Everett as the unfortunate Marlowe.

For other date movies about actors, see *America's Sweethearts* in Chapter 6 and *Tootsie* in this chapter. For another fictional tale of a famous writer finding inspiration, see *A Knight's Tale* in Chapter 3.

Do Try This at Home: Let your love inspire works of art.

Paltrow or Pfeiffer?
5. Did Gwyneth Paltrow or Michelle Pfeiffer have a small role
in the Steven Spielberg movie *Hook* (1991)?
Answer on page 207

CLASSIC DATE MOVIE SELECTION

❧ *Some Like It Hot* (1959)

Marilyn Monroe, Tony Curtis, Jack Lemmon, George Raft
DIRECTED BY BILLY WILDER
114 minutes; in black and white; not rated, comparable to PG
Intimacy Comfort Level: First Date, Going Steady, Committed/Married
Make-Out Meter: ▌▌
Just for Her: Curing a "mental block"
Just for Him: Old Chicago gangland style shoot-outs; slinky dresses with
    lots of Sugar spilling out

Set in 1929, this gender-bending farce features two out-of-work musicians, Joe (Curtis) on saxophone and Jerry (Lemmon) on bow fiddle, who accidentally witness a mob hit and become targets themselves. Needing the money, but more important, needing disguises, Joe and Jerry wear dresses, wigs, and makeup to become Josephine and Daphne, respectively. The two "women" join Sweet Sue and Her Society Syncopators, a women's band en route to a gig in Florida. The story begins in snowy Chicago and ends in sunny Miami, not because they like it hot but because they want to get as far away as possible from a Chicago mob boss (Raft).

The plot thickens when both men develop a craving for Sugar Kane (Monroe), a singer and ukulele player who looks like "Jello on springs" when she walks. The shapely Sugar admits that she's got a little problem with drinking and a big problem with men. Always stuck with the "fuzzy end of the lollypop," the unlucky-at-love twenty-four-year-old has a soft spot for male musicians, especially (as she privately confides to Josephine) for saxophone players. To break the spell, she now seeks a millionaire with thick glasses who won't leave her alone with a broken heart and an empty tube of toothpaste.

Sugar also freely admits that she's "not very bright," and who could argue with that? When Joe/Josephine disguises himself (yet again) as a frigid, near-sighted, Cary Grant–talking heir to the Shell Oil fortune, Sugar falls hook, line, and sinker for the phony yachtsman. Meanwhile, the real owner of the yacht, an aging playboy named Osgood Fielding III (Joe E. Brown), becomes enamored with Daphne and her shapely ankles.

The focus of *Some Like It Hot* is mainly on laughs about gender differences and on showcasing the singing/shimmying/jiggling talents of Monroe. However, the romance between Joe and Sugar certainly has lots of chemistry. (Offscreen, it was bad chemistry, apparently, as Curtis and Wilder publicly complained about Monroe's tardiness, inability to learn lines, and overall bad behavior on the set.) This tension works well in the romantic yacht scene where Joe pretends to be unresponsive to Sugar's sexual advances.

Check out *Children of a Lesser God* (Chapter 6), in which the sexiest scene from *Some Like It Hot* is used as a date movie within a date movie. For more characters chilling out in Chicago, see *While You Were Sleeping* in Chapter 4 and *What Women Want* in Chapter 8; and for characters basking in the Miami sun, see *Notorious* and *Out of Sight* in Chapter 7 and *There's Something About Mary* in this chapter.

Do Try This at Home: Enjoy a late-night dinner on a yacht.

In *Spider-Man*, Peter Parker (Tobey Maguire) and Mary Jane (Kirsten Dunst) both have much to hide. (Courtesy of Photofest)

❥ *Spider-Man* (2001)

Tobey Maguire, Kirsten Dunst, Willem Dafoe, James Franco
DIRECTED BY SAM RAIMI
121 minutes; in color; PG-13
Intimacy Comfort Level: First Date, Going Steady, Committed/Married
Make-Out Meter: ❚❚
Just for Her: Peter's description of when he looks into M.J.'s eyes
Just for Him: Superhero rescues

A comic-book character brought to life (with a little CGI enhancement), *Spider-Man* tells the story of a nerdy high school senior who gets bitten by a radioactive spider and undergoes an amazing physical transformation. Lighter and brighter than *Batman* and more sophisticated than *Superman: The Movie*, this is the story of a boy becoming a man, of an average guy turning into a superhero, and of good battling evil. But mostly, as Peter Parker (Maguire) is quick to point out, this is really just a story about a girl.

This particular girl is Mary Jane Watson (Dunst), a.k.a. M.J., Peter's pretty neighbor whose sunny disposition hides her abusive home life. Peter knows the truth, however, and feels her vulnerability as an additional attraction. A shy, awkward science whiz often terrorized by his classmates, Peter has only one friend, Harry (Franco), a spoiled rich kid who has flunked out of every private school in the city. Harry's father, Norman Osborn (Dafoe), is an industrial tycoon who undergoes his own transformation.

Although M.J. goes out with the class bully in high school, Peter and Harry want to date her after graduation and a move to the big city. Naturally, only Harry has the courage to actually ask. Afraid to admit the depth of his feelings for M.J.—even to the aunt and uncle who take care of him—introverted Peter is adept at hiding his true identity and his feelings. Not exactly someone who shoots straight from the hip, he learns to shoot straight from the wrist after his bizarre spider bite. He can shoot a strong, sticky web out of his wrists that allows him to swing through the air, close the mouths of obnoxious editors, and cover the eyes of villains.

Wearing a disguise to hide his secret identity is crucial to Peter's survival, both as a newspaper photographer shooting exclusive shots of Spider-Man and as the superhero himself. The fickle public shows little loyalty to its heroes, making Peter's gift an occasional curse. One day, he's considered the city's savior; the next day, people are demanding his arrest. Poor Peter has three things working against him: his nemesis, the Green Goblin; editor J. J. Jameson's suspicions about Spider-Man; and his own inability to express his feelings.

In addition to terrific special effects and heroic rescues, *Spider-Man* is full of secretive characters. Spider-Man and The Green Goblin hide their identities beneath masks and costumes in order to carry out their respective businesses of good and evil. M.J. hides her troubled past and tries to keep her current waitressing job a secret, instead bragging to others about her (imaginary) acting career. As Peter's roommate, Harry purposely keeps his romance with M.J. a secret because he knows his friend has loved her since the fourth grade.

Thanks to his uncle's dying words, Peter realizes that "with great power comes great responsibility," and he therefore keeps a rein on his emotions. Even so, Maguire does a nice job conveying those tingling spider senses whenever M.J. is around.

For another movie with a comic-book superhero, see *The Mask* in Chapter 8.

Do Try This at Home: Remember how you felt the first time you met.

In *There's Something About Mary*, the title character (Cameron Diaz) is surrounded by four men who claim to love her, but each of them is pretending to be someone or something that he's not. (From left to right: Ben Stiller, Matt Dillon, Chris Elliott, and Lee Evans.) (Glenn Watson/Copyright © 1998 Twentieth Century-Fox; courtesy of Photofest)

❧ *There's Something About Mary* (1998)

Cameron Diaz, Ben Stiller, Matt Dillon, Chris Elliot
DIRECTED BY PETER FARRELLY AND BOBBY FARRELLY
119 minutes; in color; R
Intimacy Comfort Level: Going Steady, Committed/Married
Make-Out Meter: ❚❚
Just for Her: Romantic confessions
Just for Him: Frank and beans; monkey spanking

This is the original gross-out date movie that dared to go where no date movie had gone before. The Farrelly brothers explore and exploit almost every taboo subject imaginable. Cruelty to animals, abusing the mentally and physically disabled, gay hangouts, interracial marriage, genitalia, sex toys, and body fluids are just a few of the subjects that serve as visual punch lines in the huge box-office hit *There's Something About Mary*.

In addition to all the joking around, the movie tells the story of two wonderful people who should be together. Ted (Stiller) is an unlucky guy who always manages to be at the wrong place at the wrong time doing the wrong thing (despite his lucky rabbit's foot key chain). Underneath his geeky exterior and uninspired writing career, he is a genuinely nice guy who cares about people and tries to do what's right. In this case, he believes that it's right to pursue Mary, his high school crush whom he's been craving for thirteen years since she moved away from Rhode Island to Florida.

On the surface, Mary (Diaz) is the opposite of Ted. She's a beautiful orthopedic surgeon who intrigues everyone—especially the men—she meets. Beneath her lovely exterior is an equally lovely interior. Devoted to her disabled brother Warren (W. Earl Brown), she's a little shy with men and wants to find one who is self-employed and willing to spend time with her and Warren.

After an ill-fated trip to Miami, Ted searches for Mary in an attempt to rekindle the flame. Thwarting his efforts, however, are his best friend (Elliot), a sleazy private detective (Dillon), and a disabled architect (Lee Evans), each of whom hides behind some kind of disguise. Although Ted wears no disguise, he is withholding information from Mary and misrepresenting his situation. Only the irresistible, irrepressible Mary is who she seems to be.

This quirky film raised the bar in terms of comedic date movies and considerably lowered the bar in terms of political correctness. It's still funny after repeated viewings.

For more Farrelly brothers films, see *Shallow Hal* in Chapter 6 and *Me, Myself & Irene* in Chapter 7.

Do Try This at Home: Know who makes you happy.

❧ *Tootsie* (1982)

Dustin Hoffman, Jessica Lange, Teri Garr, Dabney Coleman
DIRECTED BY SYDNEY POLLACK
116 minutes; in color; PG
Intimacy Comfort Level: First Date, Going Steady, Committed/Married
Make-Out Meter: ❙❙
Just for Her: A man who's really in touch with his feminine side
Just for Him: Ladies' dressing room; Dorothy's lustful admirers

When difficult but talented actor Michael Dorsey (Hoffman) can't get work in New York City (or anywhere else for that matter) because of his personal reputation as a prima donna, he transforms himself into Dorothy Michaels, a homely, hirsute middle-aged feminist actress. Although Michael's good friend Sandy (Garr) is rejected for the high-paid role of a prim hospital administrator on a popular soap opera, the feisty Dorothy is just what the doctor show ordered.

The lecherous director, Ron (Coleman), is romantically involved with one of the show's stars, Julie (Lange), a lovely single mother who plays a nurse on the show. Under the tutelage of Dorothy, Julie becomes a better actress and learns to stand up for herself against Ron, whose sexist behavior and comments overshadow the production of the soap opera.

Not only does Julie benefit from her new relationship with Dorothy, but Michael (in disguise) also grows up a little. The astute actor, always in touch with his character's emotions, finally realizes—with some degree of anguish—that his earlier behavior toward women closely resembled that of Ron's. Even as he scolds Ron publicly, Michael privately cringes as he hears Ron say sexist remarks that sound much like things he has told Sandy, his long-suffering friend.

As Dorothy, Michael really gets in touch with his feminine side and would like to be in touch with Julie's feminine parts, as well. Michael's crush on Julie is kept under wraps, until she invites Dorothy on a weekend trip home, where she shares secrets, recipes, and a bed. In addition to Julie's involvement with Ron and Michael's involvement with Sandy, Julie's lonely father (Charles Durning) develops quite a crush on Dorothy.

Overall Michael is a good man but makes a better woman. His motivation for taking the role in the soap opera was to raise $8,000 to produce his roommate's play. But it isn't until he's a woman that he recognizes how insensitive he's become toward women and children through his many years of poverty, disappointment, and unemployment. Watching all the action from a safe distance is Michael's dry-witted roommate, Jeff Slater (Bill Murray), a friend, writer, and definite scene stealer.

Lange won best supporting actress for her role as Julie, and Geena Davis made her film debut as a minor actress on the soap opera, usually appearing on screen in nothing more than panties and a bra.

For other movies in which lovers are in a New York state of mind, see *Moonstruck* and *Kate & Leopold,* both in Chapter 1; *Crossing Delancey, Sleepless in*

Seattle, Woman of the Year, and *You've Got Mail* in Chapter 2; *Splash* in Chapter 3; *The Thomas Crown Affair* in Chapter 4; *Annie Hall* and *One Fine Day* in Chapter 5; *Breakfast at Tiffany's* in Chapter 6; *Ghost* and *Serendipity* in Chapter 8; *Crocodile Dundee* in Chapter 9; and *Coming to America, Maid in Manhattan, Spider-Man*, and *Working Girl*, all in this chapter.

Do Try This at Home: Bake something together and take turns licking batter from each other's fingers.

❧ *Working Girl* (1988)

Harrison Ford, Melanie Griffith, Sigourney Weaver, Alec Baldwin
DIRECTED BY MIKE NICHOLS
115 minutes; in color; R
Intimacy Comfort Level: Going Steady, Committed/Married
Make-Out Meter: ▮▮▮
Just for Her: The scar story
Just for Him: Topless vacuuming

It's Tess McGill's (Griffith) thirtieth birthday and she has big hair and an even bigger ambition to succeed. Unfortunately, she also has a loser boyfriend (Baldwin), a secretarial job she hates, and a new back-stabbing boss named Katharine Parker (Weaver). Tess looks and sounds like a bimbo but aspires to corporate greatness at the New York brokerage house where she works. She describes herself as possessing "a head for business and a bod for sin."

When Katharine breaks her leg during a skiing accident, Tess takes over in a big way. She moves into Katharine's apartment, wears her clothes and perfume, works in her office, and assumes Katharine's other positions—*all* her other positions.

During her charade as a professional in acquisitions and mergers, Tess forms a personal/professional relationship with handsome investment banker Jack Trainer (Ford), who finds himself drawn to her ideas and, of course, her made-for-sin bod. You can always count on Harrison Ford to turn up the heat in any romantic date movie, and *Working Girl* is no exception.

In her transition from secretary to executive, she takes voice lessons to lose her accent, cuts her hair into a "serious" style, and tones down her jewelry and clothes from flashy to classy. (This isn't hard to do with Katharine's extravagant wardrobe at her disposal.)

The movie won an Academy Award for the Carly Simon song "Let the River Run," and Nichols certainly got plenty of use out of the music. Brief appearances by Joan Cusack, Oliver Platt, Olympia Dukakis, Nora Dunn, and Kevin Spacey are a bonus.

Although an enjoyable romantic romp featuring lovers in disguise, *Working Girl* leaves a few questions unanswered. For instance, why would Katharine's boyfriend put up with her for as long as he did or, for that matter, even date her in the first place? Why would a headstrong woman like Tess live with an abusive loser? How could an uneducated, lower-class secretary with no formal training fool so many people for so long? And, finally, why does Melanie Griffith clear her throat constantly throughout the film—is this acting or allergy?

For inevitable comparisons, see *Pretty Woman* in Chapter 5 and *Maid in Manhattan* in this chapter.

Do Try This at Home: Play a discreet game of footsies at an inappropriate time.

For more lovers in disguise, see *A Knight's Tale, The Princess Bride,* and *Roman Holiday* in Chapter 3; *Casablanca* in Chapter 4; *Kindergarten Cop, True Lies,* and *Two Mules for Sister Sara* in Chapter 7; and *All of Me* and *The Mask* in Chapter 8.

Afterword

DURING THE YEAR I spent writing *Reel Romance*, people expressed much interest and enthusiasm regarding a guidebook to romantic date movies. Men and women of all ages and in all stages of relationships had suggestions for movies that they thought I should include. Their suggestions ranged from *Rambo* (where's the love?) to *Rocky* (a sure winner, see Chapter 6), from *Divine Secrets of The Ya-Ya Sisterhood* (too chick flicky) to *Father of the Bride* (not romantic enough), and from *Batman* (too dark and depressing) to *Spider-Man* (you'll really get caught up in this one, see Chapter 10).

Although I never know what movie people might suggest, I'm always certain what they'll eventually ask: "So what's the best date movie of all time?"

I don't even pretend to have the answer to this question. I can analyze movies for their artistic merit and entertainment value—and even rank them on a make-out meter—to help readers determine if they'll enjoy the movie or not. However, I can't possibly predict something so subjective as which one particular movie will work as an aphrodisiac on the most people. For example, *Sleepless in Seattle* is simmering and romantic to some, slow-moving and tame to others.

Therefore, I've chosen to present 100 of the best romances that couples can watch together depending upon their taste and mood. And that's why these movies are categorized by theme, rather than ranked from 1 to 100.

The journalist in me doesn't like to leave any question unanswered, however, so I'll do here what I do when people ask me that unanswerable question. I'll list my personal favorites from each chapter that exemplify a certain theme.

From Chapter 1: Always a Wedding Planner, Never a Bride, *Moonstruck* is a striking example of a seemingly perfect romantic union beset by seemingly insurmountable obstacles. Cher is utterly delightful as the superstitious widow whose repressed passions emerge with a vengeance with the slightest encouragement. Beautifully written and acted, the story features growth and change in every major character, a good mix of humor and drama, and a heartfelt message about passion versus contentment.

Runner up: *Notting Hill* has a clever screenplay, attractive stars, quirky supporting roles, and an interesting story. It will leave you feeling very romantic.

From Chapter 2: Literate Ladies in Love, *When Harry Met Sally* should meet (and sometimes exceed) all your expectations for a great date movie. This extremely romantic movie boasts an excellent screenplay and the emerging talents of Meg Ryan and Billy Crystal. Not much action for the men, but plenty of insights that keep both sexes laughing and shaking their heads in agreement. The cast is wonderful; Nora Ephron's screenplay (which was nominated for an Academy Award) really captures human emotion and expression; music by Harry Connick Jr. and Marc Shaiman sets a perfect tone; and Rob Reiner's direction ties it all together beautifully. Classic scenes and lines make *When Harry Met Sally* a modern romantic masterpiece.

Runner up: *You've Got Mail* is one of the most romantic movies in the entire book, but its appeal is mainly for women. With a little more action and edge, it would have been my top pick in this category.

From Chapter 3: Once Upon a Time, *The Princess Bride* reigns supreme over the other selections. This delightful story within a story combines interesting characters, a clever screenplay, action, stunts, makeup effects, inspired direction by Rob Reiner, quotable dialogue, and a tale of true love. A beautiful work of art that's nearly flawless in its conceptualization and implementation. It's great for lovers of any age.

Runner up: *A Knight's Tale* has enough action, comedy, drama, music, dancing, and romance for everyone to have a good time.

From Chapter 4: Plains, Trains, Automobiles, and Ships, *Casablanca* has been transporting audiences to an exotic time and place for more than sixty years. This classic love story using transportation as a metaphor for transformation has outstanding characters whose inner turmoil mirrors that of the turbulent environment in which they live. The skillful acting, directing, and writing work together perfectly, and the famous airport scene is one of the most celebrated moments in film.

Runner up: *Risky Business* is a visually stunning portrait of adolescent urges and angst that leaves lots of questions to ponder. Highly erotic and deeply symbolic, the movie is far more than it appears on the surface, and keeps getting better the more times you watch it.

From Chapter 5: Opposites Attract (Then Repel, Then Attract Again), *Annie Hall* deserves to attract the most intellectual lovers looking for a little stimulation. Clever, poignant, funny, and innovative, this Woody Allen classic is packed with stars, one-liners, and insights into love. Although most of Allen's other movies could be described similarly, this particular film helped establish his career, displayed prominent up-and-coming actors, analyzed his real-life relationship with his costar, and explored creative cinematography to better express the message.

Runner up: *Pretty Woman* made Julia Roberts a star, and with good reason. While the story itself is a little flimsy, the stars shine and the sexual chemistry ignites the screen.

From Chapter 6: In the Eye of the Beholder, *Rocky* really goes the distance. Although looks can be deceiving, this movie proves that you don't need a big budget or famous stars to produce a blockbuster hit. It's about love, courage, and ambition, both on the screen and off, as Sylvester Stallone broke through cinematic and financial barriers to make this terrific date movie.

Runner up: *Roxanne* whimsically looks at the serious subject of beauty. Its bittersweet love story will make you laugh, cry, and sometimes squirm with embarrassment.

From Chapter 7: Is That a Pistol/Knife/Nunchak in Your Pocket?, *Witness* hits the romantic target market dead center. Harrison Ford adroitly portrays the conflicted police detective – who is literally and figuratively wounded—as he struggles with his violent and sexual tendencies. Kelly McGillis illuminates the screen as the passionate Amish widow, and Peter Weir effectively combines all the elements in a transfixing film that appeals to men and women equally.

Runner up: *Notorious* gained its notoriety for being highly suspenseful and highly erotic. This classic thriller has little physical action, but lots of intrigue and insinuation.

From Chapter 8: Love Is a Supernatural Thing, *Ghost* really works its magic. While other couples may have difficult obstacles to overcome in consummating their love, this pair really has a problem. Sam dies shortly after opening credits, and we're left with two hours of watching his anguished efforts to communicate his love (and get revenge on his killer). Patrick Swayze and Demi Moore bring to life a passionate story that's well acted and well told, making *Ghost* a movie that will live on forever.

Runner up: *The Birds* is Alfred Hitchcock's classic thriller that soars above most other tales of supernatural love because of its rising sexual tension, subtle humor, and increasing level of suspense.

From Chapter 9: Watch Out For That Tree!, *Romancing the Stone* swings out ahead of the other outdoor adventures to emerge as king of the jungle films. In this particular survival-of-the-fittest scenario, a timid writer transforms into one of the heroines from her novels. Funny, exciting, and romantic, this movie is perfectly proportioned in terms of male/female enjoyment.

Runner up: *The African Queen* may be more than fifty years old, but like Charlie Allnut's old steamer, it holds up just fine. It's great for taking us away to a different time and place where two people can fall in love against the odds.

From Chapter 10: Love in Disguise, *Shakespeare in Love* reveals itself as the star performer. Attractive actors, eloquent dialogue, gorgeous costumes, artful direction by John Madden, and passionate interludes make this film a stunning tribute to the art of love and the love of art.

Runner up: *Tootsie* takes the idea of love in disguise a little more literally than most of the other entries. Through his disguised identity, sexist pig Michael Dorsey comes as close to womanhood as possible, without actually having an operation. His enormous growth as a person is what most movies try, though unsuccessfully, to convey.

And for those people who just can't take no for an answer, I'll share my selection for what I personally consider the best date movie of all time—a movie that excels at every craft, succeeds on every level, and appeals to men and women of all ages. It's an action-packed depiction of true love that's so sweetly romantic, so naturally heartfelt, it needs no nudity, profanity, or sexual suggestiveness to make it work: *The Princess Bride*. My husband and I have watched it together more than fifty times and still laugh and get misty-eyed (although he won't admit it) at the same scenes every time. For me, any other choice for best romantic date movie would have been "absolutely, totally, and in all other ways inconceivable."

Trivia Answers

Answers to *Barrymore or Bullock?*

1. Drew Barrymore played William Hurt's daughter in *Altered States* when she was only five years old.

2. Sandra Bullock's mother, Helga Bullock, was a European opera singer, so Sandra traveled abroad frequently in her youth.

3. Drew Barrymore won a Golden Globe award for best actress in 1993 for her work in *Guncrazy*.

4. Sandra Bullock was the lead actress in the television series *Working Girl*, which was canceled soon after it was introduced.

5. Sandra Bullock was ranked number six in *The Hollywood Reporter* countdown of star salaries, which also ranked Barrymore at number three for the year 2002.

Answers to *Carrey or Cusack?*

1. John Cusack debuted in a supporting role as a prep school student in the 1983 film *Class*, in which an oversexed woman seduces her son's classmate.

2. Both. Jim Carrey costarred with Cameron Diaz in the 1994 film *The Mask*, and John Cusack costarred with her in *Being John Malkovich* in 1999.

3. John Cusack attended New York University for an education that prepared him for his later acting, writing, and producing responsibilities.

4. Jim Carrey starred in the 1985 comedy *Once Bitten*, in which Lauren Hutton wants his blood . . . and more.

5. John Cusack (and sister Joan Cusack) appeared in the 1987 comedy *Broadcast News*, starring William Hurt, Holly Hunter, and Albert Brooks. John appeared as an angry messenger.

Answers to *Ford or Fraser?*

1. Brendan Fraser played obsessive artist Julian Jons in the 1994 thriller *Dark Side of Genius,* also starring Finola Hughes.

2. Harrison Ford received both honors: *People*'s ten best-dressed and most beautiful people of 1997.

3. Harrison Ford is referenced in Adam Sandler's 1996 novelty hit "The Chanukah Song" from his *What the Hell Happened to Me!* CD and in the 1998 Barenaked Ladies song "One Week" from their *Stunt* CD.

4. Both. Harrison Ford and Brendan Fraser both played supporting roles early in their careers in Vietnam-themed movies. Ford was in *Getting Straight* (1970) starring Elliott Gould as a returning Vietnam soldier. Fraser was in *Dogfight* (1991) starring River Phoenix as a Marine going off to war in Vietnam.

5. Harrison Ford was the 2002 recipient of the Cecil B. DeMille Award at the 59th Golden Globe Awards.

Answers to *Gere or Grant?*

1. Richard Gere played a supporting role as a streetwise hood brought in for questioning when an undercover cop is killed in the 1974 drama *Report to the Commissioner.*

2. Hugh Grant received a Golden Globe award in 1994 for his starring role in *Four Weddings and a Funeral* with Andie MacDowell. This film helped establish him as a dapper fumbler and bumbler, a role that he perfects in several date films that follow. Richard Gere received a Golden Globe for best actor in 2003 for his song and dance role in *Chicago.*

3. Richard Gere received a gymnastics scholarship to the University of Massachusetts, which helps explain his ability to do perfect pushups in a jockstrap in the 1977 drama *Looking for Mr. Goodbar.*

4. Richard Gere dropped out of college (and apparently forfeited that gymnastics scholarship) to make it on Broadway but instead found himself a star in London, coincidentally the birthplace of Hugh Grant.

5. Both. Richard Gere and Hugh Grant have previous romantic ties to supermodels. Gere was married to Cindy Crawford, and Grant was the longtime partner of Elizabeth Hurley.

Answers to *Paltrow or Pfeiffer?*

1. Michelle Pfeiffer starred with Al Pacino in the 1991 drama *Frankie and Johnny* in which she played an unattractive waitress who had trouble getting

dates and finding love. This was such a stretch that Pfeiffer's beauty could only be reduced to "extremely pretty."

2. Michelle Pfeiffer studied at Whitley College for Court Reporting and worked briefly in that profession.

3. Both. Gwyneth Paltrow's brother, Jake, is an actor, and Michelle Pfeiffer's sister DeDee has been in more than a dozen movies.

4. Michelle Pfeiffer starred in *William Shakespeare's A Midsummer Night's Dream* (1999) with Kevin Kline, Calista Flockhart, and Rupert Everett. (Gwyneth Paltrow starred in the 1998 romance *Shakespeare in Love*, but that was a tale written about Shakespeare by screenwriters Marc Norman and Tom Stoppard, not a tale written by Shakespeare.)

5. While still in her teens, Gwyneth Paltrow appeared as the young Wendy in *Hook*, Steven Spielberg's 1991 version of *Peter Pan* starring Robin Williams and Dustin Hoffman.

Answers to *Roberts or Ryan?*

1. Both. Julia Roberts's character (Anna) falls in love with travel bookshop owner Hugh Grant in the 1999 romantic comedy *Notting Hill,* and Meg Ryan's character (Kathleen) falls in love with chain bookstore owner Tom Hanks in the 1998 film *You've Got Mail.*

2. Julia Roberts ranked number one of Hollywood leading ladies by earning $20 million in 2001 following her Oscar win for *Erin Brockovich* and starring turn in *America's Sweethearts.*

3. Meg Ryan owns Prufrock Pictures, a name inspired by T. S. Eliot's poem "The Love Song of J. Alfred Prufrock," once required reading in most public high schools across the country.

4. Meg Ryan played Debby, the eighteen-year-old daughter of novelist Candice Bergen in the drama *Rich and Famous.* Unknown at the time, she would eventually live up to the name of the film.

5. Meg Ryan became her high school homecoming queen when the girl originally selected was suspended from school.

Bibliography

Aylesworth, Thomas G., and John S. Bowman. *The World Almanac Who's Who of Film*. New York: Bison Books, 1987.

Bernard, Jami. *First Films*. New York: Citadel Press, 1993.

Cader, Michael, ed. *People Weekly Entertainment Almanac*. New York: Time, 1997.

Condon, Paul and Jim Sangster. *The Complete Hitchcock*. London: Virgin Publishing, 1999.

Eastman, John. *Retakes: Behind the Scenes of 500 Classic Movies*. New York: Ballantine Books, 1989.

Esar, Evan. *The Dictionary of Humorous Quotations*. New York: Dorset Press, 1989.

Falk, Kathryn. *How to Write a Romance and Get It Published*. New York: Crown Publishers, 1989.

Gardner, Chris. *The Hollywood Reporter*, December 2002, p. 35.

Gay, Peter, ed. *The Freud Reader*. New York: Norton, 1989.

Hosoda, Craig. *The Bare Facts Video Guide*. Santa Clara, Calif.: The Bare Facts, 1992.

Jung, C. G. *Modern Man in Search of a Soul*. Translated by W. S. Dell and Cary F. Baynes. New York: Harcourt Brace, 1933.

Pianka, Phyllis Taylor. *How to Write Romances*. Cincinnati, Ohio: Writer's Digest Books, 1988.

Zipes, Jack, ed. *The Great Fairy Tale Tradition*. New York: Norton, 2001.

Index

Note: Films reviewed (rather than just mentioned) have their subgenre listed in parentheses.

Index

Index

Index

Index

About the Author

A MEMBER OF Florida Freelance Writers Association and Professional Freelance Writers of Orlando, Leslie Halpern has worked as a professional entertainment writer since 1984. She is the author of *Dreams on Film: The Cinematic Struggle between Art and Science*, a book that analyzes dream sequences in more than 100 movies. She coauthored *Windows to the World*, an adult literacy book that won the Distinguished Service Award from The Florida Literacy Coalition, Inc.

Leslie has published more than 1,000 articles, including writing a monthly column about independent film for the past five years for the trade magazine *Markee*. Her work has appeared in *The Hollywood Reporter* (thirteen-year stringer), *Daily Variety*, *Storytelling*, *True Romance*, *Fitness*, *Location Update*, *Bluegrass Unlimited*, *Just for Laughs*, *The Journal of Graduate Liberal Studies*, and *The Orlando Sentinel*.

In 1997, Leslie was named the grand prize winner of The Mentor Award, a national essay contest sponsored by the publication *Mentor and Protégé* for an essay she wrote about her personal mentoring experiences while working as education coordinator for The Young Company of the Orlando-UCF Shakespeare Festival.

Her previous jobs also include working as an editor at an aerospace company and as a copywriter at a publishing house. She conducted workshops on "Interviewing Celebrities" and "Entertainment Writing" at the Florida Freelance Writers' Conference (1992), worked as a production assistant on an independent film, and currently teaches classes on writing at Edgewater Yoga & Arts Studio in Orlando. Leslie earned a B.A. in journalism from University of Kentucky and a Master of Liberal Studies degree from Rollins College.

Other Titles of Interest

LON CHANEY
The Man behind the Thousand Faces
Michael F. Blake
408 pp., 110 b/w photos
1-879511-09-6
$19.95
Vestal Press

A THOUSAND FACES
Lon Chaney's Unique Artistry in Motion Pictures
Michael F. Blake
400 pp., 103 b/w photos
1-879511-21-5
$19.95
Vestal Press

THE FILMS OF LON CHANEY
Michael F. Blake
304 pp., 117 b/w photos
1-56833-237-8
$18.95
Madison Books

AT THE CENTER OF THE FRAME
Leading Ladies of the Twenties and Thirties
William M. Drew
392 pp., 312 b/w photos
1-879511-44-4
$29.95
Vestal Press

BETTY GARRETT AND OTHER SONGS
A Life on Stage and Screen
Betty Garrett with Ron Rapoport
306 pp., 52 b/w photos
1-56833-098-7 (cloth); 1-56833-133-9 (paperback)
$23.95 (cloth); $18.95 (paperback)
Madison Books

BLACKFACE
Reflections on African Americans and the Movies
Nelson George
Expanded Edition
330 pp., 23 b/w photos
0-8154-1194-4
$16.95
Cooper Square Press

BLUE ANGEL
The Life of Marlene Dietrich
Donald Spoto
376 pp., 57 b/w photos
0-8154-1061-1
$18.95
Cooper Square Press

THE BOYS FROM SYRACUSE
The Shuberts' Theatrical Empire
Foster Hirsch
374 pp., 24 b/w photos
0-8154-1103-0
$18.95
Cooper Square Press

BROTHERHOOD IN RHYTHM
The Jazz Tap Dancing of the Nicholas Brothers
Constance Valis Hill
Foreword by Gregory Hines
New introduction by Jennifer Dunning
336 pp., 44 b/w illustrations
0-8154-1215-0
$18.95
Cooper Square Press

CHARLIE CHAPLIN AND HIS TIMES
Kenneth S. Lynn
632 pp., 66 b/w photos
0-8154-1255-X
$19.95
Cooper Square Press

THE CINEMA OF ROBERT ZEMECKIS
Norman Kagan
304 pp., 40 b/w photos
0-87833-293-6
$18.95
Taylor Trade Publishing

CLARA BOW
Runnin' Wild
David Stenn
with a new filmography
368 pp., 27 b/w photos
0-8154-1025-5
$19.95
Cooper Square Press

CONVERSATIONS WITH BRANDO
Lawrence Grobel
with a new afterword
238 pp., 17 b/w photos
0-8154-1014-X
$15.95
Cooper Square Press

FILM CULTURE READER
Edited by P. Adams Sitney
464 pp., 80 b/w photos
0-8154-1101-4
$19.95
Cooper Square Press

FRANCOIS TRUFFAUT
Correspondence, 1945-1984
Edited by Gilles Jacob and Claude de Givray
Foreword by Jean-Luc Godard
608 pp., 81 b/w photos, drawings, and facsimiles
0-8154-1024-7
$19.95
Cooper Square Press

FROM THE HOLOCAUST TO HOGAN'S HEROES
The Autobiography of Robert Clary
Robert Clary
256 pp., 48 b/w photos
1-56833-228-9
$26.95 cloth
Madison Books

GARY COOPER
American Hero
Jeffrey Meyers
404 pp., 32 b/w photos
0-8154-1140-5
$18.95
Cooper Square Press

THE GREAT GARBO
Robert Payne
308 pp., 116 b/w photos
0-8154-1223-1
$23.95 cloth
Cooper Square Press

HATTIE
The Life of Hattie McDaniel
Carlton Jackson
286 pp., 16 pp. of b/w photos
1-56833-004-9
$12.95
Madison Books

HOLLYWOOD REMEMBERED
An Oral History of Its Golden Age
Paul Zollo
416 pp., 50 b/w illustrations
0-8154-1239-8
$27.95 cloth
Cooper Square Press

HOLY TERROR
Andy Warhol Close Up
Bob Colacello
560 pp., 74 b/w photos
0-8154-1008-5
$17.95
Cooper Square Press

THE HUSTONS
The Life and Times of a Hollywood Dynasty
Lawrence Grobel
Updated Edition
872 pp., 61 b/w photos
0-8154-1026-3
$29.95
Cooper Square Press

I, FELLINI
Charlotte Chandler
Foreword by Billy Wilder
448 pp., 51 b/w photos
0-8154-1143-X
$19.95
Cooper Square Press

JOSEPHINE
The Hungry Heart
Jean-Claude Baker and Chris Chase
592 pp., 84 b/w photos
0-8154-1172-3
$21.95
Cooper Square Press

THE LAST LAUGH
The World of Stand-Up Comics
Phil Berger
Updated Edition
464 pp., 38 b/w photos
0-8154-1096-4
$18.95
Cooper Square Press

LAURENCE OLIVIER
A Biography
Donald Spoto
528 pp., 110 b/w photos
0-8154-1146-4
$21.95
Cooper Square Press

LEGEND
The Life and Death of Marilyn Monroe
Fred Lawrence Guiles
534 pp.
0-8128-8525-2
$16.95
Scarborough House

LOU'S ON FIRST
A Biography of Lou Costello
Chris Costello with Raymond Strait
288 pp., 31 b/w photos
0-8154-1073-2
$17.95
Cooper Square Press

MARILYN MONROE
The Biography
Donald Spoto
752 pp., 50 b/w photos
0-8154-1183-98
$24.95
Cooper Square Press

MCQUEEN
The Biography
Christopher Sandford
536 pp., 24 b/w photos
0-87833-307-X
$22.95
Taylor Trade Publishing

MEMOIRS OF MY LIFE
John Charles Frémont
Explorer of the American West
New introduction by Charles M. Robinson
696 pp., 84 b/w illustrations
0-8154-1164-2
$24.95
Cooper Square Press

MY LIFE IS IN YOUR HANDS & TAKE MY LIFE
The Autobiographies of Eddie Cantor
Eddie Cantor with David Freedman / Jane Kesner Ardmore
Foreword by Will Rogers
New introduction by Leonard Maltin
650 pp., 63 b/w photos
0-8154-1057-3
$25.95
Cooper Square Press

MY STORY
Marilyn Monroe
Coauthored by Ben Hecht
New introduction by Andrea Dworkin
176 pp., 14 b/w & 4 color photos
0-8154-1102-2
$22.95 cloth
Cooper Square Press

MY WICKED, WICKED WAYS
The Autobiography of Errol Flynn
New Introduction by Jeffrey Meyers
464 pp., 24 b/w photos
0-8154-1250-9
$17.95
Cooper Square Press

REBEL
The Life and Legend of James Dean
Donald Spoto
352 pp., 41 b/w illustrations
0-8154-1071-9
$18.95
Cooper Square Press

REMINISCING WITH NOBLE SISSLE AND EUBIE BLAKE
Robert Kimball and William Bolcom
256 pp., 244 b/w photos
0-8154-1045-X
$24.95
Cooper Square Press

THE RUNAWAY BRIDE
Hollywood Romantic Comedy of the 1930s
Elizabeth Kendall
312 pp., 24 b/w photos
0-8154-1199-5
$18.95
Cooper Square Press

A SILENT SIREN SONG
The Aitken Brothers' Hollywood Odyssey, 1905–1926
Al P. Nelson and Mel R. Jones
288 pp., 42 b/w photos
0-8154-1069-7
$25.95 cloth
Cooper Square Press

THE STORY OF THE OUTLAW
A Study of the Western Desperado
Emerson Hough
New introduction by Larry D. Underwood
400 pp., 18 b/w illustrations
0-8154-1168-5
$18.95
Cooper Square Press

THE UNRULY LIFE OF WOODY ALLEN
A Biography
Marion Meade
404 pp., 26 b/w photos
0-8154-1149-9
$18.95
Cooper Square Press

VAMP
The Rise and Fall of Theda Bara
Eve Golden
288 pp., 124 b/w photos
1-879511-32-0
$19.95
Vestal Press

Available at bookstores; or call 1-800-462-6420

COOPER SQUARE PRESS / MADISON BOOKS / SCARBOROUGH
HOUSE / TAYLOR TRADE PUBLISHING / VESTAL PRESS
200 Park Avenue South, Suite 1109
New York, NY 10003